Muslim Youth

ALSO AVAILABLE FROM CONTINUUM

European Muslims, Civility and Public Life, Edited by Ihsan
Yilmaz and Paul Weller

Muslims and Modernity, Clinton Bennett

Young, British and Muslim, Philip Lewis

Muslim Youth

Challenges, Opportunities and Expectations

Edited by

Fauzia Ahmad and Mohammad Siddique Seddon

continuum

Continuum International Publishing Group

The Tower Building	80 Maiden Lane
11 York Road	Suite 704
London	New York
SE1 7NX	NY 10038

www.continuumbooks.com

British Library Cataloguing-in-Publication Data
A catalogue record for this book is available from the British Library.

ISBN: HB: 978-1-4411-2299-5
PB: 978-1-4411-1987-2

Library of Congress Cataloguing-in-Publication Data
Muslim youth : challenges, opportunities and expectations / edited by Mohammad Siddique Seddon and Fauzia Ahmad.
p. cm.
Includes bibliographical references and index.
ISBN 978-1-4411-1987-2 (pbk.) – ISBN 978-1-4411-2299-5 (hardcover) 1. Muslim youth. 2. Muslim youth–Conduct of life. 3. Muslim youth–Attitudes. I. Seddon, Mohammed Sidiq. II. Ahmad, Fauzia.
BP188.18.Y68M866 2011
305.235088'297–dc23
2011024515

Typeset by Deanta Global Publishing Services, Chennai, India
Printed in Great Britain

CONTENTS

CONTRIBUTORS AND EDITORS

FAUZIA AHMAD is currently a research fellow at the Institute for the Study of Muslim Cultures at the Aga Khan University in London (ISMC-AKU) and an honorary research fellow at the Centre for the Study of Ethnicity and Citizenship, University of Bristol. Her publications include *Muslim Women and Higher Education: Identities, Experiences and Prospects,* (with David Tyrer), ESF/Liverpool John Moores University, (2006); 'The Scandal of "Arranged Marriages" and the Pathologisation of BrAsian Families', in N. Ali, V. Kalra and S. Sayyid (Eds) *A Postcolonial People, South Asians in Britain*, Hurst Publications, (2005), and 'Modern Traditions? British Muslim Women and Academic Achievement', *Gender and Education*, Vol. 13 (2001). She currently sits on the advisory board of the Association of Muslim Social Scientists UK (AMSS UK).

NADER AL-REFAI has a BA in Islamic Studies and an MA in Islamic Education from Yarmouk University, Jordan, and an M.Phil degree from the University of Huddersfield, England, in Education. He is currently a teacher at KD Grammar School for Boys, Manchester, and a doctoral student in the Research Centre for Education and Professional Practice, University of Derby.

CHRISTOPHER BAGLEY is emeritus professor of Social Science, University of Southampton. He has published a number of books on education and social studies.

YAHIA BAIZA is working as research associate at the Central Asian Studies, Department of Academic Research and Publications at the Institute of Ismaili Studies (IIS), London. His current research project is entitled 'The Hazara Ismailis of Afghanistan: Their History, Religious Rites, Ceremonies and Practices'. In this study, he researches the ethnic origin of the Hazara ethnic group in Afghanistan, and explores how Shi'ism and Ismailism emerged and spread among the Hazaras of Afghanistan and how the Hazara Ismailis preserved and developed their religious rites, ceremonies and festivals. He has published numerous articles in both English and Persian.

BRIAN BELTON is a senior lecturer at London's YMCA George Williams College and has taught youth work in several countries. He was a youth worker for several years and is the author of over 20 books; he is a sociologist, critical anthropologist and social historian as well.

GILL CRESSEY is a senior lecturer in Social and Community studies at Coventry University in the School of Social and Community Studies where her research spans Muslim young people in the UK and voluntary sector organizations. She is author of *The Ultimate Separatist Cage? Youth Work with Muslim Young Women*, Leicester, National Youth Agency (2007), and *Diaspora Youth and Ancestral Homelands*, Leiden: Brill Publications (2006). She is a trustee of the Muslim Youth Foundation.

ARIF FITZSIMON has worked in various Muslim organizations within the UK and the Republic of Ireland in both paid and voluntary capacities for over 20 years. His experience includes working with Muslim youth and children within various youth organizations and in a Muslim school, interfaith work and so on. During the period between June 2008 and July 2010 he was the manager of the Muslim Youth Foundation. He holds an MA in Religious Studies (Lancaster University).

ALTAF HUSAIN has a PhD from the Howard University School of Social Work, focusing on Muslim immigrant and refugee adaptation in the United States. His research interests include the integration of immigrant and refugee families, and especially Muslim adolescents, in the United States. He is a board member of the Muslim Alliance in North America (MANA) and Islamic Social Services Association of the United States and Canada (ISSA). He is also a licensed social worker in the Commonwealth of Virginia.

SEYFEDDIN KARA has worked as a researcher and head of campaigns with the Islamic Human Rights Commission (IHRC), a London-based NGO in Special Consultative Status with the Economic and Social Council of the United Nations, from 2004 to 2010. He is currently a PhD student at the School of Government and International Affairs, University of Durham.

MUHAMMAD G. KHAN is a former youth worker and now a tutor in Youth and Community Work at Ruskin College, UK. He was the editor of a Special Edition of Youth and Policy on Muslim Youth work (2006) and was the main organizer of the two Muslim Youth Work conferences that led to the establishment of the Muslim Youth Work Foundation.

SAEED A. KHAN is a lecturer in the department of Classical and Modern Languages, Literature and Cultures, Wayne State University, United States. His research interests include ethnic identity politics and the history and development of Muslim diaspora communities in the United States and Europe, Islamic and Muslim history, and political Islam.

FATIMA Y. MIRZA, earned her master's in Social Work from Virginia Commonwealth University in 2004, and has been a student in the University of Maryland School of Social Work PhD program. Her research interests include family and child well-being, trauma and its effects on individuals and groups, the Muslim community in the United States and Community-based Participatory Research methodologies.

MOHAMMAD SIDDIQUE SEDDON is currently director of the Centre for Applied Muslim Youth and Community Studies (CAMYCS), lecturer in Muslim Studies and honorary research fellow at the Department of Theology and Religious Studies, University of Chester. He is a former research fellow at the Islamic Foundation, Leicester, and is an executive member of the Association of Muslim Social Scientists (UK). His research interests are historical and contemporary issues relating to Islam and British Muslim communities. He has published a number of related works and books including, *British Muslims: Loyalty and Belonging*, (2003), *British Muslims Between Assimilation and Segregation:*

Historical, Legal & Social Realities, (2004) (both with D. Hussain and N. Malik), and *The Illustrated Encyclopaedia of Islam* (2009, with Raana Bokhari).

M. TAQI TIRMAZI is a W. K. Kellogg postdoctoral fellow at Morgan State University, United States, in the School of Community Health and Policy. He was a Race, Ethnicity, and Migration Studies scholar at Utrecht University, in the Netherlands where he conducted a comparative study on the ethnic and religious identity of Muslim youth in the Netherlands and United States. He is currently conducting a community based participatory research project aimed to examine the contextual factors associated with the preconception and inter-conception health of African American youth

TASANEE R. WALSH is based at the University of North Carolina at Chapel Hill, United States, in the School of Social Work, where she researches on Public Health and Social Work with a focus on the mental health of refugee women. Her publications include 'Cultural and Religious Contexts of Parenting by Immigrant South Asian Muslim Mothers' (with Fariyal Ross-Sheriff and M. Taqi Tirmazi).

IHSAN YILMAZ is associate professor of Political Science at Fatih University, Istanbul as well as the director of the PhD Program in Political Science and International Relations at the Institute of Social Sciences of Fatih University. He is the author of *Muslim Laws, Politics and Society in Modern Nation States: Dynamic Legal Pluralisms in England, Turkey and Pakistan* (Ashgate, 2005), co-editor (with John L. Esposito) of *Islam and Peacebuilding: Gülen Movement Initiatives* (Blue Dome, 2010) and co-editor (with Paul Weller) of a forthcoming book "European Muslims, Civility and Public Life: Perspectives On and From the Gülen Movement" (Continuum, 2011). He is the co-editor of the *European Journal of Economic and Political Studies* (EJEPS).

ACKNOWLEDGEMENTS

Mohammad S. Seddon and Fauzia Ahmad would like to thank Dr Anas Al Sheikh Ali, Shiraz Khan, Tahira Hadi and Dr Richard Reid of the Association of Muslim Social Scientists (AMSS UK), and Rev. Robert Evans and Richard Turner, Department of Theology and Religious Studies, University of Chester, for their help and support in the organizing and hosting the International Muslim Youth Conference, Muslim Youth: Challenges, Opportunities and Expectations.

We would also like to thanks our colleagues and offer personal appreciation to Professor Emeritus, Rev. Ruth Ackroyd, Sadek Hamid, Penny Jones, colleagues the Institute for the Study of Muslim Cultures, Aga Khan University (UK), Chloe Patton and the team at Continuum Press for guidance and patience. Finally, we would both like to express our deep gratitude to our families to Raana, Mustafa and Owias Seddon, and Razia and Fahzan Ahmad for their saintly patience and unconditional love.

Mohammad Siddique Seddon and Fauzia Ahmad

FOREWORD

This edited volume is the fruition of a joint initiative between the Association of Muslim Social Scientists (AMSS UK) and the Department of Theology and Religious Studies, University of Chester, that began as an international conference, *Muslim Youth: Challenges, Opportunities and Expectations*, held at the University of Chester, 20–22 March, 2009. The remit of the original conference was to create an arena of engagement by bringing together academics, educationalists, youth work practitioners and youth work institutions and organizations at national (UK), and international levels, to discuss the central issues currently facing young Muslims both locally and globally. Muslim populations across the globe, whether minority communities in the West or majority societies in the Middle East, South Asia and the Far East, are currently experiencing a youth explosion resulting in societies where more than half of the population are under the age of 25. Further, in a rapidly changing world, accelerated by global technologies and communications, young Muslims find themselves confronted by a series of challenges that have disrupted their traditional religious *weltanshuung*, cultural practices and social order. However, not all of these challenges are experienced as negative phenomena and, conversely, some present themselves as self-empowering opportunities for positive change. This is perhaps best witnessed by the 'Facebook generation' that has precipitated the so called 'Arab Spring' pro-democracy movements across the Middle East. Pitted against this powerful force for change is the reality of disenfranchised young Muslims who hold the belief that their religious values are under threat by a perceived imposition of western culture upon traditional Muslim spaces and societies. This sense of an increasing spiritual void often gives way to alienation, rejectionism and religious fanaticism, sometimes manifest through violent extremism. However, between these two opposing experiences are a multitude of complex and diverse Muslim youth narratives that deserve to be heard. This publication aims to present nuanced articulations of the possibilities and expectations for young Muslims in contemporary societies. In doing so, it has brought together an eclectic mix of contributors with expertise in Muslim youth issues from very divergent perspectives. The Association of Muslim Social Scientist and the Department of Theology and Religious Studies, University of Chester, are extremely pleased to see the publication of this collection. We are indebted to all of the authors for their informative contributions to this edited volume. We would also like to express our gratitude to the editors Mohammad S. Seddon and Fauzia Ahmad for their work in bringing this publication together and we hope that this book will be a positive contribution to the on-going debates on Muslim youth.

Dr Anas Al-Shaikh-Ali, CBE, Chair, AMSS (UK)
Professor Robert E. Warner, Dean of Humanities,
University of Chester

1

Introduction

MOHAMMAD S. SEDDON & FAUZIA AHMAD

The modern world presents a series of complex, conflicting scenarios and possibilities for young people, and for young Muslims in particular. Many Muslim societies display a 'youth bulge', where more than half of their populations are under the age of 25, a demographic reality mirrored in minority Muslim communities living in the West. An increasingly globalized western culture is rapidly eroding traditional ideas about society, from the family to the state. At the same time, rampant materialism is creating a culture of spiritual emptiness in which demoralization and pessimism easily find root. For young Muslims, these challenges are compounded by a growing sense of alienation as they face competing ideologies and divergent lifestyles. Muslim youth are often idealized as the 'future of Islam' or stigmatized as rebelling against their parental values and suffering 'identity crises'. These experiences can produce both positive and negative reactions, from intellectual engagement, social interaction and increasing spiritual maturity to emotional rejectionism, immersion in narrow identity politics and violent extremism. However, it is clear that the optimism of most young Muslims is best nurtured in an environment of opportunity, where ambitions and aspirations can exist as an achievable reality. But at the social and political levels, opportunity crucially depends on the existence of both equality and inclusivity, as well as the vision and determination within the community and the establishment to tackle educational underachievement. This publication is a collection of chapters largely based on original conference papers delivered at the international conference, 'Muslim Youth: Challenges, Opportunities and Expectations', organized jointly by the Association of Muslim Social Scientists (AMSS UK) and the Department of Theology and

Religious Studies, University of Chester, and held at the University of Chester from 20 to 22 March 2009. The featured chapters in this edited volume seek to discuss the central issues currently facing young Muslims, both locally and globally, and the contributors include academics, educationalists, youth work practitioners and youth work institutions and organizations at national (UK) and international levels.

Much has been researched and written on issues relating to Muslim youth, but relatively little of such works has been produced *by* Muslim youth themselves. In its limited capacity, this publication, and the international conference which precipitated it, seeks to redress this imbalance. Telling young people what they should and should not do has always been a far easier pursuit than listening and responding appropriately to their actual needs, desires and aspirations. Consequently, in the absence of any listening or responding, the issues and expectations of young people remain a silent and disempowering narrative. This sad reality could not be truer than in the specific case of young Muslims. The *Zeitgeist* of the current age sees young Muslims constitute a part of the collective fears of western liberal democratic societies, whether as perceived 'fifth column' religious terrorists in the western minority context, or as pro-democracy radicals at the front line of the 'Arab Spring' revolutions sweeping across the Middle East. What is absent from the academic studies and research, political policies and legislation and the daily media reports and representations of young Muslims globally, is the youth narrative. Questions such as what exactly is it that these young people want? Why do they behave in the ways that they do? And what do we need to do to engage and re-enfranchise them? – all seem obvious and legitimate questions to ask. But who exactly answers these questions, and how do these questions avoid becoming convoluted and complex discussions largely centred on the interrelationships of authority, agency and power?

This book attempts to tackle some of these difficult questions and discussions – not by politely circumnavigating this problematic terrain, but, rather, by confronting the issues head on. The contributors who have boldly undertaken this endeavour come from a range of backgrounds: Muslims and non-Muslims, academics and youth work practitioners, the young and the young-at-heart! However, despite their diverse backgrounds, what the contributors share in common are their knowledge, expertise and their empathy towards young Muslims. Hence, this volume offers a multi-dimensional approach to the key issues affecting young Muslims. What is clear from the collected chapters is that while religiosity for young people is generally expressed as a matter of personal or even private choice, usually activated by circumstantial experiences, for young Muslims, this is no longer the case. A series of 'landmark events' which have been identified and described by Muhammad Anwar as, 'events, national and international which are specifically relevant to them' (2003, p.60) – all detrimentally negative in the socio-political 'placing' of minority Muslims – have precipitated a particular form of 'anti-Muslimness', which is now understood by the generally accepted definition 'Islamophobia'. The framing of Muslims through the ever-expanding Islamophobic discourses no longer affords Muslim identity the secular privilege of being latent or private. The cumulative effects of Islamophobia is manifest in the complex issues of Muslim youth identity constructions, religiosity, education, employment, loyalty and belonging, cultural difference and resistance, racism, discrimination, social exclusion, integration, assimilation and segregation, to name but a few of the pertinent issues studied in this volume. The eidetic approaches adopted in this publication, beyond the specifics and particularities of the individual studies, all seek to offer an empowering 'self-narrative' for young Muslims and the complex and diverse challenges, opportunities and expectations that they experience and articulate.

This publication is presented in four parts, each representing broad areas of youth-related issues covered by the contributors. Part I, 'Muslim Youth: Negotiating Local and Global Contexts', begins with Saeed A. Khan's chapter, 'The phenomenon of serial nihilism among the British Muslim youth of Bradford, England', which engages with the complex issue of identity constructions among young British Muslims, asserting that the identity crisis facing British Muslim youth is often framed as a proverbial 'tug-of-war' between Muslim society and the dominant British culture. The chapter argues that such a compelling 'choice' for a generation that has only known one religion, one nationality and one country of domicile, leads to identity schizophrenia. Khan's study notes that for the majority who are unable to choose between religion and the dominant culture, there appears to be a growing trend among British Muslim youth in rejecting both Muslim faith tradition and British culture, what he terms a 'dual nihilism'. Such an analysis refutes the commonly held trope of British Muslim alienation being an entirely 'Islamist' narrative. Conversely, the chapter analyses dual nihilism among young British Muslims in Bradford, tracing the emergence of a double sense of alienation, explored through a series of interviews with Muslim youths of South Asian origin. The study investigates the causes of this sense of alienation, the ideological and intellectual influences and the opinions of the youth themselves as to possible solutions. The chapter also examines the challenges facing both British society and the Muslim community to reintegrate and re-enfranchise the youth. Attention is given to the common factors and the approaches that communities may take in an effort to re-engage young British Muslims.

The second chapter, written by Ihsan Yilmaz, 'An analysis of the factors that pave the way for the radicalization of British Muslim youth in Britain *vis-à-vis* vulnerability to extremist ideologies with a specific focus on the Hizb-ut Tahrir, contrasting the British case with the Uzbek, Turkish and Egyptian cases. In the British case, Yilmaz asks why the Hizb-ut Tahrir, which has had limited influence on the hearts and minds of the Muslim youth in autocratic countries, has been more influential in a western democracy where moderation of extremist ideologies through democratic learning should normally take place as the political science literature suggests. From a comparative perspective, the chapter looks at the issues of detraditionalization, alienation, marginalization, discrimination, socio-economic and political deprivation and the impact of the British foreign policy on young British Muslim minds. Moreover, the lack of production of any relevant contemporary Islamic knowledge and the dearth of local Islamic leaders with compatible discourses that can appeal to the Muslim youth in today's Britain are also analysed in the context of the chapter.

Moving from the global to the local, Part II, 'Identity and Belonging', explores the complex issues of Muslim youth identity constructions and begins with the chapter 'Muslim migrant youth: descriptive factors related to acculturation and psychosocial adaptation', written by M. Taqi Tirmazi, Altaf Husain, Fatima Mirza and Tasanee R. Walsh. This chapter explores how recent events have spawned increased scrutiny of the Muslim community, but very little is known about the mental health and well-being of Muslim migrant youth in the US. The chapter is based on empirical research that employed a mixed method study in order to explore the experiences of Muslim migrant youth in the US. The research sample included 175 Muslim youths between the ages of 13 and 21. The survey utilized standardized instruments to assess family cohesion, social support, religiosity, perceived discrimination, acculturation, self-esteem and depression in the sample. Following the self-administered survey, focus groups were conducted to attain an in-depth understanding of their experience. The data suggests that Muslim migrant youth had normal levels of family cohesion, social support and self-esteem while having high levels of religiosity, perceived discrimination and depressive symptoms. The data also revealed that Muslim youth face challenges in their identity development, socialization with peers, in educational settings and in the ethnic culture of their family and religious community. This chapter provides insight into the adaptation of Muslim youths within their perceived environmental settings, and also suggests that culturally sensitive programs and future research on this unique and understudied population is greatly needed.

From the particularities of Muslim youth issues in the US, Yahia Baiza's chapter 'Religion, language or ethnicity? Hybridized identity among the Isma'ili youth of Afghanistan in Germany', examines youth identity constructions among Afghan Isma'ili Muslims in Germany. Germany is home to the largest number of Afghan migrants in Europe, which is composed of various ethnic, linguistic and religious groups. Ethnically, these are divided between the major groups of Pashtun, Tajik, Hazara, Uzbek, Turkoman, and Hindus; each possessing its own language, such as Pashto (Pashtun), Farsi (Tajiks and Hazaras), Uzbeki and Turkomani (Uzbeks and Turkoman), and Panjabi (Hindu). Baiza's paper examines the role of religion, language and ethnicity in the formation of identity among the Afghan Isma'ili community in the city of Essen – the largest concentration in Germany – and examines whether factors such as religion, language and ethnicity have an influence in shaping the youth identity among the Afghan Isma'ili community in Germany. His chapter begins with a hypothesis that the Afghan Isma'ili youth in Essen possess a hybridized identity, which could be understood as the combination of an emerging identity in Germany and the existing indigenous identity transferred to them through their parents and community. However, the chapter does not aim to determine or take for granted either of the two identities, and instead explores if such a hybridized identity exists among the Afghan Isma'ili youth and how the youth generation in the Afghan Isma'ili community define their own identity. The chapter then examines which of the three factors – religion, language and ethnicity – has a determining influence on the formation of identity among the targeted community.

In Chapter 6, 'Turning to my Religion', Muhammad G. Khan's explores key inter-relational issues of allegiance, alliance and authority in the context of an apparent heightened religiosity among young British Muslims. Khan asserts that the phrase 'turning to religion' denotes the confessional and physical dimensions of religiosity as a new manifestation of what he terms the 'intrinsic and extrinsic' motivations that inform this visible Muslim youth paradigm shift. In his examination of the subtle dichotomies involved in developing work with young people, Khan scrutinizes youth work practices, policies, management and developing youth work approaches, as well as the issues and realities that affect young people's lives, as revealed by such practices. By employing an analytical approach, Khan posits that key insights which help to articulate 'what is happening in them and to them' can be gleaned. This chapter maintains that the questions that youth work asks should be relevant to the questions that young Muslims ask of themselves in the context of the 'push and pull' factors – namely, family, media, society, peers and so on – that constantly disrupt their identity facets. The backdrop to these 'intrinsic and extrinsic' religious and cultural identity formations – for instance, 9/11 and 7/7, radicalism/terrorism, the 'Islamification' [sic] of UK and Europe, headscarves, Danish cartoons – are used to typify the cause of division and moral panic that challenge the values of liberal democratic societies. In such societies, where religion is in danger of becoming a 'faded cultural memory', Khan's chapter seeks to explain why young Muslims appear to constantly challenge a supposedly secular society and the liberal values that underpin it.

Part III, 'Education and New Media', examines Muslim youth achievements, pedagogy and representations in both tertiary and higher education, and begins with Fauzia Ahmad's chapter, '"Growing up under lockdown" or "educational pioneers"? Challenging stereotypes of British Muslim women in higher education', which engages with young British Muslim women and how they are received through their experiences and achievements in higher education. Beyond the often rigid stereotypes of the identities of women of South Asian origin and their families, which frequently situate the women as 'victims' and recipients of patriarchal family impositions and the patriarchs as being oppressive and restrictive of their daughters' education, Ahmad's study instead explores Muslim women's motivations and routes into higher education, arguing that higher education provides an empowering personal and social commodity and a means to upward social mobility. Ahmad asserts that the value that Muslim women attribute to their higher education experiences offers new challenges to unfounded perceptions of such women. This chapter is informed through an ethnographic study which includes semi-structured interviews that explore Muslim women's pathways into higher education and the impact of educational success on their families. In doing so, Ahmad's study seeks to interrogate the legitimacy of deterministic and racist binarized discursive formations; as women with fixed religious and cultural identities or as rebels and 'tearaways' from their families, cultures and religion. Consequently, this chapter asserts that the recognition of some of the barriers young British Muslim women can experience in their educational journeys should no longer be viewed through the under-researched and misguided representations, and that more needs to be done to ensure that those responsible for the admission of students into higher education and careers guidance do not rely on outmoded stereotypes of Muslim women.

Seyfeddin Kara's chapter, 'Muslim youth at university: a critical examination of the British higher education experience', is a reflection of research that was conducted by the Islamic Human Rights Commission (IHRC), published in 2009. The research followed a sociological approach based on a quantitative survey and qualitative interviews. All the respondents were from diverse ethnic backgrounds and the level of their religiosity and identification with Islam was also diverse, ranging from devout practitioners to cultural and secular Muslims. The chapter, based on the findings of the original research project, reflects the experiences of Muslim youths in the British higher education system and challenges that they face being members of a faith community. The chapter critically examines 'British multiculturalism' in terms of dealing with Muslims in general and with Muslim youths in particular. In the process, the traditional understanding of 'secularism' and 'race' (ism) are examined as the chief obstacles to understanding the feelings of British Muslim students, and thus, to creating a harmonious society wherein every component of a multicultural society is represented and accommodated on equal terms.

Continuing the subject of young Muslims and education, Christopher Bagley and Nader Al-Refai's chapter, 'Muslim youth and citizenship education: idealism, Islam and prospects for successful citizenship education', focuses on the report findings from five 'best practice' Muslim secondary schools, and five state schools attended by a number of Muslim pupils in North-West England. These are 'best practice' schools with regard to their delivery of Citizenship Education (CE) following guidelines of the Crick Report, and the Qualifications and Curriculum Authority (QCA). Their study, conducted through questionnaires and interviews completed by pupils, teachers and a number of community leaders, looks at how Muslim and state school pupils (both Muslim and non-Muslim) perceive CE, and how it influences their views of society and their role within it. The chapter examines the teaching of Islam and whether it is suited to the principles of CE, arguing that it can produce pupils who are idealistic about their participation in society as moral individuals. The study asserts that, in state schools, Muslim pupils bring to CE an ethos which often reflects their religious background, concluding that CE can be successfully delivered in secondary-level Muslim faith schools. However, the chapter cautiously argues that citizenship as a subject needs a more prominent place in the curriculum, requiring further definition in terms of curriculum materials and in its integration with Islamic studies.

The final section of this edited volume, Part IV, 'Methodologies of Engaging', offers insights into 'best practices' of engaging with young Muslims, ranging from professional youth work practices and methods to reflective self-narratives and traditional approaches from Islamic primary sources. It opens with Gill Cressey's chapter, 'Activity and alterity: youth work with Muslim "girls"', which examines how young Muslim women in the UK are trapped in dominant narratives that stereotype and diminish them as 'other' in European society. For many, this alterity is compounded with other ways in which they are treated as different. Alterity means categorizing someone and thereby labelling and diminishing them; whereas recognition involves being aware of issues of similarity and difference individually and culturally and being confident and respectful in the process. Drawing on constructivist theories, this chapter critiques the activity programmes designed by youth workers for young Muslim women, who are frequently referred to as 'girls'. The object of such curricula is explored against the socio-cultural context of Muslim communities in the UK. Discourses that assign social positions to Muslim 'girls' are critically debated and case-studies of activity programmes form the empirical base of the chapter. This chapter argues that while some activities fall into the trap of providing entertainment and learning that perpetuate stereotypes, others attempt to flout stereotypes in such an obvious way that the stereotypes remain a reference point. The chapter concludes with a discussion of what constitutes an approach that affords positive recognition and personal development to young Muslim women.

In his chapter, 'Youth work and Islam: a growing tradition', Brian Belton seeks to generate a sense of the development of youth work with young Muslims in North and East London over the last 40 years via autobiographical and narrative research, which includes analysis of the life-stories of Muslims growing up in the area and their encounters with youth provision. Belton recalls how some of the respondents have become youth work professionals, and his chapter draws particular attention to the relatively long history, engagement and relationship that Muslims have had with youth work provision in these areas of London, largely with the 'mainstream' of local youth services. The chapter offers an analysis of the impact that youth work has had on those concerned, and it highlights how Islam has influenced the sphere of practice of particular workers and the way in which insights drawn from Islamic teachings can reshape current practice on a generic basis. In so doing, this chapter posits that Muslim beliefs are more relevant and appropriate than some of the more dated theories and deficit-oriented philosophies which can be found in the literature surrounding the practice of informal education and youth work.

Arif Fitzsimon's chapter, 'Training Muslim Youth to be "*Khateebs*"', introduces the growing phenomenon of voluntary *khataa'ib* (plural of *khateeb*), meaning a person who delivers the religious sermon (*khutbah*) of the Friday congregational prayer of the Islamic faith, to state schools and higher educational institutes across Britain and Europe. His chapter focuses on the *khateeb* provision offered by the Muslim Youth Foundation in Manchester, UK. The Muslim Youth Foundation was founded in 1983 in the heart of Manchester's city centre, and it initiated two groundbreaking approaches in Muslim youth work. The first was in establishing that all of its youth programmes are in the English

language in order to facilitate a common communication in the
lingua franca of the diverse Muslim youths of the city, whose
cultural origins include South Asia, Arabia, Africa, Turkey and
Eastern Europe. The second was in its approach to the facilitation
of youth programmes; study circles, karate, *qiyam ul- layl* ('night
prayer' vigil) programmes and youth camps. Over the years,
several Muslims who were active in voluntary Muslim youth work
within Manchester later became organizers and trustees of the
Muslim Youth Foundation, and the work of the organization has
recently become largely project-based. One of its more significant
projects is the *Khateeb* Rota, which was established in the late
1980s, providing regular speakers (*khaata'ib*) to prayer halls,
universities, hospitals and schools across Manchester for Friday
prayers. All the Friday *khutabaat* (sermons) are in English in a
total of eight locations which cater for more than 4000 Muslims
with the average age being 23. Fitzsimon's chapter informs us
that the Muslim Youth Foundation is currently developing a next
generation of *khataa'ib* by providing training for local Muslim
youths ranging from university students to the local Muslim
communities. The chapter presents an overview of the work of
the Muslim Youth Foundation and its achievements in faith-based
approaches in youth work, with a particular focus and specific
exploration on the training potential for new *khataa'ib*.

In the final chapter, 'Engaging with young Muslims: some
paradigms from the Qur'an and *Sunnah*', Mohammad S. Seddon
undertakes a 'time-space' application of Islam's primary sources. The
chapter engages with a textual analysis of how theological paradigms
can be applied to specific contemporary issues facing young Muslims,
particularly within the western minority community context. His
chapter endeavours to harmonize traditional approaches in *usul
al-fiqh* (Islamic theological jurisprudence) and 'best practices' within
current models of Muslim youth work practices. Seddon examines
two key areas pertinent to the experiences of a significant number
of Muslim youths: alcohol and drugs, and sex and relationships. By
employing Qur'anic and Prophetic examples in dealing with such
sensitive issues, the chapter argues that the paradigms contained
within Islam's primary sources, when understood and engaged with
through the specificity of a 'time and space' context, allow for an
empathetic, religiously and culturally sensitive and incremental
approach to Muslim youth work.

The editors hope that this collection will be a constructive addition to the continuing discourses on Muslim youth, and that this publication will serve to offer a variety of perspectives on some of the contemporary debates on the subject matter. Finally, we would like to offer our thanks to all of the contributors for their efforts in this volume; we are sure that their collective work will serve as a useful reference source for those interested in engaging with Muslim youth issues.

Reference

Anwar, M. (2003), 'British Muslims: socio-economic position', in M. S. Seddon, D. Hussein and N Malik (eds), *British Muslims: Loyalty and Belonging*. Markfield: The Islamic Foundation.

PART ONE

Muslim Youth: Negotiating Local and Global Contexts

2

The phenomenon of serial nihilism among British Muslim youth of Bradford, England

SAEED A. KHAN

Introduction

The identity crisis facing British Muslim youth is often framed as a proverbial tug-of-war between Muslim society and the dominant British culture. There are voices in each community that espouse the incompatibility of the two significant markers of the youths' identities, leading to calls for the rejection of one paradigm in favour of the other. For a generation that has only known one religion, one nationality and one country of domicile, such a compelled 'choice' leads to identity schizophrenia. Unable to choose between religion and the dominant culture, there appears to be a growing trend among British Muslim youth to reject both their Muslim faith tradition as well as their British culture. Created by a resignation that the two aspects of their life may indeed be irreconcilable, these youth are now engaged in a dual nihilism. Such an analysis refutes the commonly held trope of British Muslim alienation being an entirely 'Islamist' narrative.

This chapter seeks to provide an analysis of the phenomenon of serial nihilism among British Muslim youth in Bradford. The emergence of a multi-layered sense of alienation, explored through a series of interviews with the South Asian Muslim youth in the city, provides a microcosm for British society as a whole, and investigates the causes, the ideological and intellectual influences and the opinions of the youth themselves as to possible solutions to this sense of alienation. This paper shall also examine the issues facing both British society as a whole and the Muslim community in particular, in their attempts to reintegrate and re-enfranchise the youth. Attention shall be paid to the common factors and approaches that the communities share and may take, and will also assess the distinctive challenges of the groups and the impact of these differences on re-enfranchisement of British Muslim youth. These assertions about the identity negotiations of the subject community are based upon this author's research and are localized to the Bradford area. Given the diversity and complexities of Asian Muslim life in the UK and its variations from one city to the other, this research should not be construed to essentialize the Asian Muslim experience throughout the UK.

Geographical area of research

The research was conducted in the Metropolitan Bradford area in Great Britain during the summer of 2006. The region is situated in the northern industrial epicentre of Britain with a population size (according to the 2001 Census) at nearly half a million. Bradford has one of the largest Muslim populations outside London at just over sixteen per cent. Social deprivation in the area is significant with high unemployment rates despite a strong manufacturing base.[1] The overwhelming majority of this community is Pakistani in origin, and more specifically, from Mirpur. Many families migrated to Bradford in the 1950s and 1960s due to certain push factors that emerged in Pakistan, namely, the construction of dams near many people's homes. The result was the flooding of several hundred villages and the displacement of their denizens. The demand for menial labour in

Britain at the time, coupled with the relative ease of movement within the Commonwealth, served as pull factors and facilitated the migration of thousands of Mirpuris to Bradford, a city in need of workers.

Study sample and methodology

The field work for this project was conducted in the Bradford area and spanned a period of several days in July 2006. Data were collected through interviews with several young Muslim people of Pakistani heritage. These interviews were conducted using a sample of 52 second-generation young British Muslim men living in Bradford. It is acknowledged that this sample does not reflect the diversity of the Asian Muslim experience in the UK, though one may argue that it is a representative group of young Bradford Asian Muslim men. The topics covered in these interviews included the interviewees' perceptions of their lives a year after the '7/7' bombings; their opinions of British society and their interaction with both other Muslims as well as non-Muslims; their level of interaction within Islamic centres, such as mosques and social gatherings; and their relationship with their parents and interaction within their respective homes. Most were born and raised in Britain (all others immigrated to Britain before the age of five), and were in their early 20s. All identified themselves as Sunni Muslim according to the religious tradition practised in their households. Each interviewee was fluent in English, although each spoke a patois of working class northern, industrial English, punctuated and interspersed with several Punjabi colloquialisms. I encountered these individuals randomly while walking through Bradford and, after gaining their confidence, engaged in several conversations, ranging from one to two hours each. Initial apprehension during these interviews was due to a suspicion on the part of the interviewees as to my true intentions. Some were concerned that I was with one of the security or intelligence services, either British or American. After assuring them that I was merely an academic and researcher, they felt comfortable enough to engage in conversation.

The South Asian Muslim community in Great Britain

Despite a centuries-old legacy of interaction and encounter between Britain and Islam, Muslim settlement in palpable and measurable terms has occurred only since the middle of the nineteenth century (Gilliat-Ray, 2010). These communities, especially those from colonial India, began to develop throughout the twentieth century. Although the presence of South Asian Muslims in Great Britain predates the independence and subsequent partition of India, the community did not develop a critical mass until after World War II, when large numbers of Pakistanis arrived to avail of Britain's need for menial labour. Many workers came alone, leaving their families behind. Economic realities, alien culture and restrictive immigration policies all contributed to family disruption and detachment. The reality of being 'strangers in a strange land' was exacerbated by the fact that many Pakistani labourers ended their workday and returned to an empty home where consortium and family support were notably absent. As all emotional bonds were located in Pakistan, many workers never oriented themselves to consider Britain to be home, whether in an indefinite or in a permanent manner.[2] They maintained the economic necessity to remain in Britain only to the extent that it would yield financial benefit, most of which was immediately sent back to family members a continent away.

Opportunities for upward mobility were scarce for Pakistani workers, given the wage limitations and the difficulty to effectively save funds that could be used to acquire financial roots in Great Britain. A significant portion of each pay check would find its way to Pakistan, leaving little remaining to invest in anything beyond the austere rental flat that epitomized living conditions for many labourers. (Khan, 1990) Without a financial stake in the country and local community, many Pakistanis living in Britain during the 1960s and 1970s grew more alienated and isolated, and began to regard Britain as being less a home than as merely a temporary 'host' country.[3] However, this attitude of alienation among the (mostly male) Pakistani workers changed with evolving job opportunities and economic conditions, as well as with the repatriation of their wives and children in Britain. The establishment of rela- tively stronger roots and the support system of a now burgeoning

Pakistani community mitigated the sense of dislocation, even if it did not necessarily cultivate a greater sense of belonging to Britain (Shaw, 2000).

Postcolonialism and perceptions of Asians in Great Britain

Muslims have been present in Great Britain for over 200 years (Ansari, 2004). British exposure to the Islamic world became pronounced at this time through the nation's colonial campaigns, which took British control and rule to many areas inhabited by Muslims. British attitudes towards Muslims were primarily a function of ethnic, racial and class factors, not necessarily born of religious-based difference. The subjugation of South Asians during the colonial era demonstrated an air of British superiority in the face of ruling a population for whom the resources of the land were of paramount importance. British ethno-chauvinism continued even after the independence of Pakistan and India in 1947 (Ahmed, 1994). As with its other former colonies, the newly founded South Asian nations were welcomed into the British Commonwealth to secure amicable relations for trade and diplomatic purposes. Members of the Commonwealth enjoyed certain privileges *vis-à-vis* Great Britain in matters such as travel and commerce within the former empire. The acculturation to a British paradigm left an indelible mark on former subjects of the realm, notwithstanding the treatment they received under British colonial rule. Despite challenges and adversities caused by their colonial rulers, many South Asian Muslims living in former colonies throughout Asia and Africa still instinctively and reflexively regarded Great Britain in idealistic terms,(Ahmed, 2004).

The colonial legacy and the steady shift in the demographic realities of British society have tested the parameters of multiculturalism in Great Britain (Harris, 1995). Over the past 30 years, an entire generation of South Asian Muslims has been born and reared in the country, with scant first-hand reference to the country of its ethnic heritage.[4]

Instead, decades of reticence and/or hostility towards South Asian Muslims has yielded responses that were both natural and, arguably, inevitable. Despite an outward promotion of multiculturalism, many South Asian Muslims have felt disenfranchised from British society. Job discrimination and barriers to social mobility have been rampant. At the same time, however, there has been an effort by some sectors of Muslim Britain to repel what is perceived to be a society with attitudes that are inimical to Islamic tenets, thereby further relegating British Muslims into virtual ghettos (Haddad, 2002).

Many Asian Muslims wax nostalgic about a bygone era and, especially, a bygone place – namely, their former homeland. The difficult economic conditions in Britain, the fear of losing cultural, and perhaps religious, identity as well as experiences and encounters with xenophobia all influenced an emotional and psychological orientation that looked eastward (Poole, 2002). In the process, they maintained romanticized views of India and Pakistan as they recalled a more idyllic time when they were younger and the era was one of innocence and social harmony (Brah, 1996). The distance between Great Britain and the Indian subcontinent would conceivably allow many British Muslims to travel back and forth with relative ease and frequency, but the wage scale and limited opportunities for social mobility impeded its fruition. Even though the South Asia of their youth had generally disappeared or was unattainable financially, these migrants would still see their former homelands through a very narrow lens, ignoring many of the obvious flaws that existed in those societies. This myopia often accompanied the wholesale essentialization of societies: 'Britain is corrupt and South Asia is pure' (Lewis, 2002). As a result, many Asian immigrants felt little incentive to integrate or assimilate into British society in any meaningful way:

> I would never say I am English because I am not, and I am sure my daughter will grow up with her Pakistani identity because that is what life is. You have to look at what makes up that identity being Muslim. How many times do you hear about Britain accepting Muslims as part of their community . . . but if you start talking to young people they will say they are British Muslim even more so now I think. (Khalid Hussain, age 30, in Abbas, 2005)

The pre-existing racial, ethnic and cultural chasm between Asian Muslims and Britons was further exacerbated by the Asians' focus on an imagined and idealized South Asia.

Perceptions of British Muslim youth in Bradford

Asian Muslims face considerable backlash and anti-migrant rhetoric from significant sectors of mainstream British society. Nativist discourse is commonplace, rampant and, in many cases, institutionalized. However, second-generation migrants also face a backlash from within their own community, which regards them as being as inauthentic to their cultural identity as the dominant society views them. The Bradford youth who were the subject of this research study epitomize the various confusions, complexities and contestations in the area of identity construction for the British Muslim, especially for those who fall within the ethno-religious profile of the 7/7 bombers. Their perceptions of British society, their ethnic community and themselves is expositive on the issue of identity and even more revealing in understanding the role of Islam as a primary identity and ideological marker.

The Bradford riots of 2001 occurred three months before the 9/11 attacks in the United States. Although there is no connection between these two incidents, the proximity of these two events shone a particular light of scrutiny upon the Muslim youth involved in the violence in Bradford. While these troubles were inherently precipitated within the context of racial politics, a religious impetus was also explored within the backdrop of Islamic political radicalization. Research examining the Bradford community, however, asserted that while some participants in the riots may have identified themselves as religious, their faith was not a motivating factor in their actions, especially as the majority of rioters were not religious (Abbas, 2007). In the case of the present research, this assessment does not appear to be relevant. None of the individuals interviewed participated in the 2001 riots; they characterized themselves as being neither violent *nor* religious. Nonetheless, the current climate that tends to reduce British Muslim youth to solely a security issue has led to an exploration of religious explanations where none seem to exist (Gilliat-Ray, 2010).

A common debate focuses upon whether British Muslim youth find themselves caught between two cultures: their ethno-religious Pakistani Muslim culture and that of the dominant British society around them (Ali, Kalra and Sayyid 2008). A relatively parochial community, the Bradford Muslim youth have been the subject of considerable analysis by researchers, especially to ascertain whether they conform to such general theoretical constructs. Yet it appears as though the young people encountered for this research project do not readily fit this paradigm. The 'between two cultures' model implies a metaphoric tug-of-war in which these individuals are consciously contending and feeling the pull that each side, qua culture, is exerting (Seddon, Hussain and Malik, 2004). The model also suggests that the two cultures acting upon these young people are doing so with the goal, 'conscious' or not, of attracting the youth to their respective side. If the quality and scope of engagement of the state and the families of these individuals may serve as any metric, it appears that both are quite ambivalent regarding the acceptance of their respective cultural offerings by the youth.

Regionality is an overlooked identity marker in British discourse. Strong feelings dividing North from South, particularly exemplified by London, separate British non-Muslims just as they may British Muslim youth. In fact, for the Bradford youth, regionality trumps religion as a primary identity marker. It is the source of pride and affirmation of a cursory level of affinity and solidarity with others from the industrial heartland of the country. In addition, the contemporary infatuation with celebrity and notoriety is a compelling and often overlooked dynamic in shaping perception:

> Did you know three out of four of them were from up here, mate? They're famous and they made us famous too, yeah? I mean, no one gives two shits about the North, except for Man U and Oasis, man. These guys made the news, right. (Interview with Samir, age 22: Bradford, July 2006)

Samir's opinion of the London bombers was fascinating in that his admiration for the bombers was not based on ethnic, religious or especially ideological commonality or affinity. Samir did not view the bombers as being martyrs or committing a religious or political act. Rather, Samir was most impressed by his geographic commonality with the bombers. For Samir, they represented 'local boys made good'. Here were a few 'local lads' who got their name in the papers. They had garnered their 15 minutes of fame. Samir was enamoured by the fact that his relationship with the bombers was more neighbourly than brotherly. He exhibited an affinity for them as one would were they to live near a celebrity. A similar reaction may arguably have occurred were Samir to have been speaking about living close to a famous footballer. Samir had no contact with the London bombers, nor did he share any opinions or perspectives with them. It was enough that the often marginalized North in the British imagination had not only produced notoriety for itself, but that it had perpetrated a major act on London – the metropole relative to the provinces.

Identity politics for migrant groups often revolve around the dialectic of assimilation versus segregation or isolation. For second-generation British Muslim youth, such a dynamic would arguably result in a synthetic compromise, where some level of assimilation is coupled with selective separation of cultural space. Yet this compromise is predicated on the agency of the individual in making the choice as to where the line between such a space exists. In the case of the Bradford youth, such agency is deprived as British society has already made the decision *vis-à-vis* the level of acceptability they have, and whether assimilation is even feasible:

> Oh, they're a bunch of wankers, yeah? They keep telling us to sod off. I don't know if there's a single day that I don't hear, 'Paki go home', or 'Fuck off, you wog'. They don't get that I was born here, I've lived here all my life man. I've only been to Pakistan twice in my life cuz of a wedding and me daadi died. I'm gonna live here in Bradford and I'll probably die here too. (Basid: Bradford, July 2006)

Basid's experiences corroborate and confirm similar experiences shared by many Asian Muslims in Britain. Continuing a decades-long legacy of anti-Pakistani, anti-Muslim attitudes by the metropole in both colonial times and the post-colonial era, Basid reacts with a fatalistic acknowledgement of both the reality of racism as well as the reality of his own life situation. He is resigned to the fact that he will not be accepted as British, as a visible minority, no matter what his birth certificate and identity card state (Bhabha, 1996). He knows that 'they' will never accept him and so he chooses to reject them as a pre-emptive reaction to the inevitable and very real alienation that he has, does and will continue to experience. Basid makes some effort to distinguish himself from other Asians who have stronger ties to Pakistan, e.g. those who make more frequent trips to the country of their ethnic heritage, but he realizes that it is futile. There is a presumption by the dominant society, inaccurate though it may be, that Basid is yet another Asian who spends summers, Christmas holidays and perhaps even the long weekend, if financially feasible, in the 'homeland'.

Inclination toward jihadism implies some level of connectivity with Muslim institutions, be they local or transnational. The mosque is commonly such a locus or, at the very least, a conduit for the orientation towards a particular ideological strain. Yet the Bradford youth appear to not follow such a trajectory, in fact rejecting it altogether and thus eschewing jihadist tendencies as well:

> Who goes to the mosque, mate? Do you? The mullah don't speak our language, yeah? They bring some fuckin' villager over here and he get up there and tell us every Friday that we're shite and we're a bunch of wankers and we chase birds all day long and we aren't good Muslims. Who needs it man? I know my shit . . . I know how to live in the UK. That fucker hasn't been here for more than a few years and he thinks he knows where it's at? He can fuck off, yeah? He can't tell me what to do. Me and my mates like it out here better, yeah? (Interview with Jaleel, age 22, Bradford, July 2006)

Contrary to conventional tropes of British Muslim youth flocking to the mosque for ideological succour and radicalization, the above-stated quotation asserts an alternative narrative. Many youths feel alienated from the messages espoused from the pulpit. Mosque culture may appear ethnically similar, but the differences begin to appear from that point onward. The imam is a migrant, but is more of a migrant than the youth are. There is a linguistic as well as a cultural disconnection between the religious leader and the younger segment of the congregation, as thick accents and sermons privileging Pakistani issues leave the youth with an abject lack of contextuality. Lamentations over a great and lost civilization, coupled with a continued contempt for the British believed to be responsible for the post-colonial Pakistani morass, leave the youth with little inspiration. Perhaps worst is the derision from the community's leadership of a lost, wayward and barely redeemable youth who are consigning their futures and afterlife to doom by descending further into the British cultural abyss. For many youths, the answer is quite simple: disengagement from the mosque and all it represents.

While it may be questionable as to how obligatory mosque attendance may be among the youth of Bradford, there remains the belief that at least the home provides sanctuary from alienation. Such a scenario is not always the case, and for many British Muslim youth in Bradford, the home brings hostility and trauma:

> Me mum loves that PTV shite, man. She watch [sic] it all day long. All I get at home is what some fucker is doing in Lahore or Multan or some shite village . . . I got to call me mates to get the footie scores, man cuz I don't get no telly time at home. I mean, I don't care fuck all what's going on in some shite village in that shite country. I wanna know what's outside my door; me mum's only caring about what's happing over there. She call that her home and I says to her, 'what the fuck you call this place, mum?' It don't feel like home for me, yeah? I mean it's like a little Pakistan in the middle of Bradford. You know what them limeys call this place, yeah? Those fuckers call it Bradistan. That's how me mum's home is, man, all the smells and TV and other shite, yeah? (Interview with Asfhaq, Bradford, July 2006)

Ashfaq's home life is a place of tension and identity crisis. Far from being considered a refuge from a hostile public space, the home is just as inhospitable and unrelated to Asfhaq's experiential reality. Not only is there a pronounced dichotomy between the culture of Britain and the culture of the home, there is, for all intents and purposes, a geographic chasm that is separated only by the front door, though it may as well be the thousands of real miles that lie between Britain and Pakistan. Parental attention is clearly focused on all issues emanating from and occurring in Pakistan, while Asfhaq's mother and father remain ignorant to their immediate surroundings. Given the opportunity cost of selecting ethnic satellite television over local programming, Asfhaq's family is oblivious to its proximal, real world, in favour of the distant, imagined world. Put another way, the imagined Pakistan has become real in the minds of the viewer. Although ethnic TV had its origins and impetus in providing cultural programming for its target audience, it now serves as a categorical substitute for culture itself; that is, local British culture, and even pertinent news that would ostensibly affect their daily lives on a much more personal and profound level. In a sense, Asfhaq's parents are practising their own form of nihilism, rejecting the culture of their domicile. Although their rejection of culture constitutes a rejection of British society *in toto*, it is nonetheless a singular nihilism. They are not only maintaining another identity, i.e. Pakistani-Muslim identity, they are embracing it all the more tightly. Part of this is based on the belief that Pakistan still represents a locus of return, at present as an imagined ideal, but more importantly, as the reified terminus of a life journey, either as a place of retirement or as the site of burial. Neither is deemed to be a viable option for Asfhaq. Pakistan is, at best, the destination for a laborious family village, where he is considered to be inauthentic in the eyes of Pakistanis – a thin simulacrum of what is the 'true Pakistani' who is born, reared and steeped in Pakistan, its culture and its customs. Asfhaq has a rudimentary knowledge of Urdu or Punjabi at best. Attempts to speak the language subject him either to ridicule or the earnest effort of incorporation of choice words, usually profane, with his English. It is here that Ashfaq achieves his closest approach to cultural synthesis – working-class Northern English, with a smattering of Punjabi four-letter words. Language barriers and embarrassment of 'native' culture are two reasons that militate against Asfhaq's receptivity towards the ethnic television that dominates his home. His only option is to withdraw further from both the living room as well as the house, now deemed hostile to his own cultural sensitivities. Rejected from home and, conversely, rejecting what it represents, Ashfaq seeks sanctuary with his 'mates' on the streets of Bradford, enjoying the late sunsets and long evenings of a Bradford summer. This fraternity of similarly situated youths is a function not of religious or ideological affiliation, but, rather, common biographies of alienation and nihilism.

The perception of the Muslim youth of Bradford being 'bad boys' permeates well beyond Yorkshire. Around Britain, the Bradford youth have a reputation for being 'rough' (Hopkins, 2009). Clearly, the manner by which the Bradford youth conduct themselves, especially before the uninitiated and unsuspecting, affirms this sentiment. Those who were interviewed appeared to relish belonging to this construction of a contemporary 'Droog', complete with a patois language and holding dominion over the streets of Bradford.[5]

The identity construction of Bradford Muslim youth is complex and sometimes appears contradictory. After the 2001 race riots and the 9/11 US attacks, the Bradford youth seemed to embrace their cultural and religious heritage, while simultaneously demonstrating their pride for England's placement in the 2002 World Cup, enthusiastically displaying the St George flag publicly. At the same time, however, these youths rejected the Union Jack due to its identification with the British National Party (Abbas, 2005). The effort to reconcile ethno-religious identity with nationality and citizenship was noteworthy, given the aftermath of a particularly turbulent part of Bradford's history. Yet, a year after the 7/7 London bombings in 2005, such attempts to bridge cultural and identity markers seemed absent among the youth interviewed. Instead, a disavowal of both tropes was the common trajectory.

Prospects for improvement: The correlation between engagement and belonging

While the sense of alienation among the Muslim youth of Bradford runs quite high, there exists a sense of optimism that the situation may be rectified by cultivating among the youth a greater feeling of belonging, especially to the British society in which they reside. A key component to the fostering of this greater sense of belonging is civic engagement. In fact, there is evidence that greater religio-communal collaboration has some success in ameliorating the alienation felt by so many Muslims in Britain (Modood and Werbner, 2005).

In addition to civic engagement, there is speculation as to whether the religious leadership can reach the youth. With guarded optimism and an acknowledgement of the arduous task at hand, hope remains that greater cultural literacy and engagement by the ulama will lead to greater receptivity by the Muslim youth. This, in turn, will cultivate a sense of belonging in at least one of their areas of identity contestation (Lewis, 2007). Given the attitudes of the Bradford youth interviewed towards the religious establishment in their community, such hope seems fleeting at best. The level of cynicism and disdain that the youth exhibit towards the mullahs implies that such rapprochement is impossible, not merely improbable.

Other possible enfranchising mechanisms for British Muslim youth would include greater involvement in the country's political process, whether at the grassroots level or beyond. Political participation could serve as a viable counter movement to conventional interactions with mosque leadership (Abbas, 2005). While there are several examples of Muslim involvement in British electoral and political processes, e.g. the number of Muslim MPs, the ability to engage within the system is difficult and even more so for the parochial Bradford community, where many of the youth lack sufficient education credentials.

Conclusion

The current analysis of the disenfranchisement of Muslim youth in Britain is not only incomplete, it is also dangerously misdirected. The events of 7 July 2005 placed attention firmly within conventional tropes of politico-religious discourse. For many British Muslim youths, the issue is not a contestation of Islam versus the West; rather, it is a conflict with both Islam *and* the West. There is a sense of alienation felt from the dominant society. The legacy of postcolonial racism in Britain in relation to the Asian community is well documented and palpable, despite superficial platitudes on multiculturalism. Despite sharing a birthplace and domicile with their fellow non-Asian British citizens, these youths are not considered to be full citizens, fully British and, sometimes, even fully human. The aftermath of 7/7 has further exacerbated the alienation from the dominant society. Despite considering Britain to be 'home' because it is the only home they have known, many British Muslim youth are deprived of their right to feel enfranchised, thereby causing a sense of dislocation from their surroundings. In addition, British Muslim youth feel alienated from their own ethnic/religious community, due in part to a generation gap as well as to a communications chasm between them and their parents. The cultural disparity strongly determines and dictates the relationship across generational lines. For their parents, 'home' is still Pakistan, be it real or an imagined ideal. The youth know only British society as their birthplace and their sole domicile. Parental focus, bordering on obsession, with the 'homeland' manifests itself in anti-British rhetoric, often exclusive consumption of ethnic satellite television in the home and other cultural disassociation with British society.

Within such a domestic milieu, many British Muslim youths are made to feel dislocated from their home life – thereby, in essence, creating the perception that they are no more welcome at home than in Britain as a whole. The discomfort felt within the home space leads many of the male youths to 'hang out on the streets', as evidenced by the ease in finding these individuals to interview. In addition to the cultural chasm that exists between them and their parents, exacerbated by the dominance of Pakistani satellite television in the household, overcrowding and the primacy of feminine modalities in the home are cited as alienating factors (Gilliat-Ray, 2010).

The multi-levelled sense of dislocation felt by British Muslim youth has caused them to develop a rejectionist defence mechanism against both components of their society. This serial nihilism has its antecedent in Nietzsche rather than within an Islamic theological predicate.[6] For these youths, the expressed nihilism resembles a liberation theology, where they consider themselves untethered by any authority, whether socially or theologically. There are therefore no religious leaders or authority figures – be they the local imam or a transnational terrorist 'jihadist' entity such as Al Qaeda – that will necessarily hold appeal or influence over these youths. Similarly, dislocation from one's family and community, as well as from dominant society, augurs the continued inability and ineffectiveness of community and political leaders to have influence over the youth.

The post-7/7 policy implementation by the British government, in particular the PREVENT strategy, produced results that were opposite to those intended. Rather than foster a deeper sense of trust and cooperation between the government and the Muslim community, the chasm of mistrust widened and a greater perception of alienation was internalized by Muslim youth. In fact, these young people were subjected to a further essentialization by media, civic and political voices, who perceived them primarily, if not solely, as a security issue, bereft of complexity and even humanity.[7] Similarly, other voices of criticism emerged about what was seen as a misdirection of public funds for an ultimately ineffective attempt to curb radicalization, which they felt had intensified since the 7/7 attacks.[8]

While a variety of measures have been proposed to facilitate engagement with British Muslim youth in civic, religious and even political arenas, such efforts have either fallen woefully short of the intended objectives or have paradoxically increased feelings of alienation. These measures have attempted to address the three areas of dislocation confronting the youth: state, religious community and family, but with little cause for optimism at present. Due to the fact that some British Muslim youths have succeeded in becoming marginalized from all social boundaries, the ability to re-enfranchise them with the hope of wielding any level of authoritative influence is an open question.

References

Abbas, T. (2005), *Muslim Britain*. London: Zed Books.
—(2007) (ed.), *Islamic Political Radicalism*. Edinburgh: Edinburgh University Press.
Ahmed, A. (1994), *Islam, Globalization and Postmodernity*. London: Routledge.
—(2004), *Postmodernism and Islam*. London: Routledge.
Ali, N., Kalra, V. S., and Sayyid, S. (2008) (eds), *A Postcolonial People*. London: Hurst and Co.
Ansari, H. (2004), *The Infidel Within*. London: Hurst & Company.
Anwar, M. (1979), *The Myth of Return*. London: Heinemann.
—(1998), *Between Cultures: Continuity and Change in the Lives of Young Asians*. London: Routledge.
Bhabha, H. (1996), 'Unsatisfied: notes on vernacular composition', in L. Moreno, and P. Pfeiffer (eds), *Text and Nation: Cross-Disciplinary Essays on Cultural and National Identities*. New York: Camden House.
Brah, A. (1996), *Cartographies of Diaspora*. London: Routledge.
Haddad, Y. (2002) (ed.), *Muslims in the West*. New York: Oxford University Press.
Harris, D. (1995) (ed.), *Multiculturalism from the Margins*. Westport: Bergin & Garvey.
Hopkins, P., and Gale, R. (2009) (eds), *Muslims in Britain*. Edinburgh: Edinburgh University Press.
Khan, M. (1990), 'Macroeconomic policies and the balance of payment in Pakistan: 1972–1986'. International Monetary Fund Working Paper: WP/90/78. Washington, D.C: International Monetary Fund.
Lewis, P. (2002), *Islamic Britain: Religion, Politics and Identity Among British Muslims*. London: I.B. Tauris.

—(2007), *Young, British and Muslim*. London: Continuum.
Modood, T. (2005), *Multicultural Politics*. Minneapolis: University of Minnesota Press.
Modood, T., and Werbner, P. (2005) (eds), *The Politics of Multiculturalism in the New Europe*. Minneapolis: University of Minnesota Press.
Poole, E. (2002), *Reporting Islam: Media Representations and British Muslims*. London: I.B. Tauris.
Seddon, M. S., Hussain, D., and Malik, N. (2004) (eds), *British Muslims Between Assimilation and Segregation*. Leicester: The Islamic Foundation.
Shaw, A. (2000), *Kinship and Continuity: Pakistani Families in Britain*. Amsterdam: Harwood Academic Publisher.

3

An analysis of the factors that pave the way for the radicalization of British Muslim youth from a comparative perspective

IHSAN YILMAZ

Introduction

Disaffection, disenfranchisement and isolation are said to be some of the reasons why some young British Muslims have been radicalized (Abbas, 2007a), and against the backdrop of social alienation and internal disorder, 'Islam has become a template for the culturally confused, a language of protest for the politically frustrated' (Murphy, 2002, p.276).[1] Hizb ut-Tahrir (The Party of Liberation, hereinafter, 'HT') targets frustrated youth who have lost faith in their home country's 'system' (Gruen, 2004, p.116). The party's propaganda was especially attuned to the 'underprivileged, suffering from poor housing, high unemployment and racial discrimination ... [and] the party gives [these] alienated young Muslims a sense of belonging, and an unequivocal answer to their search for an identity' (Taji-Farouki, 1996, p.177). The modern language of HT is more attractive to these young, secularized men than the complex religious formulas of the more traditional mullahs. HT is much less demanding in terms of religious knowledge than other Islamic sects: there is no need to learn Arabic or study the many books of religious scholars deeply. All that a member needs to know is already distilled in a short list of books and pamphlets written in easy-to-understand contemporary idiom (International Crisis Group [ICG], 2003, p.16–17). The main reason for joining seems to be the lack of anything else to do, and the sheer pointlessness of many young men's lives (ibid, p.15). There is no single issue, but there is often a psychological response related to loss of social status, lack of belief in the future and a desire to 'do something' about changes in society that deeply affect people's lives (ibid, p.14). Both radical Islamist groups and white ethno-nationalists are known to focus their efforts on young men between the approximate ages of 16 and 22, and they have analysed the interests of this demographic and have found that much of their time is spent online in chat groups, game-and music-related sites where they can either download music or chat about a particular band (Gruen, 2004).

According to one of its official documents published on its UK website, HT is a global Islamic political organization established in 1953 under the leadership of Taqiuddin an-Nabhani. The current leader of the organization is Ata ibn Khaleel Abu Rushta (HT, 2010; see also Taji-Farouki, 1996). The leader of HT Britain, Jalaluddin Patel, stated in an interview in 2004 that:

> In the UK, HT works on two levels. Firstly with the Muslim community, explaining the duty to work for the Khilafah (Caliphate) state, living by Islam in the West without losing our identity and projecting a positive image of Islam in Western society. Secondly, with the wider community, by articulating the cause of the Muslim world, presenting a case for the Khilafah state as a valid model for the Muslim world.[2]

The official document of the party also confirms:

> In the Muslim world, Hizb ut-Tahrir works at all levels of society to restore to the Muslims a means of living an Islamic way of life under the shade of the Khilafah State (Caliphate) following an exclusively political method. In the West, Hizb ut-Tahrir works to cultivate a Muslim community that lives by Islam in thought and deed, whereby adhering to the rules of Islam and preserving a strong Islamic identity (HT 2010, p. 2).

HT rejects the concept of the modern nation state and has divided the world into provinces (*Wilayah*); a province can coincide with a nation state or a particular region within a state. At the provincial level, there is a committee headed by a provincial representative (Mu'tamad) who oversees group activities. The Mu'tamad is appointed by the central committee (lajnat al-qiyada) of the international party, headed by the supreme leader (Amir) of HT (Taji-Farouki, 1996). Whereas several states have banned HT (for example, Russia and Germany) or made it illegal by non-registration (Uzbekistan), others have a more liberal approach (for example, the United States, Australia, Denmark, the United Kingdom and Switzerland) (Keller and Sigron, 2010).

The party does not find democracy compatible with Islam and also opposes the idea of nation states and opts for a global state, or *ummah* (represented by a *caliphate*), for example:

> Hizb ut-Tahrir is working for an accountable government in the Muslim world, where authority lies with the people, but not for a democracy – where sovereignty is not for the Shariah and the process of legislation is open to external interference . . . Democracy in capitalist states is undoubtedly a ruling system that is distinct from the Islamic ruling system . . . While the capitalist system advocates sovereignty in legislation for humankind, the Islamic system advocates sovereignty in legislation for the Creator (HT, 2010, p. 12).

Nabhani has provided a scheme for achieving the very specific objective for Muslims that he defined, beginning with a small group of committed elite individuals and ending with their successful conversion of the Muslim masses to their vision so that an Islamic revolution could take place (Commins, 1991). The discourse of HT is radical, and there is an uncompromising dimension in its ideology, emphasizing the Islamic legitimacy of offensive (in addition to defensive) *jihad*, thus contradicting the attempts by many Muslim thinkers to present a softer view of Islam (Mayer, 2004).[3] In HT's vision, gradualism is wrong and, similarly, democratic participation is an obstacle in the way towards the caliphate (HT, 2000). HT strongly rejects: 'the error of 'gradualism': the gradual approach to implement Islam is not acceptable in its eyes and betrays a faulty understanding of Islam, since it would mean that Allah has sent something impractical that has to be made practical by Muslims' (HT, 2000, p. 65).

Our analysis here starts with a short elaboration of the socio-economic, political and theological deprivation that the Muslim youth suffers from in Britain, to be followed by brief analyses of Uzbekistan, Egypt and Turkey.

The rise of HT in Britain

Under the leadership of Omar Bakri Muhammad, during the late 1980s and early 1990s, HT grew from a very small organization in Britain to one of the most active Islamist groups in the country (Valentine, 2010). The party has grown by actively recruiting second-generation Muslim immigrants. Since these young Muslims 'did not themselves flee tyrannical states as many of their parents did, they are often more critical of democracy and the inequalities of capitalism and correspondingly attracted to Hizb ut Tahrir's message of a just Islamic order' (International Crisis Group, 2003, p. 11). HT now 'dominates the British Scene' with some 8,500 members in the UK (Leiken and Brooke, 2007, p. 120). It targets British Muslims at further education colleges and institutions of higher education (Ahmed and Stuart, 2009). Since its inception in 1986, HT has followed a centralized recruitment protocol of localized *halaqaat* (small circles consisting of five people) (Taji-Farouki, 1996). In September 1993, HT began openly targeting young second-generation British Muslims on UK campuses and at mosques.[4] It also started holding fortnightly seminars in London in 1989, and in the early 1990s published fortnightly and

quarterly magazines in Arabic, *Al-Khilafa*, and in English, *Al-fajr*
(Taji-Farouki, 1996). In recent years HT's tactics on UK campuses
have become more sophisticated, and the party operates covertly
through front groups (Ahmed and Stuart, 2009). In university
campuses, HT has often operated in groups under other names
such as the 'Thought Society', 'Debating Society', '1924 Society',
'One Nation Society', or the 'Pakistan Society' (Valentine, 2010,
p.7). The party also uses pre-existing networks within British
Muslim communities to propagate its ideology, including the Islam
Channel and Press TV (Ahmed and Stuart, 2009), and it is active
at a grassroots level within British Muslim communities. A party
tactic is to set up small front organizations in local areas in order
to anonymously propagate HT ideology (Ahmed and Stuart, 2009).
Since 2000, the party has further established schools and youth
groups in order to target young British Muslims. It has tended to use
pre-existing networks within British Muslim communities to further
disseminate its message (Ahmed and Stuart, 2009). According to
one of its former senior members:

> The organization's method is to access the individual through
> existing grievances, and then build an ideological framework in
> the recruit's mind. Each recruit must participate in the process
> of 'culturing', which consists of at least one two-hour discussion
> every week that addresses broader political and theological
> matters. (Nawaz, 2008)

Omar Bakri Mohammed, who effectively re-founded HT in London
after he moved there in 1987, broke with HT in 1997 over 'the
methodology'. Omar Bakri, who then founded Al-Muhajiroun
(the Migrants) in London in 1997, disagreed with HT's official view,
which sought to establish 'the Khilafah only in a specific Muslim
country'. By contrast, Al-Muhajiroun 'engage in the divine method
to establish the Khilafah wherever they have members' (Jones and
Smith, 2010, p. 247; Taji-Farouki, 1996, p. 30–1). This implied
that Al-Muhajiroun, with a predominately UK based membership,
aimed to establish a caliphate on UK soil (Connor, 2005). Most
importantly, Al-Muhajiroun believed in 'twinning Da'wa (the
call to Islam) and *jihad*', and for Al-Muhajiroun, *jihad* was an
individual duty beholden on each Muslim, whereas HT holds to
a more traditional conception which stresses the importance of

legitimate authority (Connor, 2005). The present leaders of HT in the UK present a much more moderate message, and have been careful to play down any possible misinterpretation of their ideas, but the basic ideological message remains the same (International Crisis Group, 2003).[5]

Socio-Economic, political and theological deprivation of the British youth in Britain

Socio-Economic deprivation

There is a vast literature that reiterates that socio-economic deprivation is an everyday reality for many Muslims in Britain. The Muslim population in Britain is young and rapidly growing; its socio-economic profile is depressed, marked by the low participation rate of women in the formal labour market, and by high concentration in areas of multiple deprivations (see Peach, 2006). Muslims generally live in areas that are facing high levels of social tension and economic deprivation through direct discrimination and racial hostility (Abbas, 2007a). Evidence from the 2001 Census and Labour Force Surveys shows that the unemployment rate for Muslims was almost three times as high as the rate for whites (Anwar, 2008), or the majority Christian group (Briggs and Birdwell, 2009). Bangladeshis and Pakistanis are two-and-a-half times more likely to be unemployed than the white population and three times more likely to be in low-paid jobs (Samad and Sen, 2007). Muslims also have the youngest age profile of all faith groups; in 2001, one-third (33.8 per cent) were under the age of 16, compared to one-fifth of the population overall (20.2 per cent). The average age is 28, 13 years below the national average (see, in detail, Samad and Sen, 2007). This has a bearing on the extent of political activism within the community, with most being youth-led. Muslims constitute some of the most deprived communities in the UK. Almost one-third of Muslims of working age have no qualifications – the highest proportion for any faith group (Bunglawala et al., 2004). Muslim children experience high levels of the risk factors associated with child poverty (national average figures are shown in brackets): 42 per cent live in crowded accommodation (12 per cent); 12 per cent live in households without central heating (6 per cent) and over one-third – 35 per cent – are growing up in households where there are no adults in employment (17 per cent) (Bunglawala et al., 2004). Muslims are over-represented in the prison system – they constitute 3 per cent of the general population but 9 per cent of the prison population (Briggs and Birdwell, 2009).

It is easy to see that young British Muslims face exclusion, marginalization, disempowerment, media bias, political rhetoric and far right hostility (Abbas, 2007b). A 2001 report from Britain's Home Office shows that Muslims feel discriminated against and that discrimination is becoming more prevalent. For example, 'The majority of Muslim respondents thought that hostility, verbal abuse and unfair media coverage had become more frequent' (Weller, Feldman and Purdam, 2001, p. vi–vii). A consistently higher level of unfair treatment was reported by Muslim organizations than by most other religious groups, and in 2001 the majority of Muslim organizations reported that their members experienced unfair treatment in every aspect of education, employment, housing, law and order and in all the local government services (ibid, p. vii). But little attention is being paid to the widening economic, social and cultural polarities, and continued focus on culture, identity, ethnicity and religiosity *per se* takes attention away from issues such as alienation, exclusion, disempowerment and all sorts of deprivations (Abbas, 2007c). Thus, British Muslim youth experience a sense of dislocation and alienation, perceived or real, which negatively affects their outlook, and these experiences motivate them to seek to 'resolve' domestic and global Muslim issues (Abbas, 2007a, p. 291). Post-9/11 and 7/7 anti-terror legislation has contributed negatively to the British Muslim community. The National Council for Civil Liberties, known simply as Liberty, concluded in a 2004 report that:

> Police powers have been used disproportionately against the Muslim population in the UK. The majority of arrests have been Muslims . . . The way in which anti-terror powers are being used, has led to feelings of isolation amongst many of the 1.6 million Muslims in the UK. There is disillusionment with a Government which, rather than protecting them from this backlash, is effectively criminalizing them as a community. The group as a whole is stigmatized, and Muslims have often described

themselves as feeling 'under siege' . . . The relationship between British Muslims and the authorities is at an all time low . . . The way in which Muslims are being treated by the authorities . . . is making them reluctant to come forward and assist. In addition, the mood of resentment which has developed can foster and encourage extremism amongst a small number of an increasingly marginalized group. (Liberty, 2004, p. 8–9)

As a result, 'the people who are engaging with the fierce debates in and around the mosques of Britain and around the dining tables of Muslim homes are already alienated from white, secular society' (Farrar, 2006, p.104).

Political deprivation

Political deprivation of the British Muslim community is also conspicuous. There were only four Muslim Members of Parliament (MPs) in the House of Commons out of a total of 646 MPs before the most recent elections took place (in May 2010). After the elections, the number of Muslim MPs in the House of Commons doubled – to eight – with the Conservatives gaining their first two Muslim MPs and the Muslim community their first three women MPs, all Labour. However, to reflect the number of Muslims in Britain there should be more than 20 MPs of Muslim origin. There are nine members of Muslim origin in the House of Lords. Again, to reflect the Muslim population there should be at least another 18. Muslims do not feel that they take part in political decision-making processes. That is why a European Union think-tank (European Monitoring Centre of Racism and Xenophobia) recommended in 2005 that 'Member States and the European Institutions should encourage and promote the active involvement of Muslim communities in institutionalized procedures of policy-making and include them in more informal channels of dialogue at European, national and local level' (EMCRX, 2005, p. 6).

British foreign policy is also a contributing factor to political deprivation. International ideas and events impact upon the course and effectiveness of Muslim political activity in Britain for better or for worse (Radcliffe, 2004). There is a feeling among many young Muslims that British and US foreign policy has impacted on the perceptions of already much maligned and disenfranchised young Muslim males who feel they have no voice (Abbas, 2007a). Many Muslims link their perception of discrimination with international affairs, pointing towards a British bias in favour of Israel and against Palestinians (Baran, 2004b). In fact, many within the Muslim community argue that they have failed to effect real change in British foreign policy (Radcliffe, 2004).

This is confirmed by Majid Nawaz who was a long-time member of the British leadership committee of HT. After talking about the socio-economic deprivations that he suffered, he goes on to underline that:

> In addition to these local experiences, there was the international context. In the early 1990s, I associated all of my problems with racism, but the ethnic violence in Bosnia brought religious identity problems to the forefront. As a result, I was confronted with an identity crisis and began to wonder, 'Am I British? Am I Pakistani? Am I Muslim?' At this point, when I was sixteen years old, I encountered a member of Hizb al-Tahrir (HT) who answered these questions by saying that I was a part of the global Muslim community. (Nawaz, 2008)

In many young British Muslims' eyes, 'their imagined *ummah* is besieged and under threat. Foreign policy grievances, coupled with social and cultural, as opposed to purely economic, marginalization supply the fuel that ignites terrorist activities worldwide' (Gerges, 2005, p. 242). Mayer (2004) writes that a party activist explained to him how, 'his political consciousness had been awakened by his attendance as a teenager at Friday prayers in mosques in England, listening to the ever-growing list of Muslims suffering around the world and being prayed for: in Palestine, Afghanistan, Somalia, Chechnya, Kosovo' (p. 23).

As Baran (2004b) underlines, Muslim attitudes towards the US began to change with the declaration of Israel's independence as a state in 1948, and increasingly worsened as more and more Muslims perceived the US to be improperly backing Israel and their own corrupt, repressive rulers. Pakistanis in Britain identify deeply with the plight of Palestinians, Bosnians, Kashmiris, Afghans or Iraqis. The Gulf War, Bosnia, Palestine, Kashmir, Chechnya, September 11, the nuclear confrontation between

India and Pakistan, the wars in Afghanistan and Iraq, have all mobilized young Pakistanis and other Muslims on to the streets of Britain (Werbner, 2004). The major shift in popular opinion against the US started with the Bosnian War. Even secular, non-political Muslims were furious about Western indifference to the mass killings of their co-religionists. The slaughter of Muslims in the heart of Europe was a major turning point for the global Muslim consciousness (Baran, 2004b). US actions in the Israeli–Palestinian conflict were increasingly perceived as biased (ibid). The failure of the international community to effect a resolution of the Palestinian claim has provided an influential, if not vital, recruitment tool for the extremists (Connor, 2005).

HT benefits from the foreign policies of the Western powers. As an official HT document highlights:

'We work to direct the sentiments of Muslims regarding events in the Muslim world into non-violent political work – such as channelling the anger and frustration over events in the Muslim world towards positive political work. Our activities include public protests, petitions, conferences, seminars and roundtable discussions and have been attended by thousands of people. In recent times we have held panel discussions with non-Muslim politicians, thinkers and personalities. These events have helped to overcome the intellectual entrenchment that characterises most of today's debate (HT, 2010, p. 4).

HT claims that the first Gulf War in Iraq, the persecution of Muslims in Bosnia, Somalia, the impact of sanctions on Iraq, a number of confrontations between the West and the Muslim world, current hostilities in Afghanistan and Iraq following the onset of the War on Terror, have all impacted Muslim thinking in Britain and, 'have acted to awaken a consciousness in the Muslim community, triggering concerns about Muslims from either their countries of origin or those to whom they have a sense of religious affiliation' (HT, 2007, p. 12).

While the US has so far not advanced any convincing arguments for either its invasion of Iraq or its subsequent management of the occupation, HT, for its part, has built a strong ideological case (Baran, 2004b). Many Muslims were outraged by President Bush's reference to the war on terrorism as a 'crusade' in September 2001 (ibid, p. 19).

A research report on HT, prepared for a Washingtonian think-tank, advances a number of key foreign policy recommendations to the US, showing that at least some analysts agree that western foreign policy has had an impact on radicalism. First, the report recommends that the US needs to rehabilitate its credibility and moral authority so that Muslims can once again be inspired by the ideals for which the US stands. Second, to change the perception that American foreign policy is 'unjust', the most important step that the US can take is to ensure a two-state solution to the Israeli-Palestinian conflict that will be seen as fair by a majority of Muslims. Third, the US needs to help Muslims improve their socio-economic conditions in visible ways, and in particular should focus on eradicating inequitable wealth distribution, corruption and cronyism (ibid). The US, in many quarters, is no longer seen as a just and moral power and its actions in Iraq are creating, for the first time, a truly global *umma* that shares HT's political views (ibid).

It is striking that in a refusal letter to Zeyno Baran, who argued that HT was a conveyor belt to terrorism, a member of the HT (Abdullah Robin) stated that:

> Were the production of terrorists our goal, we would find it hard to compete with American foreign policy, which Muslims perceive in the same way that Americans perceive the brutal tactics of the English during the War of Independence. A picture, it is said, tells a thousand words; and Muslims have many pictures of US foreign policy in action, from many theatres, over many years. I tend to agree with a recent headline from Robert Fisk, 'What better recruiting sergeant could Bin Laden have than the President of the United States' (HT, 2010, p. 16).

The difficulty in situating UK foreign policy within an account of the radicalization towards violence of some British Muslims, as a means of objectively assessing how it has or has not contributed to that radicalization, pervades many of the analyses that followed the London attacks (Brighton, 2007). Chatham House claimed directly after 7/7 that the war in Iraq made the UK a target and many within the UK domestic security services often express their exasperation for having to pay for what they view as mistakes in British foreign policy (Hellyer, 2008).

Theological deprivation

In addition to socio-economic and political deprivations, theological deprivation is also a major influence in the radicalization of the young British-born Muslims. HT has turned some alienated and disenfranchised young Muslims into, 'fellow radicals in places such as mosques, bookstores, fitness halls, backrooms, garages, basements, prisons and universities where radicals mobilize, socialize, and speak to alienated youths who are engaged in discussion to "catalyze initial interest"' (Wiktorowicz, 2005, p. 5). Lacking social, cultural and economic opportunities, and being disengaged from the political process, these young Muslims find it very difficult to 'connect with rural-born uneducated leaders and elders whose attention is on matters elsewhere' (Abbas, 2007c, p. 731). Muslim 'community' leaders in Britain have usually been 'lay' rather than religious specialists (McLoughlin, 2005, p.58).[6] In the British context, where a majority of ulema and mosque imams are imported from Pakistan, only a few are sophisticated Islamic scholars and their social status is modest (Lewis, 2006, p. 274). Negative perceptions are the staple of many Islamic websites, commenting that teaching methods of imams are characterized by 'the stick not love' (Lewis, 2006, p. 276). However, given that many of them lack a strong understanding of theology, and that the communities in which they live lack a theological infrastructure, many are left to self-declared religious leaders, who provide them with a quick fix for their identity crises while pushing them slowly towards radicalism (Baran, 2004b, p. 59). In general, local Islamic institutions are not fit for purpose, leaving some young Muslims to 'download problematic *fatwas* from websites, with the medium of English used to communicate fanatic ideals with much effect' (Abbas, 2007c, p. 724). Being underserved by mosques and imams, young Muslims go on to form their own study circles, use the internet to access alternative sources of information and utilize modes of communication, such as English, which are familiar to them (Abbas, 2007a, p. 297). According to Abbas (2007c), there are numerous Muslim social scientists and humanities experts, but one cannot easily count on one hand the number of high-profile Muslim theologians who could be regarded as notable. A former senior member of HT also concurs with this: 'Another factor exacerbating my identity crisis was the language barrier between the local imams and me. They were not fluent in English, making it difficult to relate or communicate with them' (Nawaz, 2008). He highlights that:

> My experience in prison was a critical step in my de-radicalization. While in prison, I learned Arabic and was able to read classical Islamic texts as well as interact with intellectuals and dissidents, such as Egyptian opposition leader Ayman Noor who challenged and debated my ideas. (Nawaz, 2008)

Its literature clearly shows that HT is well aware of the above-mentioned socio-economic, political and theological deprivations, and has made use of them:

> We believe our model offers an alternative to these failed strategies of isolation and (varying degrees of) assimilation. Moreover, we offer an alternative to the frustration felt by some people, tasting injustice here, and seeing it in the Muslim world. (HT, 2009, 10)

HT in Uzbekistan, Egypt and Turkey

While 'Uzbekistan is the hub of Hizb ut-Tahrir's activities in Central Asia' (Karagiannis and McCauley, 2006, p. 316), there is not much literature about HT in Egypt and Turkey. Several scholars have noted HT's meteoric rise in popularity in Uzbekistan (Keller and Sigron, 2010). In the country, HT has 'had considerable success in promoting anti-government frames portraying Uzbekistan's political system as illegitimate and corrupted' (Karagiannis and McCauley, 2006, p. 323). Since it operates clandestinely, its membership in Uzbekistan is unknown, but rough estimates of its strength range from 20,000 to 100,000 in Central Asia, most of them being in Uzbekistan (ibid, p. 316). In general, like other Islamist movements, HT has been less successful in recruiting nomadic peoples (such as Turkmen and Kazakhstani), who traditionally have been less religious, and are more successful among the more settled Uzbekistani, Kyrgyzstani and Tajikistani peoples. It is therefore not surprising that HT is strongest in Uzbekistan, with estimates ranging from 7,000 up to 60,000 (Baran, 2004b). Even though 'it has never been proven that Hizb ut-Tahrir has performed any violent or terrorist act in

Central Asia', thousands of HT members have been imprisoned in Uzbekistan (Keller and Sigron, 2010, p. 159).

In totalitarian Uzbekistan, where there is no political opposition, HT has sought to occupy the vacuum in the socio-political sphere (Whine, 2004). The repression of all civilian groupings by the Uzbek state ensured that little religious plurality emerged; instead, the way was prepared for radical groups such as HT (International Crisis Group, 2003). In comparison to the other Islamist groups, HT has offered the most comprehensive and easy to understand answers to a myriad of complex questions resulting from the collapse of the Soviet Union. It has provided a holistic answer to the socio-economic challenges, such as extreme poverty, high unemployment, corruption among government officials, drug addiction, prostitution and lack of education (Baran, 2004b). When HT draws attention to the illegitimacy of the existing political order, the group is making a point that resonates with people of many different political perspectives, social classes, ethnic groups and educational backgrounds (Baran, 2004b). HT activists convey their message in simple terms: poverty and inequality can be addressed once corrupt governments are replaced with the Islamic law. There is widespread support for the criticism that HT levels against corruption, inequality and the repression of devout Muslims. The call for social justice strikes a chord with hundreds of thousands of people (Mukhametrakhimova, 2006).

HT also serves more immediate needs, filling the serious psychological holes of loneliness and aimlessness left in the lives of many Central Asians. In particular, the young acutely feel the lack of a social network, which is neatly provided by HT study circles (Baran 2004b, p. 78–81). HT attracts:

> [. . .] disaffected youth who seek to make a great difference in life. Many may come from the rural and large impoverished families of the hinterland, but many also hail from comfortable urban families. Far from desperation uniting these forces, it is the sincere belief that only they may alter the course of society for the good of all under God's watchful eye. Rebellious youth suffer only from the inability to see the vitality of past practice as well as the meaning with which people imbue old and well-respected practices. (Zanca, 2004, p. 104–5)

Many people, especially the young, have joined HT to learn about Islam (Baran, 2004b). Although 92 per cent of the Uzbeks consider themselves as Muslim, almost half of them have either no religious education or very little knowledge of Islam (Chaudet, 2006). Limited popular knowledge of the traditional and classical orthodox Islam and the post-Soviet identity crisis have benefited political, radical, extremist and unorthodox Islamic movements (Olcott and Ziyaeva, 2008). Due to the Soviet-era repression, there were an insufficient number of native imams and Islamic scholars to instruct people about their indigenous Islamic culture and traditions. The radicals were able to succeed as the rapid Islamization of the region occurred without any oversight or regulation (Baran, 2004b). There was an extensive dissemination of religious extremist publications by international groups seeking to take advantage of the desire for knowledge of Islam among the population (Khusnidinov, 2004). The lack of well-trained imams, capable of refuting the arguments of Islamists, still continues to be one of the major difficulties in confronting their message today (Kalonov and Alonso, 2008).

The Islamist[7] revival in Egypt began in the 1920s but rapidly spread after the early 1970s, reaching its peak in the early 1990s. It consists of several groups, from violent militants to non-violent and gradualist Islamic coalition, and from the individualist Sufi orders to the state's Al-Azhar, the Ministry of Awqaf and the Supreme Islamic Council (Bayat, 1998). Islamism emerged as a reaction to the perceived causes of such a state of deprivation – economic dependency, cultural sell out, and national humiliation, and in view of all the failed ideologies and of the western cultural, political and economic onslaught, Islam was seen as the only doctrine that could bring about a change (ibid). The Society of Muslim Brotherhood (MB) emerged in 1928 when the secular-nationalist Wafdist Party and the Royal family ruled the country. The MB was founded by Hassan al-Banna, in whose view the MB had to be organized as a 'movement' rather than as a 'party', as al-Banna espoused a bottom–up approach and did not believe in the forceful transformation of society by using state power (Haqqani and Fradkin, 2008, p. 14–15).

In Egypt, if the MB is a conservative movement, HT has been 'its opposite: radical and dedicated to the resurrection of the caliphate by overthrowing corrupt Arab states' (Milton-Edwards,

1996, p. 65). HT was banned in Egypt after being implicated in the 1974 coup attempt (International Crisis Group, 2003, 10). The Egyptian government has since arrested suspected party members; and in 1983 the government arrested and charged 60 HT members with working to overthrow the regime, with the aim of establishing the caliphate[8]. Further arrests took place in 2002 for attempting to revive the party in Egypt (International Crisis Group, 2003).

In general, however, party support in Egypt remains weak when compared to competing Islamist groups, such as the MB. HT has not managed to build a large following among Arab Muslims, and its influence in Egypt – where it has managed to survive and operate despite the difficulties – has diminished due to the dominance of the MB (Baran, 2004a). A 1996 analysis states that HT's influence in Egypt has been overshadowed by the wider support that the MB receives, and a 2007 analysis confirms that the MB receives mass support, especially from young people and student activists in Egypt (Zambelis, 2007; see also Taji-Farouki, 1996). Another study concurs that the results of HT work in the Middle East have been largely negligible, and among well-educated Muslims it is seen as a heterodox group with an unacceptable interpretation of much of the original Islamic sources (International Crisis Group, 2003).

HT could not be influential in Egypt as it is in Uzbekistan. Similar to Uzbekistan, while the socio–economic and political deprivation and authoritarianism exist also in Egypt, there is no theological vacuum where the MB has been a solid opposition force with a more or less contemporary, competent and global discourse. In that respect, the Turkish case also shows similarities with the Egyptian one.

In Turkey, the party has been active but has faced repression by the state (International Crisis Group, 2003). HT first made itself known in Turkey in 1967 when it sent some of its publications such as ('HT Presents', 'The Constitution of the Islamic State', 'The Islamic Order' and 'The Vital Problem of Muslims') to journalists, intellectuals and political personalities advocating, *inter alia*, the restoration of the Islamic caliphate.[9] The group had also distributed leaflets in different parts of the country. Security forces moved quickly and soon arrested several Jordanian citizens studying in

different Ankara universities, as well as a group of Turkish citizens
(Cakir, 2004). HT members have been frequently arrested. As early
as 1967, leaders of HT Turkey were arrested. In 1985 and 1986,
security forces captured 42 HT activists distributing booklets
entitled 'The Constitution of HT', in Ankara, Istanbul and Çorum,
and four HT members received four-year prison sentences (ibid,
p. 37). In 2003, Turkish HT 's leader, Yilmaz Celik, 10 and 93
others were arrested (ibid). Despite the setbacks, HT never gave up
on Turkey and continued to maintain a presence in the country.[11] In
July 2009, 200 suspected HT members were arrested and detained.
Some are allegedly linked to the neo-nationalist group Ergenekon,
which was declared a terrorist organization by the Istanbul Chief
Prosecutor's Office, and some of whose members are currently
facing charges of plotting a coup against the government. Thirty-
three out of the 200 detained were arrested as the Istanbul anti-
terrorist unit held a press conference saying they had confiscated
a number of documents linking the suspects to the Islamist group.
Police officials revealed some of the suspects' links with Ergenekon
(Sariibrahimoglu, 2009).

The Turkish case resembles the Egyptian one. Since the practising
Muslims do not suffer from theological deprivation and they benefit
from the political opportunity structures, HT's influence has been
very minimal among the youth. During the last decade, Turkish
political life, Turkish believers and Turkish Islamic movements have
all experienced major changes. HT, in contrast, is structurally resistant
to change. It might use the latest technological advances, such as the
internet, or transfer its headquarters to the West, but it still insists on
advocating the Islamism of the Cold War and, as a result, appears
out of fashion. The state was providing religious education through
the Imam Hatip Schools (IHL) and the High Institute of Islam.
This constituted an important bulwark against HT's considerable
transnational resources, preventing them from influencing or tainting
the education of the children of conservative and lower-class families
(Cakir, 2004). Beginning in the 1980s, Islamic mobilization increased,
but for several reasons HT did not experience a revival. Some Islamic
communities entered the media, and in the 1990s they came to
own newspapers, magazines and radio and television stations. HT's
'Islamic alternative' had become obsolete in comparison to the
platforms of other Islamist groups. Turkish Islamists produce their

own values, intellectuals, leaders and institutions, thus making it difficult for outside groups to gain a foothold (ibid).

Conclusion

Our analysis of four countries (Britain, Uzbekistan, Egypt and Turkey) elaborated on the socio-economic, political and theological deprivations. While in Britain and Uzbekistan, HT is influential and has successfully radicalized thousands of young Muslims, it has not been influential in Egypt and Turkey. As far as the British youth is concerned, all three of these deprivations are mundane realities of daily life, the political deprivation factor being strengthened by foreign policy of the UK. Even though Uzbekistan is a Muslim majority country and the state is not overtly secular and has established several Islamic institutions similar to Britain, these three deprivations still exist. In Egypt and Turkey, while socio–economic and political deprivations have existed for at least some strata of society, theological deprivation has never been a case, showing that if socio-economic and political deprivations are not accompanied by theological deprivation, radicalization of the Muslim youth is highly unlikely.

This paper's analysis has confirmed also, to a certain extent, the International Crisis Group's argument that 'Hizb ut-Tahrir seems to have an advantage in societies where there is only limited religious knowledge among Muslims, where the state itself is overtly secular, such as those in Central Asia, or among Muslim communities in Western Europe' (International Crisis Group, 2003, p. 11). However, our analysis differs from the ICG report in the sense that the state's overt secularism is not so important and the emphasis should be on theological deprivation instead of political structures. The Turkish case shows that in a country where the state is aggressively secular, if not anti-Islam, civil society has been able to fill the theological gap in myriad ways. Thus, HT has not been influential. This is a positive sign as far as the Muslims in the West, which the ICG report also refers to in the context of theological deprivation, are concerned. The secular political structures are not influential as long as Muslim civil society institutions and actors can skilfully challenge the theological deprivation in tune with the temporal and spatial conditions so that the Muslim youth's radicalization can be eradicated.

References

Abbas, T. (2007a), 'Muslim minorities in Britain: integration, multiculturalism and radicalism in the post-7/7 period', *Journal of Intercultural Studies*, 28, (3), pp. 287–300.

—(2007b), 'Ethno-Religious identities and Islamic political radicalism in the UK: A Case Study', *Journal of Muslim Minority Affairs*, 27, (3), pp. 429–42.

—(2007c), 'British muslim minorities today: challenges and opportunities to Europeanism, Multiculturalism and Islamism', *Sociology Compass*, 1, (2), pp. 720–36.

Ahmed, H and Stuart, H. (2009), *Hizb ut-Tahrir: Ideology and Strategy*. London: The Centre for Social Cohesion.

Anwar, M (2008), 'Muslims in western states: The British experience and the way forward', *Journal of Muslim Minority Affairs*, 28, (1), pp. 125–37.

Baran, Z. (2004a) (ed.), *The Challenge of Hizb ut-Tahrir: Deciphering and Combating Radical Islamist Ideology*. Washington DC: The Nixon Centre.

—(2004b), *Hizb ut-Tahrir: Islam's Political Insurgency*. Washington DC: The Nixon Centre.

Bayat, A. (1998), 'Revolution without movement, movement without revolution: Comparing Islamic activism in Iran and Egypt', *Comparative Studies in Society and History*, 40, (1), pp. 136–69.

Briggs, R. and Birdwell, J. (2009), *Radicalisation among Muslims in the UK. MICROCON Policy Working Paper 7*. Brighton: MICROCON.

Brighton, S. (2007), 'British Muslims, multiculturalism and UK foreign policy: "integration" and "cohesion" in and beyond the state', *International Affairs*, 83, (1), pp. 1–17.

Bunglawala, Z., Halstead, M., Malik, M., and Spalek, B. (2004), 'Muslims in the UK: Policies for engaged citizens', Open Society Institute, EU Monitoring and Advocacy Program.

Cakir, R. (2004), 'The rise and fall of Turkish Hizb ut-Tahrir', in Z. Baran (ed.), *The Challenge of Hizb ut-Tahrir: Deciphering and Combating Radical Islamist Ideology*. Washington DC: The Nixon Centre, pp. 37–9.

Chaudet, D. (2006), 'Hizb ut-Tahrir: An Islamist threat to central Asia?', *Journal of Muslim Minority Affairs*, 26, (1), pp. 113–25.

Commins, D. (1991), 'Taqi Al-Din Al-Nabhani and The Islamic liberation party', *The Muslim World*, 81, (3–4), pp. 194–211.

Connor, K. (2005), 'Islamism' in the west? the life-span of the Al-Muhajiroun in the United Kingdom', *Journal of Muslim Minority Affairs*, 25, (1), pp. 119–35.

EMCRX (2005), *The Impact of 7 July 2005 European Monitoring Centre of Racism and Xenophobia, 2005. London Bomb Attacks on Muslim Communities in The EU*. Vienna: European Monitoring Centre of Racism and Xenophobia.

Farrar, M. (2006), 'When alienation turns to nihilism: The dilemmas posed for diversity post 7/7', *Conversations in Religion and Theology*, 4, (1), pp. 99–109.

Gerges, F. A. (2005), *The Far Enemy: Why Jihad Went Global*. New York: Cambridge University Press.

Gruen, M. (2004), 'Demographics and methods of recruitment', in Z. Baran (ed.), *The Challenge of Hizb ut-Tahrir: Deciphering and Combating Radical Islamist Ideology*. Washington DC: The Nixon Centr, pp. 116–23.

Haqqani, H., and Hillel, F. (2008), 'Islamist parties: Going back to the origins', *Journal of Democracy*, 19, (3), pp. 13–18.

Hellyer, H. A. (2008), 'Engaging British Muslim communities in counter-terrorism strategies', *The RUSI Journal*, 153, (2), pp. 8–13.

HT (2000), *The Method to Re-establish the Khilafah and Resume the Islamic Way of Life*. London: Al-Khilafah Publications.

—(2002), *The Inevitability of the Clash of Civilisation*. London: Al-Khilafah Publications.

— (2007), *Radicalisation, Extremism & 'Islamism' Realities and Myths in the 'War on Terror: A report by Hizb ut-Tahrir Britain'*. London: HT.

— (2009), *A Positive Agenda for Muslims in Britain*. London: HT.

— (2010), *Media Pack*. London: HT.

International Crisis Group (2003), *Radical Islam in Central Asia: Responding To Hizb ut-Tahrir, ICG Asia Report No.58*. Osh/Brussels: ICG.

Jones, D. M., and Smith, M. L. R. (2010), 'Beyond belief: Islamist strategic thinking and international relations theory', *Terrorism and Political Violence*, 22, (2), pp. 242–66.

Kalonov, K. and Alonso, A. (2008), *Sacred Places and 'Folk Islam', in Central Asia, UNISCI Discussion Papers 17*. Zurich: UNISCI.

Karagiannis, E., and McCauley, C. (2006), 'Hizb ut-Tahrir al-Islami: Evaluating the threat posed by a radical Islamic group that remains nonviolent', *Terrorism and Political Violence*, 18, (2), pp. 315–34.

Keller, H., and Sigron, M. (2010), 'State security v. freedom of expression: legitimate fight against terrorism or suppression of political opposition?', *Human Rights Law Review*, 10, (1), pp. 151–68.

Khusnidinov, Z. (2004), 'The Uzbek response,' in Z Baran (ed.), *The Challenge of Hizb ut-Tahrir: Deciphering and Combating Radical Islamist Ideology*. Washington DC: The Nixon Centre, pp. 140–50.

Leiken, R. S., and Brooke, S. (2007), 'The moderate muslim brotherhood', *Foreign Affairs Journal*, 86, (2), pp. 107–21.

Lewis, P. (2006), 'Imams, ulema and Sufis: providers of bridging social capital for British Pakistanis?', *Contemporary South Asia*, 15, (3), pp. 273–87.

Liberty. (2004), *Reconciling Security and Liberty in an Open Society– Liberty Response*. London: Liberty.

Mayer, J. (2004), *Hizb ut-Tahrir - The Next Al-Qaida, Really? PSIO Occasional Paper 4*. Geneva: IUHEI.

McLoughlin, S. (2005), 'The state, "new" Muslim leaderships and Islam as a "resource" for public engagement in Britain', in J. Cesari and S. McLoughlin (eds), *European Muslims and the Secular State*. Aldershot: Ashgate, pp. 55–69.

Milton-Edwards, B. (1996), *Islamic Politics in Palestine*. London and New York: Tauris.

Mukhametrakhimova, S. (2006), *Dealing With Hizb-ut-Tahrir*. London: Institute of War and Peace Reporting (IWPR).

Murphy, C. (2002), *Passion for Islam*. New York: Simon & Schuster.

Nawaz, M. (2008), *The Way Back from Islamism, PolicyWatch #1390: Special Forum Report*. Washington DC: Washington Institute for Near East Policy (WINEP). http://www.washingtoninstitute.org/ templateC05.php?CID = 2911 [accessed 24.10.2010].

Olcott, M. B., and Ziyaeva, D. (2008), *Islam in Uzbekistan: Religious Education and State Ideology*. Washington DC: Carnegie Endowment for International Peace.

Peach, C. (2006), 'Muslims in the 2001 Census of England and Wales: Gender and economic disadvantage', *Ethnic and Racial Studies*, 29, (4), pp. 629–55.

Radcliffe, L. (2004), 'A Muslim lobby at Whitehall? Examining the role of the Muslim minority in British foreign policy making', *Islam and Christian-Muslim Relations*, 15, (3), pp. 365–86.

Roy, O. (2008), *Al Qaeda in the West as a Youth Movement: The Power of a Narrative. MICROCON Policy Working Paper 2*. Brighton: MICROCON.

Samad, Y. and Sen, K. (2007), *Islam in the European Union: Transnationalism, Youth and the War on Terror*. Oxford: Oxford University Press.

Sariibrahimoglu, L. (2009), 'Turkish Counter-Terrorist Police Allege Hizb-ut-Tahrir Link with Ergenekon', *Eurasia Daily Monitor*, 6, 147. Washington DC: The Jamestown Foundation. http://www.jamestown. org/programs/edm/single/?tx_ttnews%5Btt_news%5D = 35349&tx_ ttnews%5BbackPid%5D = 485&no_cache = 1 [accessed 24.10.2010].

Taji-Farouki, S. (1996), *A Fundamental Quest: Hizb ut-Tahrir and the Search for the Islamic Caliphate*. London: Grey Seal.

Valentine, S R. (2010), 'Monitoring Islamic Militancy: Hizb-ut-Tahrir: "The party of liberation"', *Policing*, 4, (3), pp. 1–10.

Weller, P., Feldman, A., and Purdam, K. (2001), *Religious discrimination in England and Wales*. London: Home Office Research, Development and Statistics Directorate.

Werbner, P. (2004), 'Theorising Complex Diasporas: Purity and Hybridity in the South Asian Public Sphere in Britain', *Journal of Ethnic and Migration Studies*, 30, (5), pp. 895–911.

Whine, M. (2004), 'Hizb ut-Tahrir in Open Societies', in Z Baran (ed.), *The Challenge of Hizb ut-Tahrir: Deciphering and Combating Radical Islamist Ideology*. Washington DC: The Nixon Centre.

Wiktorowicz, Q. (2005), *Radical Islam Rising: Muslim Extremism in the West*. Oxford: Rowman and Littlefield Publishers.

Zambelis, C. (2007), 'Egypt's Muslim Brotherhood: Political Islam Without al-Qaeda', Jamestown Foundation, *Terrorism Monitor*, 5, 22. http://www.jamestown.org/programs/gta/single/?tx_ttnews%5Btt_news%5D = 4568&tx_ttnews%5BbackPid%5D = 182&no_cache = 1 [accessed 24.10.2010].

Zanca, Rl. (2004), 'Explaining Islam in Central Asia: An Anthropological Approach for Uzbekistan', *Journal of Muslim Affairs*, 24, (1), pp. 99–107.

PART TWO

Identity and Belonging

4

Muslim migrant youth: descriptive factors related to acculturation and psychosocial adaptation

M. TAQI TIRMAZI, ALTAF HUSAIN, FATIMA Y. MIRZA, TASANEE R. WALSH

Introduction

A critical mass of Muslim youth of migrant backgrounds is coming of age in the United States but little is known about their culture, religious distinctiveness, social and educational experience, multigenerational acculturation and psychosocial adaptation. Even less is known about the challenges of adaptation that these Muslim American youth encounter related to their status as an ethnic and religious minority.

President Barack Obama, in his inaugural address, acknowledged the religious diversity of the US when he stated that 'we are a nation of Christians and Muslims, Jews and Hindus, and non-believers'.

Scholars suggest that Islam is one of the fastest growing religions in the US (Haddad, 1997; Maloof and Ross-Sheriff, 2003; Smith, 1999). However, it is difficult to estimate the Muslim population in the US. As a result, estimates vary greatly, anywhere from 1.9 million to eight million (Bagby et al., 2001; Ba-Yanus and Siddiqui, 1998; Center for American Islamic Relations, 2001; Eck, 1997; Kosmin et al., 2001; Power, 1998; Smith, 1999; Strum, 2003). The most commonly referenced estimates suggest that there are six to seven million Muslims in the US (Center for American Islamic Relations, 2006; Forman, 2001; Smith, 1999; Power, 1998). Consequently, there are no estimates of the number of migrant Muslim youth in the US.

Muslims have been a part of the US population long before the country was founded. Evidence suggests that Muslims were present in Spanish Colonial America before 1550 (Maloof and Ross-Sheriff, 2003), and that significant numbers of African slaves brought to the US were Muslim (Smith, 2005; Maloof and Ross-Sheriff, 2003). The voluntary migration of Muslims to the US occurred in a series of distinguishable periods, also known as 'waves'. The first occurred during the post-Civil War period; the second took place at the end of World War I; the third lasted from 1947 to 1960; and the fourth and most recent wave of Muslim immigration began after the passage of the 1965 Immigration Act (P.L. 89–236, Smith, 2005). Several factors spurred Muslim migration after 1965, including the voluntary migration in pursuit of education, a better quality of life and family reunification, and the scores of refugees sponsored by the US government for resettlement in the US following civil war and internal strife in their own homelands (Maloof and Ross-Sheriff, 2003; Smith, 1999, 2005).

A little more than a third (36 per cent) of Muslim Americans polled report being born in the US (Bukhari, 2001), and others estimate that migrant Muslims and their descendents make up two-thirds of the Muslim American population (Haddad and Lummis, 1987). However, sampling techniques may not adequately represent those Muslims with traditional Euro-American surnames. Migrant Muslim populations usually come to the US from the Middle-East, North Africa and South and South-East Asia – where Islam is the predominant religion (Denny, 1995) – and enter into an American context where they are both ethnic and religious minorities. Migrant Muslims in America are divided among three major ethnic groups:

32–33 per cent of them are South Asians; 25–26 per cent are Arabs; and 20–30 per cent are African Americans (Bukhari, 2001; Center for American Islamic Relations, 2001). As a result, it is not surprising that migrant Muslim American youth are an extremely diverse group and may even represent over 75 different ethnicities and nationalities (Maloof and Ross-Sheriff, 2003).

The Muslim community in the United States is fairly young, educated and prosperous. According to the Muslims in the American Public Square (MAPS) project, 75 per cent of Muslims are less than 50 years of age, 58 per cent are college graduates in various professional fields, and 50 per cent have an annual household income of over $50,000 (Bukhari, 2001). Most Muslims in the US live in major cosmopolitan areas: 20 per cent in California; 16 per cent in New York; 8 per cent in Illinois; 4 per cent in New Jersey and Indiana; and 3 per cent in other states such as Michigan, Virginia, Texas and Ohio (Nu'man, 1992). According to the American Arab Institute (2003), the average household size for a Muslim family in the US is 4.9 people. In addition, it is estimated that 5 per cent of students in the public school system are Muslim (Carter and El Hindi, 1999).

Scholars suggest that migration presents myriad challenges to youth development and adaptation (Pine and Drachman, 2005; Portes and Rumbaut, 2001; Suarez-Orozco, 2004; Tartar, 1998; Ulman and Tartar, 2001). However, a distinction is not drawn in the literature between the experiences of migrant Muslim youth and other migrant youth in the US. Yet, preliminary studies indicate that the acculturative and psychosocial adaptations of migrant Muslim youth are unique due to their cultural and religious differences (e.g. Amer and Hovey, 2007).

In addition, socio–political events such as the tragedy of 11 September 2001 ('9/11'), resulted in a dramatic rise in the interest in Muslims, both in the US and internationally. Not only has the social fabric of America changed after the tragedy of 9/11, but the Muslim communities and Muslims have been changing and evolving as well. However, the impact of 9/11, and subsequent reactions and challenges for Muslims in the US, remain understudied. Subsequent events, such as the ongoing wars in Afghanistan and Iraq, the continued Israeli–Palestinian conflict, military focus in Pakistan and other isolated incidents involving Muslims have resulted in Muslims being eyed with suspicion in Western countries, including the US. Many citizens in the West have difficulty comprehending the distinct cultures and religion of Muslims, and often prefer that Muslims assimilate into societal norms and values of mainstream America rather than 'integrate' as Muslims.

Such scrutiny, paired with the increased 'Islamophobia' and assimilationist discourses, have resulted in a fierce public debate about American, Muslim and ethnic identities. In fact, some report a shift in the acculturation strategies[1] employed by Muslim Americans in response to anti-Muslim sentiment, which has resulted in a two-fold effect (Abdo, 2006a). First, many Muslims have become more committed to their faith. Second, many Muslims have developed a sense that they do not belong in the US. These developments may be due to feelings of alienation produced in response to defending their faith, ethnicity and culture from criticisms. Muslim American youth may therefore encounter more frequent and more intense adaptation challenges than other first- and second-generation migrant youth. However, it is also important to remember that the present discourse about the acculturation and psychosocial adaptation experiences of Muslim youth in the United States is largely based on western-oriented conceptual assumptions which research findings do not support. These conceptual arguments and rhetoric are based on stereotypical myths and assumptions rather than on research specifically focusing on migrant Muslim youth.

Although there is increased attention on Muslims around the world and in the US, unlike research conducted in Canada and Europe (Aswat and Malcarne, 2007; Verkuyten and Yildiz, 2007), research has neglected to examine the overall experience and adaptation of Muslim Americans. Scholars (Al-Johar, 2005; Hodge, 2002; Mahmoud, 1996; Ross-Sheriff and Husain, 2001) have begun to address the experience of migrant Muslim youth in the US and have produced significant findings. The modest literature on migrant Muslim youth has produced mixed findings regarding to their experiences in the US. Much of the previous literature on migrant Muslim youth focused attention on adaptation in regard to their Islamic values and beliefs, participation in Western culture, family relations and assimilation (Barazangi, 1988, 1991, 1996; Cox, 1983; Ghuman, 1997; Ross-Sheriff and Husain, 2001), while some research focused on the experience of migrant Muslim youth in educational settings (Carter and El Hindi, 1999; Hodge, 2002;

Mahmoud, 1996; Shaikh, 1995; Zine, 2000, 2007). However, many of the studies have methodological limitations regarding sample size and are not guided by theory. Furthermore, several of these studies fail to consider critical demographic and ecological factors[1] associated with the psychosocial adaptation of migrant Muslim youth. Most of these studies were conducted before the events of 9/11, and should be generalized with caution due to the shift in the social and political climate in the US. A more comprehensive study, guided by theories of acculturation/adaptation and employing a large sample, which assesses critical demographic and ecological variables, needs to be conducted in order to study the adaptation of migrant Muslim youth in the US.

This chapter, therefore, describes the acculturation and psychosocial adaptation of 175 migrant Muslim youth residing in the US. It provides information about their demographic characteristics, (gender, age, ethnic origin, migration status, birth country and educational level), ecological factors (family and friends social support, religiosity, family cohesion, native language proficiency, and perceived discrimination), experience with acculturation and mental health and the impact on acculturation, self-esteem and depression. What follows is a short summary of the literature that guided the development of this study.

Acculturation of migrant Muslim American youth

Scholars have generally noted that the process of adaptation has been associated with some negative effects on individual psychosocial well-being (Aronowitz, 1985; Harker, 2001; Portes and Rumbaut, 1996; Suarez-Orozco, 2004). Despite the increasing numbers, the relative economic well-being of their parents and the achievements of migrant Muslim youth, little is known about their acculturation and psychosocial health. Over the last several decades, there have been a few studies that have attempted to explore, describe and explain the adaptation experience of migrant Muslim youth. A few leading scholars (Al-Johar, 2005; Amer and Hovey, 2007; Aswat and Malcarne, 2007; Barazangi, 1996; Hodge, 2002; Mahmoud, 1996; Peek, 2005; Ross-Sheriff and Husain, 2001) have begun the groundwork for addressing the challenges of migrant Muslim youth in the US and Canada.

Muslim youth appear to follow the trend among migrant youth in that they tend to adapt to the host culture faster than their parents (Barazangi, 1988). In an illustrative case-study, Ross-Sheriff and Husain (2001) discovered the existence of parent–child conflict due to Pakistani Muslim parents misunderstanding their adolescent daughter's behaviour which was reflective of age-graded expectations (Newman and Newman, 2011) for American youth. This case-study exemplifies the fear of many Muslim parents that their children will be socialized into western secular values that will do little to advance their children's well-being in this world or, from a Muslim perspective, the next (Smith, 1999). These studies suggest that Muslim youth may be more likely to utilize an assimilative acculturation strategy rather than strategies of integration, separation, individualism or marginalization. However, it is important to note that assimilation into western culture may not be a viable strategy for the youth because it would threaten family cohesion, which in turn may affect their psychosocial adaptation.

Muslim youth may be less likely to assimilate than youth from other religious backgrounds (Cox, 1983). Studies conducted in the UK that examined the strategies employed by students of different ethnic groups found that Arab Muslims were less likely to assimilate than Arab Christians (Amer and Hovey, 2007), that Saudi adolescents had differing values than British adolescents (Simmons et al., 1994) and that South Asian Muslims were more likely to retain their own values than South Asian Hindu or Sikh adolescents (Ghuman, 1997). Among North American Muslim youth, they desired to retain their Islamic values (Barzangi, 1991) and tended to identify with the cultural heritage of their migrant parents, which influenced the decisions they made with regard to their future marital decisions (Al-Johar, 2005). These studies indicate that migrant Muslim youth tend to identify with their parents' culture and are concerned with adhering to Islamic values. Furthermore, the literature suggests that when it comes to ethnic, cultural and religious values, Muslim youth are likely to utilize separation strategies towards acculturating rather than assimilative, integrated or individualistic acculturation strategies (Al-Johar, 2005; Barzangi, 1991; Cox, 1983; Ghuman, 1997; Simmons et al., 1994).

Transitioning into a new school setting for migrant Muslim youth can also be difficult. Practising Islam in the public school system can lead to conflict for migrant Muslim youth where secular discourse predominates (Carter and El Hindi, 1999; Shaikh, 1995). The difficulties can be more challenging for those youth who choose to adhere to certain practices associated with Islamic religious beliefs. For example, it is difficult for Muslim youth to pray and fast during the month of Ramadan if schools are not cooperative (Mahmoud, 1996).

Muslim migrant youth also experience peer pressure because they may not follow the age-graded expectations of mainstream American society. Many adolescent Muslim females are ridiculed because they choose to wear a *hijab*, which covers their hair, ears and neck (Mahmoud, 1996). Further, young Muslim adolescent females prefer to wear sweat pants and long-sleeved T-shirts instead of shorts and tank tops in physical education classes even if they have to face being ridiculed by their peers (Shaikh, 1995). Reports of Muslim youth being harassed because of their religious beliefs and stereotypes that have been perpetuated by the media are not uncommon (The Arab American Institute, 2003). This perceived discrimination may impact the psychosocial adaptation of migrant Muslim youth, and some research has begun to connect it with eating disorders among some Muslim girls (Iyer and Haslam, 2003).

In addition, many migrant Muslim youth encounter conflicts because of differences in the sexual values of their families and the larger American society (Shaikh, 1995). Secular dating habits are incompatible with Islamic values and many migrant Muslim youths feel pressured to conform to secular beliefs. Certain aspects of sex education can also conflict with Islamic belief relating to modesty (Hodge, 2002). These studies illustrate the challenges that young Muslim women face in particular, but which impacts the acculturation and psychosocial well-being of migrant Muslim youth in general.

Methodology

This cross-sectional study utilized an ecological perspective (Bronfenbrenner, 1989) and acculturation theory (Phinney et al., 2006;

Berry, 1997; Gordon, 1964; Graves, 1967; James, 1997; Liebkind, 2001; Berry, 1986) along with quantitative methods to describe and examine the demographic characteristics, ecological factors, acculturation, and psychosocial adaptation among a sample of 175 migrant Muslim youth in the US. Multi-stage sampling methods were used to select the sites (Masjids/Mosques, Islamic schools, community centres, and Muslim Student Associations), followed by purposive sampling to select migrant Muslim youth from these sites.

Participants were between 12 and 22 years of age, either migrants or second-generation Americans, and Muslims who identify with their Islamic faith. Power analyses indicate that this study was sufficiently powered to detect medium-effect sizes (Abu-Bader, 2006; Tabachnick and Fidell, 2007). A self-administered survey (Muslim Youth Questionnaire or MYQ) was utilized during the quantitative phase of the research study. The first part of the survey included demographic questions related to participant age, gender, educational level, ethnic origin, immigration status and native language. The second part of the survey asked participants to respond to questions regarding family cohesion, family and friends social support, religiosity and perceived discrimination. The third part of the survey asked participants to share information about acculturation and psychosocial variables and included instruments to measure acculturation strategies, self-esteem and depression. The MYQ was administered only in English.

Upon completion of the data collection, the data was checked for accuracy and completeness. Additional tests on data collected via standardized measures allowed researchers to determine if data collected were reliable. (For the most part, these checks revealed no problems that needed to be accounted for.)

Demographic characteristics of Muslim youth

The MYQ was distributed to 240 Muslim youth, of which 175 Muslim youth completed the questionnaire for a response rate of 73 per cent, which is considered excellent (Rubbin and Babbie, 2008). Information on the demographic characteristics of the sample is provided in Table 1.

Table 4.1 Sample Description: Categorical Data

Variable	Female		Male		Total		χ^2	p
	n	%	n	%	n	%		
Age								
Early Adolescence	37	21.8	31	18.2	68	40	3.19	.203
Middle Adolescence	40	23.5	29	17.1	69	40.6		
Later Adolescence	24	14.1	9	5.3	33	19.4		
Ethnicity								
Arab/Middle-Eastern	32	18.6	26	15.1	58	33.7	3.55	.616
South Asian	30	17.4	18	10.5	48	27.9		
African	8	4.7	3	1.7	11	6.4		
Mixed	13	7.6	13	7.6	26	15.1		
Muslim	10	5.8	4	2.3	14	8.1		
Total	103	59.9	69	40.1	172	100		
Birth Country								
United States	75	43.4	52	30.1	127	73.4	.54	.463
Foreign Born	30	17.3	16	9.2	46	26.6		
Total	105	60.7	68	39.3	173	100		
School								
Middle School	27	15.5	19	10.9	46	26.4	.28	.871
High School	50	28.7	34	19.5	84	48.3		
College	28	16.1	16	9.2	44	25.3		
Total	105	60.3	69	39.7	174	100		
Status								
Citizen	86	49.7	61	35.3	147	85	1.96	.751
Green Card	10	5.8	5	2.9	15	8.7		
Other	8	4.7	3	1.6	11	6.3		
Total	104	60.1	69	39.9	173	100		

The sample was 60 per cent female (n = 104) and 40 per cent male (n = 69), with two respondents not answering the question regarding gender. The participants' ages ranged from 12 to 22 years age, with a mean age of 15.75 years. For data analysis purposes, age ranges were divided into three categories: 12–14 (early adolescence), 15–18 (middle adolescence), and 19–22 (later adolescence). Of the 104 females that participated in the study, 22 per cent (n = 37) of the females were between 12 and 14 years of age; while another 24 per cent (n = 40) were between 15 and 18 years of age, and 14 per cent (n = 24) were between 18 and 22 years of age. Of the 69 males that participated in the study, 18 per cent (n = 31) were between 12 and 14 years of age; while another 17 per cent (n = 29) were between 15 and 18 years of age, and another 5 per cent (n = 9) were between 18 and 22 years of age.

A majority of the participants attended high school (49 per cent, n = 84); while 25 per cent (n = 44) attended college, and 26 per cent (n = 46) attended middle school. In addition, the majority of the participants in the sample were from Arab (34 per cent, n = 58) or South Asian (27 per cent, n = 48) origin, while another 7 per cent (n = 11) identified themselves as African, and 15 per cent (n = 26) as of ethnically mixed origin, and 8 per cent (n = 14) of the participants identified their ethnicity as being Muslim.

Most participants (73 per cent, n = 127) were born in the US. Of the 27 per cent (n = 46) that were born in a foreign country, the average age of migration to the US was five. A majority of the participants in the sample were US citizens (84 per cent, n = 147), while 9 per cent (n = 15) had green cards, and a small percentage of the participants did not know of their status (7 per cent, n = 11). A chi-square test of association was run to examine the association between age, gender, ethnicity, educational level and immigration status. There were no significant differences between females and males, age, ethnic breakdown, educational level and immigration status, which means that the respondents were evenly distributed between these categories.

In addition to the demographic characteristics, data were collected for 12 subscales: Ethnic Language Proficiency Measure, Santa Clara Strengths of Religious Faith Questionnaire, Family Cohesion Scale, Perceived Social Support–Family and Friends Scale, Perceived Racism Scale, Immigrant Acculturation Scale, Center for Epidemiological Studies Depression Scale for Children, and Rosenberg Self-Esteem

Scale. Descriptive statistics were run to determine the extent of ecological (ethnic language, family support, friends support, family cohesion, religiosity, and perceived discrimination); acculturation (separation, assimilation, marginalization, and individualism); and psychosocial (self-esteem and depression) indices among the sample of Muslim youth.

Native language proficiency

This study utilized a 13-item language proficiency scale consisting of six questions related to participant's native and English language use, and proficiency with family and friends. This particular scale is structured where higher scores reflect a relatively stronger preference of using ethnic language, whereas lower scores reflect a relatively low preference for using ethnic language. The English questions were used to attain descriptive information and were used as a criterion to ensure students could comprehend the questionnaire. The native language proficiency questions were used in the analysis. All of the participants had acceptable English proficiency.

Participants spoke various native languages, including Swahili, Urdu, Arabic, Farsi, Spanish, among others. Thirty per cent (n = 53) of the study participants spoke three languages: their language of origin, and English and Spanish. The language proficiency scale posed six questions about participant's native language, and scores ranged from 6 to 25, with higher scores indicating higher levels of native language proficiency. Of the 171 participants who answered the ethnic language proficiency questions, 30 per cent (n = 53) of the respondents stated that they use their ethnic language half of the time when speaking with their parents. Thirty per cent (n = 53) of the respondents also stated that they use English when speaking with their parents half of the time as well. Participants appeared to be more proficient in English than in their own ethnic language.

Family and friends social support

The family and friends support scale is a 40-item measure, of which 20 yes–no questions assess perceived social support from family, and 20 questions assess perceived social support from friends. The scores on the family social support can measure range from 0 to 20, and the scores on the friends social support measure can range from 0 to 18, with higher scores reflecting higher perceived social support (Procidano and Heller, 1983). Of the 173 participants who answered the family support questions, the mean score was 11.94. For example, when asked whether they agree with the statement, 'Members of my family are good at helping me solve problems', 64 per cent (n = 112) of the participants stated 'yes', while 32 per cent (n = 56) said 'no'. Of the 173 participants who answered the friends support questions, the mean score was 11.58. For instance, when asked whether they agree with the statement, 'I rely on my friends for emotional support', 70 per cent (n = 121) of participants stated 'no' and 30 per cent (n = 52) responded 'yes'.

Family cohesion

The family cohesion scale consists of 20 questions that ask about an individual's perception of family cohesiveness. Scores on the family cohesion scale can range from 49 to 100, with higher scores indicating higher family enmeshment (Olson et al., 1985). Of the 163 participants who answered the family cohesion questions, the mean score was 71.83, indicating moderate levels of family cohesion. For instance when asked about their level of agreement with the statement 'Family members feel close to each other', 26 per cent (n = 45) of the participants stated 'almost always', another 26 per cent (n = 45) responded 'frequently', and 32 per cent (n = 56) said 'sometimes'.

Religiosity

A modified version of the Santa Clara Strengths of Religious Faith Questionnaire (SCSRF) was utilized to ask participant about their Islamic faith. There were a total of ten questions which were summed, and scores ranged between 14 and 40. Higher scores are associated with stronger levels of religious faith (Plante and Boccaccini, 1997a, 1997b). When asked, if 'Islam is important to me', 59 per cent (n = 103) of the participants, 'strongly agree', while another 36 per cent (n = 63) agreed. In another question that asked the degree to which 'My relationship with Allah is extremely important to me',

73 per cent (n = 128) of the participants claimed that they strongly agreed and 25 per cent (n = 44) agreed. Overall, the mean average for religiosity was 33.72, indicating that the sample of Muslim youth had high levels of religiosity.

Perceived discrimination

Perceived discrimination was measured using a modification of the International Comparative Study on Ethno-cultural Youth (ICSEY) perceived discrimination scale, consisting of five items. Scores ranged from 5 to 24. The scale was scored so that higher scores indicate stronger perceived discrimination. Of the 172 individuals that answered the perceived racism questions, 34 per cent (n = 60) of participants strongly agreed and 36 (n = 63) per cent of the participants agreed when asked, 'I think others have behaved in an unfair or negative way towards Muslims'. However, only 9 per cent (n = 16) of the participants strongly agreed and 25 per cent (n = 44) of the participants agreed when asked, 'I have been teased or insulted because of being a Muslim'. The overall mean average for racism was 13.86, which indicates that the sample perceived mild levels of discrimination.

Acculturation

This study used a modified version of the Bourhis and Barette (2004) Immigrant Acculturation Scale to evaluate participants' attitudes about their religion, culture, marriage and language. The scale consisted of five questions for each of the aforementioned domains totalling 25 items. Questions assessed the five acculturation styles (integration, assimilation, marginalization, separation and individualism) that participants may adopt. The scores for the five styles ranged as follows: integration 5–28; assimilation 3–24; marginalization 1–28; separation 2–28; individualism 3–24. The five subscales were scored whereas higher scores on each scale indicate stronger acculturative attitudes. However, due to an unacceptable reliability coefficient (.38), integration was not utilized in the analysis. Of the 164 participants that answered the acculturation questions, the mean scores were: 10.50 for assimilation, 9.04 for marginalization, 19.71 for separation and 13.07 for individualism. Also, there was no statistically significant acculturative difference in relation to age, gender and ethnicity.

Depression

Depression was measured using the Center for Epidemiological Studies Depression Scale for Children (CES-DC). The 20-item scale's scores ranged between 4 and 53 in this study. Higher scores indicate increasing levels of depression where the cut-off score of 15 indicates a significant level of depressive symptomatology (Weissman et al., 1980). However, Nebbitt and Lombe (2007) explain that numerous studies suggest that a cut-off score of 24 should be used among minority youth because within this group a score of 0–15 indicates minimal depressive symptoms, a score of 16–23 suggests mild depressive symptoms, and a score of above 24 reveals moderate/severe depressive symptoms.

Of the 174 participants that answered the CES-DC questions, 45 per cent (n = 78) of the participants had a score of 24 or higher on the CES-DC. Overall, the mean score on the CES-DC was 23.60. For example when asked, 'I am fearful', 46 per cent (n = 80) of the participants stated 'no', 34 per cent (n = 60) stated 'a little', 12 per cent (n = 21) stated 'some', and 8 per cent (n = 14) stated 'a lot'. In another statement, 'I enjoy life', 36 per cent (n = 63) stated 'a lot', 37 per cent (n = 65) stated 'some', 12 per cent (n = 21) stated 'a little', 8 per cent (n = 14) stated 'not at all'. Females had a mean score of 22.49, while males had a mean score of 25.49. Thus, the findings of this study reveal that the average score was 23.60, which indicates between mild and moderate depressive symptoms. However, over 45 per cent (n = 78) of the participants had a score of above 24, which suggests moderate/severe depressive symptoms. Moreover, there was no statistically significant difference in depression in regard to age, gender and ethnicity.

Self-Esteem

This study used the Rosenberg Self-Esteem scale, which consists of ten questions, with higher scores indicating higher levels of self-esteem. Of the 172 participants that answered the questions

Table 4.2   Descriptive Statistics for Subscales

Variable	N	Mean	Median	SD	Range
Ethnic Language	171	16.49	16.00	4.43	6–25
Friends Social Support	173	11.58	12.00	5.54	0–18
Family Social Support	173	11.94	12.00	4.38	0–20
Family Cohesion	163	71.83	74.00	15.45	49–100
Religiosity	173	33.72	35.00	5.45	14–40
Perceived Discrimination	172	13.86	13.00	4.43	5–25
Acculturation	164				
Assimilation		10.50	9.50	4.81	3–24
Separation		19.71	21.00	4.80	3–28
Marginalization		9.04	9.00	4.64	1–28
Individualism		13.07	5.78	5.78	3–28
Depression	174	23.60	22.00	9.56	4–53
Self-Esteem	172	20.10	21.00	5.00	9–35

regarding self-esteem, 27 per cent (n = 47) strongly agreed and 55 per cent (n = 97) agreed with the statement 'On the whole I am satisfied with myself'. While 27 per cent (n = 47) strongly agreed and 31 per cent (n = 55) agreed with the statement 'I certainly feel useless at times'. The overall mean score on the self-esteem scale was 20.10. Females had mean score of 20.25 (SD = 4.92) while males had a mean score of 19.88. The scores ranged between 9 and 35. The scores indicate that the sample of Muslim youth in this study had scores within the normal range of 15–25. In addition, there was no statistically significant difference in self-esteem in relation to age, gender and ethnicity.

Conclusions

The results of this study indicate that first- and second-generation Muslim American youth tend to report moderate to high family cohesion, moderate comfort with their ethnic languages and high religiosity. However, they also tend to report high levels of negative perceptions of Muslims by the larger American community, even though few in this sample report having directly experienced religion-based teasing. This tendency may account for the slightly higher propensity to employ an acculturation style of separation. However, the acculturation measure used needs refinement to more accurately capture the attitudes of young American Muslims. Depression scores reported by the respondents were startlingly high, while self-esteem and friend and family social support measures were all in the moderate range. Further exploration is needed to better determine the source of these elevated scores.

This research study had numerous strengths. First, respondents in this study were diverse in ethnicity and age, and were fairly representative of the Muslim American community. Second, both males and females were adequately represented in each age group, and were recruited from several organizations. Third, the sample size was also relatively large. All of these features strengthen the generalizablility of results to other US Muslim youth. As such, this article is a significant contribution to a literature that is devoid of quantitative research that describes the well-being and acculturation among Muslim youth of a variety of ethnic backgrounds.

The research had some limitations as well. Though multi-stage sampling techniques were utilized to recruit a representative sample, the only sites at which these youth could be accessed were religiously-affiliated organizations. As a result, respondents were likely to be more religious than those who are not affiliated with such organizations. Therefore, caution must be employed when making statements about US Muslim youth based on these results. Additionally, many of the measures utilized in this study have not been adequately tested among Muslims, leaving room for error. The acculturation scale is one that had a noticeably weak alpha in one of its subscales. The other standardized measures performed reliably in this sample but were not tested for construct validity. The high scores on the CES-DC paired with the moderate scores on the self-esteem and social support scales indicate that further construct validity testing for this group needs to be conducted before the scores can be accepted at face value.

The findings from this study highlight ecological factors that are associated with the psychosocial adaptation of migrant Muslim youth. The relatively high levels of depression among migrant Muslim youth suggest that there is a need for social work interventions that address depression. In addition, cultural sensitivity training for social workers and educators who work with Muslim youth should revolve around ecological factors and social determinants of mental health and health behaviours. Furthermore, the findings of this study raise a red flag for Muslim communities to be aware of depressive symptoms among their youth, and to be receptive to accessing mental health services. Muslim communities should employ preventative measures to address depressive symptoms among their youth.

References

Abdo, G. (2006), 'America's Muslims aren't as assimilated as you think', *Washington Post Sunday*, August 27, B30.

Abu-Bader, S. (2006), *Using Statistical Methods In Social Work Practice*. Chicago: Lyceum Books Inc.

Al-Johar, D. (2005), 'Muslim marriages in America', *The Muslim World*, 95, pp. 557–74.

Amer, M. M., and Hovey, J. D. (2007), 'Socio-demographic differences in acculturation and mental health for a sample of 2nd generation/early immigrant Arab Americans', *Journal of Immigrant and Minority Health*, 9, pp. 335–47.

Arab American Institute (2003), *Healing the Nation: The Arab American experience after September 11*, Retrieved from http://aai.3cdn.net/64de7330dc475fe470_h1m6b0yk4.pdf.(accessed January 2, 2001)

Aronowitz, M. (1985), 'The social and economical adjustment of immigrant children. A review of literature', *International Migration Review*, 18, (2), pp. 237–57.

Aswat, Y., and Malcarne, V. L. (2007), 'Acculturation and depressive symptoms in Muslim University students: Personal-family acculturation match', *International Journal of Psychology*, 1, (11), pp. 1–11.

Ba-Yanus, B. and Siddiqui, M. M. (1998), 'A report on the Muslim population in the United States of America'. New York: Center for American Muslim Research and Information.

Bagby, I., Perl, M. P., and Froehle, B. T. (2001), *The Mosque in America: A National Portrait*. Washington, DC: Council on American–Islamic Relations, Washington, DC.

Barazangi, N. H. (1988), 'Perceptions of the Islamic belief system: The Muslims in North America', Ph.D. Thesis, Cornell University, Ithaca.

—(1991), 'Islamic education in the United States and Canada: conception and practice of the Islamic belief system', in Y. Haddad (ed.), *The Muslims of America*, New York: Oxford University Press, pp. 157–74.

—(1996), 'Parents and youth: Perceiving and practicing Islam in North America', in B. C. Aswad and B. Bilge (eds), *Family and Gender Among American Muslims: Issues Facing Middle Eastern Immigrants and Their Descendants*. Philadelphia, PA: Temple University Press, pp. 129–42.

Berry, J. W. (1986), 'The acculturation process and refugee behavior', in C. L. Williams and J. Westinmeyer (eds), *Refugee Mental Health in Resettlement Countries*. Washington, D.C: Hemisphere Publishing Corp, pp. 25–37.

—(1997), 'Immigration, acculturation and adaptation', *Applied Psychology*, 46, pp. 5–68.

Berry, J. W., Phinney, J., Sam, D. L., and Vedder, P. (2006), *Immigrant Youth in Cultural Transition: Acculturation, Identity, and Adaptation across National Contexts*. Mahwah, NJ: Lawrence Erlbaum Associates, Inc.

Bourhis, R. Y. and Barrette, G. (2004), 'Notes on the immigrant acculturation scale', *Working Paper, LECRI*, Department of Psychology, University of Quebec, Montreal, Canada, November.

Bronfenbrenner, U. (1989), 'Ecological systems theory', in R. Vasta (ed.), *Six Theories of Child Development, Annals of Child Development*, 6. Greenwich, CT: JAI press, pp. 187–249.

Bukhari, Z. H. (2001), 'Demography, identity, space: defining American Muslims', in P. Strum and D. Tarantolo (eds), *Muslims in the United States*. Washington, DC: Woodrow Wilson International Center for Scholars, pp. 7–20.

Carter, R. B., and El Hindi, A. E. (1999), 'Counseling Muslim children in school settings', *Professional School Counseling*, 2, (3), pp. 183–8.

Center for American Islamic Relations. (2006), *American Muslim Voters: A Demographic Profile and Survey of Attitudes*. Washington, DC:CAIR.

Council on American-Islamic Relations (2001), *American Muslims: Population Statistics*, Retrieved June 5, 2006, from http://www.cair.com/asp/populationstats.asp.

Cox, D. R. (1983), 'Religion and the welfare of immigrants', *Australian Social Work*, 36, (1), pp. 3–10.

Denny, F. M. (1995), 'Islam in Americas', in J. L. Esposito (ed.), *The Oxford Encyclopedia of the Modern Islamic World*. New York: Oxford University Press, pp. 296–300.

Eck, D. L. (1997), *On Common Ground: World Religions in America*. New York: Columbia University Press.

Forman, M. T. (2001), 'Straight outta Mogadishu': prescribed identities and performative practices among Somali youth in North American high schools', *Topia*, 5, pp. 20–41.

Ghuman, P. A. S. (1997), 'Assimilation or integration? A study of Asian adolescents', *Education Research*, 39, (1), pp. 23–35.

Gordon, M. M. (1964), *Assimilation in American Life*. New York: Oxford University Press.

Graves, T. (1967), 'Psychological acculturation in a tri-ethnic community', *South-Western Journal of Anthropology*, 23, pp. 337–50.

Haddad, Y. Y. (1997), 'Make room for the Muslims?', in W. H. Conser Jr. and S.B. Twiss (eds), *Religious diversity and American religious history*. Athens: University of Georgia Press. pp. 218–61.

Haddad, Y. Y. and Lummis, A. T. (1987), *Islamic values in the United States*. New York: Oxford University Press.

Harker, K. (2001), 'Immigrant generation, assimilation, and adolescent psychological well-being', *Social Forces*, 79, (3), pp. 969–1004.

Hodge, D. R. (2002), 'Working with Muslim youths: understanding the values and beliefs of Islamic discourse', *Children and Schools*, 24, (1), pp. 6–20.

Iyer, D. S., and Haslam, N. (2003), 'Body image and eating disturbances among South Asian-American women: The role of racial teasing', *International Journal of Eating Disorders*, 34, pp. 142–7.

James, D. C. S. (1997), 'Coping with a new society: the unique psychosocial problems of immigrant youth', *The Journal of School Health*, 67, pp. 98–102.

Kosmin, B. A., Mayer, E., and Keysar, A. (2001), 'American Religious Identification Survey'. The Graduate Center of the City University of New York. Retrieved 5 June 2006, from http://www.gc.cuny.edu/faculty/researchstudies/aris.pdf.

Liebkind, K. (2001), 'Acculturation', in R. Brown and S. Gaetner (eds), *Blackwell Handbook of Social Psychology Vol. 3: Intergroup Processes*. Oxford, England: Blackwell, pp. 386–406.

Mahmoud, V. (1996), 'African American Muslim families', in M. McGoldrick, J. Giordano and J. K. Pearce (eds), *Ethnicity and family Therapy*. New York: Guilford Press, pp. 122–8.

Maloof, P. S., and Ross-Sheriff, F. (2003), *Muslim Refugees in the United States. A Guide for Service Providers*. Washington, D.C.: Center for Applied Linguistics.

Nebbitt, V. E., Sr., and Lombe, M. (2007), Environmental correlates of depressive symptoms among African American adolescents living in public housing. *Journal of Human Behavior in the Social Environment*, 15, (2), pp. 435–54.

Newman, B. M., and Newman, P. R. (2011), *Development Through Life: A Psychosocial Approach*. Belmont, CA: Wadsworth Cengage Learning.

Nu'man, F. H. (1992), *The Muslim Population in the United States: A Brief Statement*. Washington DC: The American Muslim Council.

Olson, D. H., Portner, J. and Lavee, Y. (1985), *FACES III*. St. Paul: University of Minnesota, Department of Family Social Science. (Also in: K. Concoran and J. Fischer [2000], *Measures for Clinical Practice*, pp. 247–9. New York: The Free Press.)

Peek, L. (2005) 'Becoming Muslim: The development of a religious identity', *Sociology of Religion*, 66, (3), pp. 215–42.

Phinney, J., Berry, J. W., Vedder, P., and Liebkind, K. (2006), 'The acculturation experience: attitudes, identities, and behaviors of immigrant youth', in J.W. Berry, J. S. Phinney, D. L. Sam, and P. Vedder (eds), *Immigrant Youth in Cultural Transition: Acculturation, Identity, and Adaptation Across National Contexts*. Mahwah, NJ: Lawrence Erlbaum Associates, Inc., pp. 71–116.

Pine, B., and Drachman, D. (2005), 'Effective child welfare practice with immigrant and refugee children and their families', *Child Welfare*, 84, (5), pp. 537–62.

Plante, T. G., and Boccaccini, M. T. (1997a), 'Reliability and validity of the Santa Clara Strength of Religious Faith Questionnaire', *Pastoral Psychology*, 45, pp. 375–87.

—(1997b), 'The Santa Clara Strength of Religious Faith Questionnaire', *Pastoral Psychology*, 45, pp. 301–15.

Portes A., and Rumbaut, R. G. (1996), *Immigrant America: A Portrait*. Berkeley: University of California Press.

—(2001), *Legacies*. Berkeley: CA. University of California Press.

Power, C. (1998), 'The new Islam', *Newsweek*, 131, pp. 34–7.

Procidano, M. E., and Heller, K. (1983), 'Measures of perceived social support from friends and from family: Three validation studies', *American Journal of Community Psychology*, 11, pp. 1–24.

Ross-Sheriff, F., and Husain, A. (2001), 'Values and ethics in social work practice with Asian Americans: A South Asian Muslim Case Example', in Fong, R and Furuto, S (eds), *Culturally Competent Practice*. Boston: Allyn and Bacon, pp. 75–88.

Rubbin, A., and Babbie, E. R. (2008), *Research Methods for Social Work*. (6th edn), California: Thompson Brooks Cole.

Shaikh, M. A. (1995), 'Teaching about Islam and Muslims in the public school classroom' (3rd edn), Mountain Valley, CA: Educational Studies, 20, (1), pp. 69–86.

Simmons, C., Simmons, C., and Allah, M. H. (1994), 'English, Israeli-Arab and Saudi Arabian adolescent values', *Educational Studies*, 20, (1), pp. 69–86.

Smith, J. I. (1999), *Islam in America*. New York: Columbia University Press.

—(2005), 'Patterns of Muslim immigration', *USINFO.STATE.GOV, International Information Programs*. Retrieved 26 June 2005 http://uninfo.state.gov/products/pubs/muslimlife/immirat.htm.

Strum, P. (2003), 'Executive summary', in P. Strum and D. Tarantolo (eds), *Muslims in the United States*. Washington, DC: Woodrow Wilson International Center for Scholars, pp. 1–4.

Suárez-Orozco, C. (2004), 'Formulating Identity in a Globalized World', in M. Suárez-Orozco and D. B. Qin-Hilliard (eds), *Globalization: Culture and Education in the New Millennium*. Berkeley: University of California Press.

Tabachnick, B. G., and Fidell, L. S. (2007), *Using Multivariate Statistic* (5th edn) Boston: Allyn and Bacon.

Tartar, M. (1998), 'Counselling Immigrants: School Contexts and Emerging Strategies', *British Journal of Guidance Counselling*, 26, pp. 337–52.

Ulman, C. and Tartar, M. (2001), 'Psychological adjustment among Israeli adolescent Immigrants: A report on life satisfaction, self-concept, and self-esteem', *Journal of Youth and Adolescence*, 30, pp. 449–63.

Verkuyten, M., and Yildiz, A. A. (2007), 'National (dis)identification, and ethnic and religious identity: A study among Turkish-Dutch Muslims', *Personality and Social Psychology Bulletin*, 33, (1448), pp. 1–15.

Weissman, M., Orvaschel, H. and Padian, N. (1980), 'Children's symptom and social function self-report scales: Comparison of mothers' and children's reports', *Journal of Nervous and Mental Disease*, 168, pp. 736–40.

Zine, J. (2000), 'Redefining resistance: Towards an Islamic subculture in schools', *Race, Ethnicity, and Education*, 3, (3), pp. 293–16.

—(2007), 'Safe havens or religious "ghettos"? Narratives of Islamic schooling in Canada', *Race, Ethnicity, and Education*, 10, (1), pp. 71–92.

5

Religion, language or ethnicity? Hybridized identity among the Isma'ili youth of Afghanistan in Germany

YAHIA BAIZA

Introduction

This chapter explores the role of religion, language and ethnicity in the formation of identity constructions among the *Shi'ah* Isma'ili youth of Afghani origin in the city of Essen in Germany. The diasporic Afghani Isma'ili community in Germany is primarily concentrated in four major regions of Essen (Nordrhein-Westfalen), Frankfurt (Hessen), Munich (Bayern) and Hamburg (or Freie und Hansestadt Hamburg). The location of the community is signalled by the presence of the *Jamat-khana* (literally, 'house of gathering'). A *Jamat-khana* is a space for devotional and congregational activity (Nanji, 2008, p. 89). The Afghani Isma'ili community of Essen includes those families that live in the city of Essen and in the neighbouring cities, from where they visit the Essen *Jamat-khana* for prayer, attending social events and gatherings and religious classes called *Bait al-'Ilm* (literally, 'the house of knowledge'), and other religious and cultural festivals. The population of the Essen region contains the largest Afghani Isma'ili diasporic community in Germany. This chapter then focuses on the development of a hybridized identity construction among the Afghani Isma'ili youth in Essen. The term 'identity' in this study is understood as something that is formed through long-term socio–political and historical processes and subjective experiences. Here, the term 'hybridized identity' refers to a compound identity derived from a mixture of parental and community influences, and the influences from the country of settlement, and is explored in order to find out (i) how the youth define their identity; (ii) the ways in which religion, language and ethnicity influence the development and construction of their identities; and (iii) which one of the three elements – religion, language or ethnicity – if any, has the greater determining influence on the formation of their identity. As I go on to show, the development of identities among Afghani Isma'ili youth in modern urban settings are complex and subjective experiences were influenced by their parents and the community as well as language, ethnicity, religion, and the cultural values of the country of settlement. The findings show that these different identity formations compete with one another for dominance in the construction of a hybridized identity, and the youth in this study attempt to resolve the competing elements by choosing the particular identity which they feel reflects strongest their personal enthusiasm and commitment. This identity facet is discussed in the wider contextual background and is presented in the findings that follow.

Contextual background

The study of diasporic communities has undergone a paradigmatic shift over the past few decades. Originally, the term 'diaspora' was used to describe the biblical displacement and migration (exodus) of Jews from their 'promised homeland'. However, as Brubaker states, the meaning of the term has been stretched to accommodate the various intellectual, cultural and political agendas which now include the semantic, conceptual and disciplinary spaces (2005, p. 1). Currently, there is a plethora of theories and studies engaged with the examination of all diasporic communities. Some of these include the study of (i) 'cultural identity', 'hybridity' and 'new' identities, as opposed to 'old' identities (Brah, 1996; Gilroy, 1987, 1997; Hall, 1994); (ii) the culture of production and reproduction, which studies the way migrant communities strive to preserve their cultural heritage in their place of settlement (Vertovec 1997); (iii) the diasporic communities' political activities (Shain, 1999; Shain and Sherman, 1998; Sheffer, 1986, 1995); (iv) integration and citizenship (Favell, 2001, 2003); (v) social organization (Mizruchi, 1996; Wahlbeck, 1999; Fennema, 2004; Vermeulen and Berger, 2008); (vi) integration and multiculturalism which float between assimilation and cultural pluralism (Kundnani, 2002; Wimmer and Schiller, 2002); and (vii) the transnational perspective of diasporic communities (Faist, 2000; Wahlbeck, 2002). In this chapter, the term 'diaspora' refers to the 'displacement' caused when one leaves one's country of origin and settles in a new country. This resettlement may have been caused by a variety of reasons, such as economic hardship, famine, war and so on. Migration from Afghanistan in the late 1980s and throughout the 1990s contributed to the largest migrant population in the world, the majority of which settled in Pakistan and Iran.

In Europe, Germany is home to the largest number of Afghani migrants who belong to various ethnic, linguistic and religious groups. Ethnically, they are divided among the major groups of Pashtun, Tajik, Hazara, Uzbek, Turkoman and Hindu. Each ethnic group possesses its own language, such as Pashto (Pashtun), Persian (Tajik and Hazara), Uzbeki and Turkomani (Uzbek and Turkoman), and Punjabi (Hindu). Islam (Sunni Hanifi, Shi'ah Imami Ithna Ashari and Shi'ah Imami Isma'ili) is the predominant religion. Brubaker states that, 'from the point of view of homeland, emigrant groups have been conceptualized as diasporas, even when they have largely been assimilated' (2005, p. 1). Brubaker's statement can be seen to apply to the case of the young Afghani Isma'ili community in Germany. Although they have been well integrated into the German society, indigenous Germans still consider them a diasporic, or 'outsider' community, a fact that has had an impact on the formation of their hybridized identity, as detailed later. The majority of Afghani Isma'ili youth in Germany belong to the Hazara ethnic community and follow the Shia'h Imami Isma'ili expression of Islam.

The Isma'ilis from Afghanistan originally migrated to Germany, gradually settling in and around the city of Essen during the Soviet occupation of Afghanistan in the 1980s and the subsequent civil war in the 1990s. Initially, the community members managed their religious and cultural events through decentralized and informal community gatherings. With the establishment of the *Jamat-khana*s and the Isma'ili institutions in Essen, Frankfurt and Munich, the community's religio–cultural life became centrally administered through the religious centres and institutions. The community members and institutions, including the *Jamat-khana*s, are supported through His Highness Prince Karim Aga Khan's Shi'ah Imami Isma'ili Council for the United Kingdom, which is guided and instructed by the Aga Khan IV. The Essen *Jamat-khana* was the first such religio–cultural centre to be established (1997), and since then it has played an important social, cultural, religious, economic and educational role in the lives of the community members.

It was my initial personal observation of the existence of a hybridized identity among the Afghani Isma'ili youth in Germany that motivated this research. I observed the way the youth behaved and socialized inside the *Jamat-khana*, at social and cultural events (e.g. New Year's celebrations, weddings, youth camps, religious festivals and family gatherings). The youths displayed a significant degree of respect to the older generation, kissing their elders' hands and allowing them, in turn, to kiss their heads. In their homes, whenever a guest arrived, they would follow their parents' behaviour in welcoming guests and in cooking meals. However, their interactions and modes of socialization are different from those of the older generation in a number of ways. For example, they are more comfortable talking to one another in German than in Persian or Hazaragi. Also, before and after the prayer, they often congregate in groups in the *Jamat-khana*'s social hall, although they do occasionally mix with the older generation. These observations motivated my exploration into how second-generation Afghani Isma'ili youth in Germany construct their identity. In conducting the research, I was conscious that the subjects of this research lived in a modern, pluralistic urban setting, in which they had continuous contact, through school, with youths from different religious, ethnic and linguistic backgrounds.

In such multi-cultural environments, students learn about the religio–cultural practices and values of one another, which also shapes their conception of 'who they are'. Conversely, since it was not possible to explore the impact of all influencing factors that contribute to the construction of identity facets among this group, this study focused exclusively on the influence of religion, language and ethnicity in the formation of a hybridized identity.

Research method

A qualitative, ethnographic approach through the use of a case-study was employed. This encompassed a combination of semi-structured interviews, documentary analysis and participatory and non-participatory observation to explore different aspects of the development of identity among Afghani Isma'ili youth. Participation in this study was voluntary, and parental consent was obtained for respondents under the age of 18. The research respondents consisted of seven young women and five young men, between the ages of 15 and 22. The collected data were analysed using an interpretative approach, which was selected from the three main theoretical approaches: positivist, interpretative and critical social inquiry (Jupp and Norris, 1996, p. 40). This method suited the qualitative nature of the research subject and questions, which also allowed me to focus on understanding and interpreting texts. In order to minimize the possibility of mistranslation, I analysed the collected data in their original languages, German or Persian, and only translated the reported sections into English.

The development of hybridized identity

The period of adolescence (youth) appears to be a critical stage in the formation of an individual's identity. Although identity is seen as an answer to the question 'who am I' (Blasi, 1988, pp. 226–7), the development of identity is more complex. It is a long-term socio–political process that gives meaning to the question of 'who am I?' From a psychological vantage, Erikson believes that personality develops primarily from the growth of the ego as a person, and in the course of one's life, confronts major obstacles (DiCaprio, 1983, p. 168). This idea became the foundation for his 'eight stages' of personality development. Since then, Erikson's developmental schema (1950) has influenced contemporary theories of adult development, despite disagreement regarding his model, method or his theory (Noam, 1988) regarding the particular stages in his proposed eight stages of the life cycle. Erikson's (1968) Stage 5 deals with the development of identity in adolescents. He terms this stage 'identity crisis' or 'confusion', which represents the development between childhood and adulthood (Erikson, 1968, p. 128), the transitional period from childhood to adolescence when the self is in need of a 'central perspective' and direction, and where the hopes and anticipations of adulthood are realized (Erikson, 1958, p. 12). At this stage, some form of crisis is necessary for the young person to resolve his or her identity (Hendry et al., 2007, p. 183). The crisis occurs when a gap emerges between the young person's burgeoning identity and the parentally given identity. The successful resolution of the identity crisis occurs through the adolescent 'having integrity and continuity and [. . .] keeping the internal and external worlds aligned to each other' (Rattansi and Phoenix, 2005, p. 101). Here, 'integrity' means the integration of one's psychological needs and the interests and defences with the cultural milieu in which one resides (Hendry et al., 2007, p. 183). This maintenance of continuity with the parentally given identity and integrity within the German cultural milieu is exemplified in interviews with Zibah and Fairoz:

> I feel myself [to be] half Afghani and half German. I have grown up here, and I cannot imagine living in Afghanistan. Therefore, I would like to say [that I am] half Afghani and half German . . . I know that I am originally from Afghanistan and have lived in Germany for a long period of time, and one has to integrate oneself in the society. Integration requires learning the language, but some [people] don't do that. (Zibah, age 15)

> I see myself [as being] fifty per cent Afghani and fifty per cent German. I have an Afghani background; and, in the same way, I am a German, because I have been grown up here, and I have German citizenship. While I speak Persian at home, I speak

German with others. The bottom line is that both [identities] are balanced. At home you are Afghani, but outside [home] you are part of the society. Therefore, I would say that both [identities] are in balance. (Fairoz, age 18)

Mastura's experience further explains how society plays a role in the formation of a hybridized identity:

I was two years old when I came [with my parents] to Germany. I grew up here. When one grows up in a country, one is naturally a part of it. I study here, I have done my schooling here and I was in kindergarten and I did [study] everything possible. I speak German. One learns the language and culture automatically . . . Therefore, I feel fifty per cent German.

YB: 'Could you please describe for me when you first felt German?'

Hmm, the question should be the other way round. It is better to ask when I first had the feeling that I was a foreigner. In kindergarten, naturally, I was small yet, exactly the same as other children. When I grew older, in the primary school, I still felt German. In the fifth or sixth grade, I noticed that I was an Afghani.

YB: 'What made you feel that you were a foreigner?'

Yes, hmm, the reaction of others had an influence, and I was also asked, 'Where do you come from?' When someone asks you, 'Where do you come from?' you know right away that you are not German. And then, when I was in the seventh grade, the other children, the German pupils, told us, 'You are foreigners.' It was said to me and a couple of my friends, and I noticed that, yes, I was a foreigner. (Mastura, age 18).

Mastura's experience echoes that of other respondents and indicates that the development of identity is a complex and subjective process, largely driven by the individual's experience. It is the interaction with others that contributes to the development of a hybridized identity. Mastura's experience provides a glimpse of such conversations, which can take place in passing but become internalized and shape one's interpretation and understanding of oneself. The literature demonstrates similar experiences among other communities. In describing his experience, Sadat states that, despite being born in Germany and having lived there for eight years, 'I was perceived as an Ausländer (foreigner)' (2008, p. 331). Sadat's experience of migration and life in the US is remarkably similar, and he states that: 'some Americans referred to us as Afghan-American, but not intending to mean Americans with an Afghan heritage but to mean second-rate American' (ibid, p. 331). Claire Dwyer's research records a similar experience among South Asian Muslim girls in Britain, who identified themselves as British/Asian/Pakistani/Muslim (Dwyer 1999). Dwyer also notes that young Muslim women identified themselves as 'British Asian', 'British Pakistani' or 'British Muslim', as opposed to just 'British' because 'Britishness' is often synonymous with 'Englishness', which is associated with 'whiteness' and Christianity (2000, p. 476). Thus, the role of society and the personal experiences of members of diasporic communities are the key elements in the development of a hybridized identity.

The cultural and communal identity of diasporic communities is sometimes analysed using an essentialist approach, which often leads to misinterpretation and incorrect analysis. This mode of analysis conceives of culture as something that can be fixed, measured and described (Mandaville, 2001, p. 171). In the context of the diasporic communities of Afghanistan, Sadat (2001, 2008), ascribes cultural and moral values to his conception of *Afghaniyat* ('Afghan-ness'), stating that Afghan-ness incorporates *akhlaq-e wejdani* (moral values), *aqa-id* (beliefs) and *ananat* (customs), all of which shape the psychosocial realms of the people of Afghanistan (2001, 2008, p. 330). However, the term *Afghaniyat* is problematic, not because such values could be attributed to any groups, or because the term 'Afghan' refers to one ethnic group (i.e. Pashtun) in the country, but because there is no such thing as 'Afghan-ness' (i.e. *Afghaniyat*). As has already been stated, Afghanistan includes many ethnic groups. Even though ethnic groups share similarities, each has its own characteristic features that differentiate it from the others. The danger of generalizing and ascribing artificial concepts results in the masking of the country's ethnic and cultural diversity. Abu-Lughod (1991), in 'Writing against culture', encourages a distancing from an essentialist mode of analysing culture and group identity, stating that:

When one generalizes from experiences and conversations with a number of specific people in a community, one tends to flatten

out differences among them and to homogenize them. The
appearance of an absence of internal differentiation makes it
easier to conceive of a group of people as a discrete, bounded
entity [. . .]who do this or that and believe such-and-such. . . . The
effort to produce general ethnographic descriptions of people's
beliefs or actions tends to smooth over contradictions, conflicts
of interest, and doubts and arguments, not to mention changing
motivations and circumstances. The erasure of time and conflict
make what is inside the boundary set up by homogenization
something essential and fixed. (Abu-Lughod, 1991, p. 152–3)

Sadat's (2008, p. 341) *Afghaniyat* further complicates diasporic
identity, particularly when arguing that the one who 'rejects his or
her *Afghaniyat* is no longer considered a cultural Afghan, Afghan-e
socha (a real Afghan)'. Ayhan Kaya's study, 'German-Turkish
Transnational Space' (2007), is another example, where the term
'Turks or the Turkish diaspora in Germany' masks the rich diversity
within Turkish diaspora communities, which include ethnic Turks
(Sunni and Alevi Muslims), Kurds, Circassians, Laz and so forth.
In counter-distinction, Hall argues that situating an individual's
subjective understanding of who they are within their ethnic context
results in the discovery of their ethnicity and origin. He goes on to
state that it is questions such as 'Who am I? Where have I come
from?' that enable individuals (and a group of people) to position
themselves, and allow them to begin to explore and experience their
true identities (1989, p. 24).

The impact of ethnicity

Like many other sociological and anthropological terms and
concepts, 'ethnicity' is embedded with a variety of meanings and
definitions. There are a multitude of definitions employed by
anthropologists, archeologists, sociologists, political and social
scientists for the term 'ethnicity', not to mention the variations
of meanings that different social groups ascribe to it and how
members of different ethnic groups view themselves. Fredrik Barth
has provided a useful, though contestable, definition for the term,
which defines an ethnic group's identity in terms of boundaries
rather than the cultural material that it encloses. For Barth,

ethnic groups are social organizations whose defining features are identified by the members themselves and are readily identifiable by others. Each group is distinguishable from other groups of the same order. In his definition, Barth describes the social processes by which ethnic groups identify themselves as distinctive entities, and as such, they maintain the boundaries that differentiate them from others. Barth's central position is that an ethnic group ought to be defined and viewed according to its own boundaries and not by its cultural characteristics (1969, 2000). However, in his criticism of Barth's definition of ethnic identity, Geoff Emberling (1997) argues for the use of the term 'difference' instead of 'boundary', because 'a boundary suggests a sharp separation between members of one group and those of another'. He adds that the term is misleading because:

> First, it may suggest that people in a single ethnic group are completely separate from members of other ethnic groups ... Second, a boundary has a physical sense that is sometimes inappropriate. The metaphor leads us to use other physical terms: ethnic groups construct and maintain boundaries, boundaries are permeable (or not), and boundaries enclose cultural traits. These associations tend to make us view ethnicity as absolute, rather than based on perceptions of difference. For these reasons, 'difference' may be a more appropriate term than boundary. (Emberling, 1997, p. 299–300)

The characteristics of ethnic groups in Afghanistan demonstrate that a definition strongly based on 'boundary' and a sharp separation between different groups is problematic. For instance, there are Shi'ah (Ithna Ashari and Isma'ili) and Sunni (Hanafi) Hazaras who speak both Persian and Hazaragi (a dialect of Persian). The Pashtun ethnic group contains orthodox and Sufi Sunnis (Hanafi) and Shi'ah (mainly Ithna Ashari) Muslims who speak both Pashto and Persian. The Tajik group contains Shi'ah (Ithna Ashari and Isma'ili) and Sunni/ Sufi (Hanafi) Muslims who speak Persian and other non-Persian languages. Thus, there are no clear boundaries among these ethnic groups; rather, the boundaries overlap. Although they share some strong areas of fusion, there remains much fission. Thus, Afghani ethnic groups can also be understood in terms of social and group solidarity among their various members. In early Muslim literature, the Arabic concept of *asabiyya* (tribal belonging), has its roots in the word '*asb*', which literally means 'nerve', and is understood as the fibre or sinew by which a group is held together (Goodman, 1972, p. 256). The term has also been translated as 'spirit of kinship, (Gabrieli, 1960, p. 681), 'group feeling' (Ibn-Khaldun, trans. Rosenthal, 1967, p. 28), 'social solidarity' (Issawi, 1950, p. 103) and 'social solidarity with a group consciousness' (Esposito, 2003, p. 25). Further, Adamec (2001, p. 49) describes *asabiyya* as social solidarity and (unconditional) loyalty and devotion to one's clan and tribe. Ibn-Khaldun, the medieval Islamic scholar describes *asabiyya* as tribal kinship and solidarity; it is a fundamental element which is formed only in groups related by blood ties, or by other ties which fulfil the same functions (Ibn-Khaldun, 1971, p. 128–9, 1980, p. 242; Issawi, 1950, p. 103). The strength of ethnic, or social and group solidarity is affected by a number of factors, such as the group's socio–economic, political and historical situation, its interaction with other groups, and the strength of kinship among its members. In Afghanistan, many forms of social injustice were imposed upon the Hazara Isma'ilis by the dominant groups in the country. In traditional societies like Afghanistan, the *asabiyya* of the dominant tribal group led to the marginalization, suppression and exclusion of smaller groups. In this study, the young people interviewed showed little ethnic solidarity. This is explained by the fact that the Hazara Isma'ili community in Germany does not face the social injustices of tribal *asabiyya* experienced in Afghanistan. Therefore, the youths in this study do not have a strong sense of solidarity with their Hazara ethnicity. Fatima's and Rafi's experiences demonstrate that ethnic solidarity has been replaced by ethnic consciousness that leads to a new, alternative form of ethnic identity:

> I was not born in Afghanistan. I don't know what the life of a Hazara is like in Afghanistan; what reputation the Hazaras have in Afghanistan. When I meet with other Afghanis, those from Kabul, Qandahar or whatever their ethnic background, I am not ashamed to tell them that I am a Hazara. I am proud of the fact that I am a Hazara and that I was born a Hazara. (Rafi, age 17)

> I have learned about some of the history of our community in Afghanistan from my parents: the injustices, the suppression, and that the Hazaras have no rights in Afghanistan. I have also

read a book about the Hazaras, *The Kite Runner*, and have the details of what was happening with the Hazaras. Fortunately, here in Germany, I have not experienced such injustices, or someone would have said to me, 'You are a Hazara, what do you want here?', or 'You are not special'. While I acknowledge [that my being a] Hazara is part of my identity, since I have not experienced injustice related to the Hazaras [in Afghanistan], I [believe it has far less of an] influence on my identity than religion, and being a German citizen. (Fatima, age 17)

Fatima's and Rafi's experiences display how the 'old' ethnicity, inherited from parents and members of the community, is expressed as a new construction of ethnicity. In this 'new ethnicity', the members are conscious of the shared experiences of the group through literature, media and oral narratives, but do not experience them in the same way as their parents. The existence of this ethnic consciousness is an important factor in the development of the youth's hybridized identity. Hall (1989) states that it is on the basis of this consciousness that one can act, talk and reflect on one's own experience, history, and cultural traditions. The youth's relationship to their traditions is partly formed through the memories of parents and community members and partly through their subjective, self-conscious experiences, the combination of which enables them to experience and express their 'true self' and 'true identity'.

The impact of language

Language connects the Isma'ili Afghani youths in this study to their past, the traditions maintained for them by their parents and members of the community. The recitation of *qasidas* (laudatory poems) is one example of the connection between the present and the past. Speaking both Persian and German enhances the development of their hybridized identity. As the research respondents were Hazara Afghanis living in Germany, they spoke Hazaragi, Persian and German. They usually spoke Hazaragi with their parents and community members and German among themselves and non-Afghani friends. Zainab's comment below reveal how she is aware of how language sets her apart from the wider German society. This awareness was common among other respondents:

One notices the difference between oneself and others when
one is young. The others, for example, are German, and we are
different and at home we speak differently, not German. One
notices such differences when one is young. (Zainab, age 15)

Language also intersects with religious practices; for example, the
Afghani Isma'ili youth perform their prayers in Arabic, although
Persian is also used in other liturgical aspects of their religious
ceremonies. This is observed in the recitation of devotional literature, such as *qasidas*, written in praise of God, Prophet Mohammad, Caliph 'Ali, and the Isma'ili Imams. *Qasidas* are written in
'high Persian', and reading and understanding *qasidas* is challenging for many respondents because they have not lived and
studied in Afghanistan and many cannot read and write Persian
well. Therefore, many of them recite *qasidas* through phonetic
German transliterations. However, they do treat *qasidas* with
respect and consider them sacred texts because they are written in praise of Allah, Prophet Mohammad, Caliph 'Ali and the
Isma'ili Imams.

The impact of religion

The *Jamat-khana* represents the physical embodiment of religious
space, where various forms of religious and spiritual expressions
and practices – such as prayers, religious rites, ceremonies,
festivals, customs, dress and so on – occur. In addition, the
Jamat-khana also serves as a focus for the social organization
and mobilization of the community – as a place for conducting
cultural activities. The culmination of these factors produces an
ambient environment in which the link between man and God,
and between material and spiritual life, is maintained, elevating
the believer's state of consciousness beyond the ordinary. The
impact of religion on identity is expressed in Hayatullah's
comment:

To be a Hazara does not mean much actually. Frankly speaking,
to be an Afghani does not mean much to me either. I could
come from another country, and it would be the same to me.
But, to be an Isma'ili is then something different. I don't know if

I could imagine having any other religion . . . it has been the most important thing to me. (Hayatullah, age 18)

For the Isma'ili Afghani youths in Germany, the *Jamat-khana* appears to heighten their religious consciousness. Fatima describes the *Jamat-khana* and the Isma'ili community as the most important factors in the construction of her identity:

I saw a film about Hazir Imam [in the *Jamat-khana*], made by the AKDN.[1] I don't know why I suddenly experienced a strong feeling [during watching the film], as it told me that the path I had chosen was the true [path]. Here, I felt that my religious path was a path of truth. Yes, here I got the strongest feeling about religion. When I attended the *didar*[2] [in London], I cried, as I had a deep spiritual emotion and could not stop my tears. I would say that this process is continuously building, and there is no end to it. (Fatima, age 17)

Fatima's experience highlights a profoundly emotional religious experience. Such an experience does not occur without a context, nor does it occur in a cultural vacuum. Rather, it is influenced by socio–cultural and historical events and experiences. The community, the place and space of the *Jamat-khana*, the religious rites and rituals, the Imam's *farman*,[3] work and face-to-face *didars* all influenced the facets of Fatima's identity. These contributory factors and events facilitated a kind of religious experience and understanding that was fostered by her personal enthusiasm and commitment to religion. Zibah's experience, expressed in the following statement, resonates with Fatima's and that of other respondents:

I would say that religion is a part of me. [I see] religion . . . as a belief and . . . as deeds. By belief, I mean that one performs prayer; that one believes in what one prays and also one understands it in one or another way. By deeds, I mean that one does not only pray and believe in it, but . . . also lives according to those principles and that one becomes a good human being and does good things. (Zibah, age 15)

It is not enough to perform prayer and attend the *Jamat-khana*. Religion is more than prayer. For example, one has to help others through voluntary works and activities. One has to help others, regardless of the person's background; one has to behave correctly in school and at home. All these are part of religious practice. (Fatima, age 17)

The research findings demonstrate that religion had both a transformational and transcending influence on the respondents, thus giving them the opportunity to rise above their ethnicity, language and other cultural limitations. Zibah's experience, which was echoed by other respondents, best summarizes this transformative and transcendental power of the spiritual experience:

First, Isma'ilism is our religion and that is important for us. Here, one's [country of] origin is no longer important. There are many Isma'ilis who come from different countries, but they have the same religion. Second, I value German [culture], because I live here in Germany and it has an influence on my identity. Third, to be a Hazara means that I am from Afghanistan. Finally, the Persian language and [being an] Afghani are mutually connected. They both are equally important to me, and all Afghanis do speak Persian . . . However, religion has contributed a lot to who I am now. I have attended *Bait al-'Ilm* classes for a quite long time now. In *Bait al-'Ilm*, I learn about how our religion began; I learn about Prophet Mohammad, etc. Yes, I also attend the *Jamat-khana* every Friday and Saturday and say my prayer. The *Jamat-khana* has an influence on my identity. (Marina, age 17)

King (1987), states that such transformative experiences can be found in every religion, while Dwyer's (2000) study of young Muslim women in Britain shows the existence of a supranational Muslim identity that connects her respondents to other Muslims across a transnational *ummah* (universal Muslim community). However, some differences between these two different diasporic youth's experiences are discernable. Dwyer states that unlike men, young women were often excluded from sites where religious knowledge is transmitted; for example, at mosque meetings (Dwyer, 1999, 2000). Marina, Fatima and Zibah's statements, however, indicate that both male and female youth in Germany have access to *Jamat-khana* activities and receive religious knowledge, and the *Bait al-'Ilm* classes provide them with religious education which they would not gain in Germany's secular education system. However, it is also interesting to note that while, in both cases, religion exercises a similar transcendental power, the youth's experience of that power needs to be contextualized. The Hazara Isma'ili youths of Afghani-origin identify with the wider global Isma'ili community, while the South Asian Muslim women identify with the wider Muslim *ummah*. The reason for this difference lies in the social history of these groups. Although the Isma'ilis contributed significantly to Muslim civilizations, particularly during the Fatimid (909–1171 CE) and Alamut (1090–1256 CE) eras, for most of Islamic history, Isma'ilis were a politically marginalized group. Frischauer (1970) states that the Isma'ilis, from an early period, were persecuted from all sides. Their support for Imam Isma'il (765–75 CE) was not only considered heretical by majority Sunni Muslims, it was also regarded as high treason by their fellow Shi'ahs who supported Musa al-Kazim. In addition, the Hazara Isma'ilis in Afghanistan were also persecuted because of their ethnic background. Thus, this double suppression has led the Hazara Isma'ilis of Afghanistan to identify with and seek support from the global Isma'ili community rather than the wider *ummah*. Fatima's comment reflects this narrative:

> I am an Isma'ili first. I was born and grew up in this community, and I am proud of it. Second . . . I am a Muslim. Being a Muslim is not as [important to me] as being an Isma'ili, because there are different Muslim groups and we do not celebrate some festivals that the other Muslims do, and they do not celebrate our festivals. (Fatima age 17)

Fatima's comment also exhibits that the wider Muslim population (the *ummah*), is a complex, diverse and heterogeneous community. In everyday life, Muslims within the wider *ummah* differentiate between one another according to religious doctrine, language, ethnicity, polity, cultural experiences and geographic location. All of these factors affect an individual's perception of religion and religious practices, and shape their identity. For the majority of respondents in this study, religion was a very personal experience which they appeared to embrace enthusiastically. Activities such as, youth camps, the annual National Sport Festival in the UK, the solar *hijri* New Year celebration of Nawroz, which were organized by Isma'ili institutions and *Jamat-khanas*, played a pivotal role in developing the youth's personal enthusiasm and commitment to religion. These events provided the Afghani Hazara Isma'ili youth in Germany with an opportunity to meet other Isma'ili youth from other cities and countries. Rafi's comments reflect his personal commitment and enthusiasm for his faith:

> I can always firmly hold onto my religion, but I can't firmly hold onto my birthplace. For example, my religion is always here for me. When I have a problem, I can pray, I can try to find contact with God. This is the most important thing for me. (Rafi, age 17)

The above comment demonstrates that religion plays the most dominant role in the construction of identity among the Isma'ili youth in Germany. The dominance of one form of identity often does resolve competing fields of multiple identities (Marshall and Read, 2003). In the context of this particular study, commitment to religious values and principles imbued the youth with a higher degree of consciousness and made them more able to rationalize competing aspects of their identities. Thus, one can conclude that religion, in this specific context, has had a much stronger impact on the youth's identity than the other factors discussed. To paraphrase Marcia (1988), when one factor influencing the development of identity is significantly stronger than others, an individual's identity becomes fixed, and is less likely to undergo further changes in the future. To conclude, the findings of this study have demonstrated that, since religion occupies such a dominant position in the hybridized identity of the diasporic Afghani Isma'ili youths in Germany, it is very likely that it will continue to influence, and remain a powerful element in, the future development of the studied youth's identity.

Conclusion

The Afghani Isma'ili community in Germany is relatively a young diasporic community. The community members have a strong interest in maintaining their cultural and traditional values and identity, and reproduce them in varied forms. The research findings outlined here demonstrate that the youths are conscious of their ethnic origins (Hazara), ethnic language (Hazaragi), their country of origin

(Afghanistan) and the Persian language, even though most youths have never been to their country of origin. The research findings show that while Afghani youth appreciate German cultural values, they are also committed to maintaining the identity that they have inherited from their parents. For example, they embrace the positive values from both communities – the freedom of expression, liberty of thought and educational opportunities from German society; and the sense of collectiveness, hospitality, respect for their elders and parents, and the sense of sharing and caring from their parents and the Isma'ili community. This research also demonstrates that religion plays the most dominant role in Afghani youth identities in Germany. This study has highlighted the complexity, subjectivity and temporal nature of religious and cultural identities for an under-researched youth group within Europe. It is a process that also involves complex power relations (Brah and Phoenix, 2004) that manifest themselves in the aligning of 'old' Afghani Isma'ili identities versus the 'newer' hybridized identities of the youth. The youth studied here developed their hybridized identities through the prism of their parental and community identities, combined with the cultural values of German society. Although the majority of respondents have never been to Afghanistan, they have learnt about the country of their origin, the living conditions there, their family and its ethnic status, the reasons for their migration and the political situation through their parents, community members, and the media.

The results of this study highlight the need for further research on the Hazara Isma'ili diasporic communities in Europe, as these have been under-researched thus far. Research on the Hazaras in Europe could also be focused on education, social integration and inclusion, pluralism, the experiences of Hazara Isma'ili women in Europe and the building of bridges between the Muslim communities internally and non-Muslims communities externally – all of which would prove to be intriguing areas for future study.

References

Abu-Lughod, L. (1991), 'Writing against culture', in Richard G. Fox (ed.), *Recapturing Anthropology: Working in the Present*. Santa Fe, NM: School of American Research, pp. 137–62.

Adamec, L. W. (2001), *Historical Dictionary of Islam*. London: The Scarecrow Press, Inc.

Barth, F. (1969), *Ethnic Groups and Boundaries*. Boston: Little, Brown and Company.

— (2000), 'Enduring and emerging issues in the analysis of ethnicity', in, H. Vermeulen and C. Govers (eds), *Anthropology of Ethnicity: Beyond 'Ethnic Groups and Boundaries'*. Amsterdam: HET Spinhuis Publishers, pp. 11–32.

Blasi, A. (1988), 'Identity and the development of the self', in D. K. Lapsley and F. C. Power (eds), *Self, Ego, and Identity: Integrative Approaches*. New York: Springer-Verlag, pp. 226–42.

—(1996), *Cartographies of Diaspora*. London: Routledge.

Brah, A., and Phoenix, A. (2004), 'Ain't I a woman? Revisiting intersectionality', *Journal of International Women's Studies*, 5, (3), pp. 75–86.

Brubaker, R. (2005), 'The "diaspora" diaspora', *Ethnic and Racial Studies*, 28, (1), pp. 1–19.

DiCaprio, N. S. (1983), *Personality Theories: A Guide to Human Nature*. (2nd edn), Winston: CBS College Publishing.

Dwyer, C. (1999), 'Contradictions of community: questions of identity for young British Muslim women', *Environment and Planning A*, 31, pp. 53–68.

—(2000), 'Negotiating diasporic identities: young British South Asian Muslim women', *Women's Studies International Forum*, 23, (4), pp. 475–86.

Emberling, G. (1997), 'Ethnicity in complex societies: archaeological perspectives', *Journal of Archaeological Research*, 5, (4), pp. 295–344.

Erikson, E. H. (1950), *Childhood and Society*. New York: Norton.

—(1958), *Young Man Luther: A Study in Psychoanalysis and History*. London: Faber & Faber Ltd.

—(1968), *Identity: Youth and Crisis*. London: Faber & Faber Ltd.

Esposito, J. L. (2003), *The Oxford Dictionary of Islam*. Oxford: Oxford University Press.

Faist, T. (2000), *The Volume and Dynamics of International Migration and Transnational Social Spaces*. Oxford: Oxford University Press.

Favell, A. (2001), 'Integration policy and integration research in Europe: a review and a critique', in T. A. Aleinikoff and D. Klusmeyer (eds), *Citizenship Today: Global Perspectives and Practices*. Massachusetts: Brookings Institution Press.

—(2003), 'Integration nations: the nation-state and research on immigrants in Western Europe', in G. Brochmann (ed.), *The Multicultural Challenge*. Oxford: Elsevier.

Fennema, M. (2004), 'The concept and measurement of ethnic community', *Journal of Ethnic and Migration Studies*, 30, (3), pp. 429–47.

Frischauer, W. (1970), *The Aga Khans*. London: The Bodley Head.

Gabrieli, F. (1960), Oriental Essays. Salvatore Sciascia Editore: Caltanissetta-Roma

Gilroy, P. (1987), *There Ain't No Black in the Union Jack*. Hutchinson: London.

—(1997), 'Diaspora and the detours of identity', in K. Woodward (ed.), *Identity and Difference*. London: Sage, pp. 299–343.

Goodman, L. E. (1972), 'Ibn Khaldun and Thucydides', *Journal of the American Oriental Society*, 92, (2), 250–70.

Hall, S. (1989), *Ethnicity: Identity and Difference*. Available from: < https://pantherfile.uwm.edu/wash/www/102/stuarthall. htm#2 > [Accessed: 20 August 2010].

—(1994), 'Cultural Identity and Diaspora', in P. Williams and L. Chrisman (eds), *Colonial Discourse and Post-Colonial Theory: A Reader*. New York: Columbia University Press.

Hendry, L. B., Mayer, P., and Kloep, M. (2007), 'Belonging or opposing? A grounded theory approach to young people's cultural identity in a majority/minority societal context', *Identity: An International Journal of Theory and Research*, 7, (3), pp. 181–204.

Ibn Khaldun, Abd al-Rahman ibn Mohammad (1967), *The Muqaddimah: An Introduction to History*. Trans. F. Rosenthal, ed. by N. J. Dawood. Princeton, NJ: Princeton University Press.

—(1971), *Al-Muqaddimah*. Bayrut: Dar Ihya'al-Turath al-Arabi.

—(1980), *Muqaddimah*. Trans. P. Gunabadi. Tehran: Bungah-e Tarjomah wa Nashr-e Kitab.

Issawi C. (1950) *An Arab Philosophy of History: Selections from the Prolegomena of Ibn Khaldun of Tunis (1332–1406)*. London: John Murray.

Jupp, V., and Norris, C. (1996), 'Traditions in documentary analysis', in M. Hamersley (ed.), *Social Research: Philosophy, Politics and Practice*. London: Sage in Association with The Open University.

Kaya, A. (2007), 'German-Turkish transnational space: a separate space of their own', *German Studies Review*, 30, (3), pp. 1–20.

King, W. L. (1987), 'Religion', in M. Eliade (ed.), *The Encyclopaedia of Religion*. 12, New York: Macmillan Publishing Company.

Kundnani, A (2002), 'The death of multiculturalism'. Institute of Race Relations. Available from: < http://www.irr.org.uk/2002/april/ ak000001.html > [Accessed: 20 August 2010].

Mandaville, P. (2001), 'Re-imagining Islam in diaspora: the politics of mediated community', *International Communication Gazette*, 63, (2–3), pp. 169–86.

Marcia, J. E. (1988), 'Ego identity, cognitive/moral development, and individuation', in D. K. Lapsley and F. C. Power (eds), *Self, Ego, and Identity: Integrative Approaches*. New York: Springer-Verlag.

Marshall, S. E., and Read, J. G. (2003), 'Identity politics among Arab-American women', *Social Science Quarterly*, 84, (4), pp. 875–91.

Mizruchi, M. S. (1996), 'What do interlocks do? An analysis, critique, and assessment of research on interlocking directorates', *Annual Review of Sociology*, 22, pp. 217–98.

Nanji, A. (2008), *Dictionary of Islam*. London: Penguin Books.

Noam, G. G. (1988), 'The self, adult development, and the theory of biography and transformation', in D. K. Lapsley and F. C. Power (eds), *Self, Ego, and Identity: Integrative Approaches*. New York: Springer-Verlag.

Rattansi, A., and Phoenix, A. (2005), 'Rethinking youth identities: modernist and postmodernist frameworks', *Identity: An International Journal of Theory and Research*, 5, (2), pp. 97–123.

Sadat, M. H. (2001), 'The quest for Afghanistan by defining Afghaniyat', *Omaid Weekly*. Available from: < http://www.omaid.com/english_section/back_issues_archive/476.htm#item2 > [Accessed: 20 August 2010].

—(2008), 'Hyphenating *Afghaniyat* (Afghan-ness) in the Afghan diaspora', *Journal of Muslim Affairs*, 28, (3), pp. 329–42.

Shain, Y. (1999), *Marketing the American Creed Abroad: Diasporas in US and their Homelands*. Cambridge: Cambridge University Press.

Shain, Y., and Sherman, M. (1998), 'Dynamics of disintegration: diaspora, secession and the paradox of nation-states', *Nations and Nationalism*, 4, (3), pp. 321–46.

Sheffer, G. (1986), 'A new field of study: modern diasporas in international politics', in G. Sheffer (ed.), *Modern Diasporas in International Politics*. London: Croom Helm, pp. 9–15.

—(1995), 'The emergence of new ethno-national diasporas'. *Migration*, 28, (2), pp. 5–28.

Vermeulen, F., and Berger, M. (2008), 'Turkish civic networks and political behaviour in Amsterdam and Berlin', in S. K. Ramakrishnan and I. Bloemraad (eds), *Civil Hopes and Political Realities: Immigrants, Community Organizations and Political Engagement*. New York: Russell Sage Foundation, pp. 160–92.

Vertovec, S. (1997), 'Three meanings of "diaspora", exemplified among South Asian religions', *Diaspora*, 6, (3), pp. 277–99.

Wahlbeck, Ö. (1999), *Kurdish Diasporas: A Comparative Study of Kurdish Refugee Communities*. London: Macmillan.

—(2002), 'The concept of diaspora as an analytical tool in the study of refugee communities', *Journal of Ethnic and Migration Studies*, 28, (2), pp. 221–38.

Wimmer, A., and Schiller, N. G. (2002), 'Methodological nationalism and beyond: nation-state building, migration and the social sciences', *Global Networks*, 2, (4), pp. 301–34.

6

Turning to my religion

MUHAMMAD G. KHAN

Introduction

This chapter explores some of the forces at play in seeking the allegiance, alliance and authority of young Muslims as they 'turn to religion'. I use this phrase as it represents both the confessional and the physical aspects of this act. The 'new' physical appearance is both a demonstration and a manifestation of the relationship between the intrinsic and extrinsic motivations that inform this *turning to*.

In this exercise, I cannot help but be informed by my experience in youth work practice, policy, management and my work in developing Muslim youth work approaches. This lens is helpful in that the subtle dichotomies involved in developing work with young people and the issues and realities that affect their lives are revealed in its practice, giving rise to key insights that help articulate what is happening both *in them* and *to them*.

The questions that youth work asks are the key questions being faced by young Muslims and should be relevant to the questions that young people are asking themselves as they consider the different pulls and pushes from family, media, society, peers and so on. As

Young (2006) notes, the issue of identity is integral to youth work in terms of:

- Self-image: a person's description of self.
- Self-esteem: a person's evaluation of self, a crucial dimension of which is a person's adherence to moral and ethical standards. (Coleman and Hendry, 1999, cited in Young, op.cit.)

She goes on to note that:

> [. . .] youth work is an exercise in moral philosophy insofar as it enables and supports young people to examine what they consider to be 'good or bad', 'right or wrong', 'desirable or undesirable' in relation to self and others – 'What sort of person am I?' 'What kind of relationships do I want?' 'What kind of community/society do I want to live in?' (Young, 2006, p. 3)

These questions about identity, which define youth work according to Young, are questions with significant contemporary relevance in a context where a recent Church of England survey suggests that Christianity has become a 'faded cultural memory' (Collins-Mayo et al., 2010) among the young, and a variety of polls listed by Zuckerman (2007) suggest that anything from 32 per cent to 44 per cent of people in Britain do not believe in God. The percentage is even higher in Sweden, France and the Netherlands. To add to this religious ambivalence, according to a 2006 *Guardian/ICM* poll, 63 per cent of people said that they were not religious (compared to 33 per cent that said they were) and 82 per cent of those questioned saw religion as a cause of division and tension between people.

It seems inevitable that in this context the presence of Muslims who identify themselves as Muslims challenge a supposedly increasingly secular society and the values that underpin it. In such circumstances Islam, and Muslims in particluar, with the variety of scripts in play – such as the attacks on the Twin Towers in the US in 2001 (commonly referred to as '9/11'), the London bombings in July 2005 (also known as '7/7'), concerns over an increase in radicalism or terrorism, the Islamification of UK and

Europe, the take up and wearing of headscarves among Muslim women and the controversy surrounding the Danish cartoons – are easily caricatured as being a source of division, a moral panic that challenges the values that inform a democratic and free society. To stand up and be seen as a Muslim and face this momentum, as described below by Allen (2010), could be seen as an act of anger, courage, conviction, a need to defend, a need for comfort or an act of solidarity. Just as being a Muslim can mean different things in different contexts (Sayyid, 2010), the reasons for this *turn to* Islam for young Muslims can also have a multitude of causes and not just as a response to the following:

> Muslims have become understood in frames that both acknowledged and perpetuated an ongoing otherness, one that is inherently foreign, alien and enemy and regularly interchanged with those populist notions of Muslims as 'terrorists' and fifth columnists. (Allen, 2010, p. 111)

This *turning to* can be described as an act that is relevant and in its time, for, as Ignatieff (1997) suggests, the core value of modernity is freedom, the purpose of which is:

> To fashion one's identity, and one's life as one wills, since the very sense of dignity and self-worth are tied into this idea of personal freedom. We tend to rank feelings of belonging to community, nation, and family much lower in our conception than in pre-industrial and pre-modern society. (p. 85–6)

With this statement, Ignatieff indicates the tensions associated with a *turning to* Islam by young Muslims; it is not only an act of freedom but also an act of association with family and community, an act that is thoroughly modern and thoroughly, according to Ignatieff, pre-modern. It is clearly an act of agency, a rejection of passively participating in the world that young people find themselves in; it is no longer a need of endurance but an act of creation, rebellion or rejection. It is this ability, and the fear it generates, that has concentrated such attention on youth participation in democratic processes (John, 2003), when young people move beyond being seen as chattels of parents or communities.

British Muslim – practising Muslim

It is not clear whether the creation of the label 'British Muslim' is as confidently used by many young Muslims today as it was to describe who they are by faith, location and culture. For instance:

- Faith – their religious identity as Muslims.
- Location – being in Britain, Germany, etc.
- Culture – being bought up in and influenced by the cultural context they surround themselves with and shape.

'British Muslim' was a term coined by young Muslims to express a symbiotic relationship that evolved between their British and religious identities. It emerged in the early 1990s as an act of self-definition in a context in which the label 'Muslim' was often preceded by Pakistani, Indian and so forth as an extension, or an aspect, of their ethnicity (Samad, 1996; Lewis, 1994). This movement from politics to culture to faith is captured by Tariq Modood (2007) when he says: 'some of those who said they were Black at the start of the 1980s might be Bangladeshi at the end of the decade and might today be British Muslim' (p. 105). This does not mean that young people have abstracted other aspects; for example, where before the term 'Black' might have been one of solidarity borne out of a shared experience of racism, today it may inform the cultural practices associated with resistance or complaint (Cooke and Lawrence, 2005).

Being a British Muslim gave legitimacy to both their location and the presence of their religious identity within it. In their most conservative form, both of these identities sought to extract, for different reasons, the 'ethno and cultural' identities sustained by the connection with relationships and practices with the points of origin of their parents or grandparents. This was, and is, an act of self-definition in the context of belonging *in* Britain. However, in the British context there is a retreat from its earlier policies of multiculturalism – as most recently evidenced by the Prime Minister David Cameron's speech in Munich in February 2011, in which he announced that 'state multiculturalism had failed' (BBC, 2011) – to more essentialized notions of Britishness (Kymlicka, 2007). This has increasingly viewed and associated a sense of belonging to Britain through the introduction of a citizenship oath and pledge (Nationality, Immigration and Asylum Act 2002), an Act which, in terms of political rhetoric at least, conflates established minority communities with new migrants.

The connection with ethnicity and ethnic roots has historically been bound up with competing concepts of assimilation and integration, which have led to notions such as that of a 'culture clash' (Anwar, 1998) and later discourses around 'Muslim enclaves' or 'ghettoes' (Cantle, 2001; Ouseley, 2001). These connections are problematic for reasons which will be explored here. I have sought to depict these 'push and pull' factors through Figure 6.1 below.

In the diagram below, Point 1 symbolizes Saudi Arabia, within which are Mecca and Medina – the most important sites of Islam and the real and aspirational meeting points for the *Ummah* (the Muslim community), and it is from Saudi Arabia that the momentum for the most conservative form of Islam, commonly known as *Wahhabism*, is resourced and exported. The *Ummah* presents itself to young Muslims as the religious aspirational sphere. The 'guardians' of the cities of Mecca and Medina, with their religious and spiritual significance, are believed to project an authentic 'Muslim' identity without the baggage of innovation that is often threaded into people's lives through culture, custom and tradition. The guardians of this space conflate this aspiration with a pejorative interpretation of custom and tradition.

Point 2 on this diagram represents the 'original' source and locale for this custom and tradition as well as being points of origin such

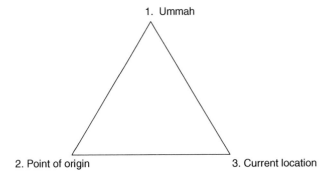

FIGURE 6. 1   Muslim youth – push and pull factors

as Kashmir, Bangladesh, Turkey, Pakistan, Somalia, Morocco and so on for those who have made their home in Britain, Germany, France and other non-Muslim countries in the West.

Point 3 represents where one could say a 'struggle for extraction' was taking place. This might be Britain or France in the 'third space', described by Gilroy (1987) as occupied by post-colonial settlers who are neither of one culture nor another. The struggle has been to extract oneself from the kind of 'folk Islam' that manifests itself in the third space and has been bought over by 'settlers' from their points of origin (Point 2). This form of Islam in the lives of young Muslims in Britain has often been presented as tainted by the religious traditions of their non-Muslim ancestors in India or Kashmir, for example. In the process of this extraction, the guardians associated with Point 1 on the diagram have often found willing converts, with young people frustrated by issues such as forced marriages or the supposed anachronism of customs associated with marriage or death whose meanings have been lost but whose form, through ritual, still remains. The need for distance from such ritualistic practices of Islam may be a response to the polarizing mechanisms often employed by racist discourses and which create feelings of shame and embarrassment among young Muslims as Pakistani's, Bangladeshis and so on.

However, customs do serve the purpose of bringing together families and communities on a regular basis, through which children are integrated and made familiar with the wider familial networks and relationships and learn how they should behave in them. This act of community preservation can be conflated with those of Point 1 in the diagram as an act of cultural preservation which becomes a struggle over the meaning and significance of either culture or religion as sources of legitimacy for ritual and custom, and therefore for behaviour and practice. This then makes its way into notions of what it is to be a 'practising Muslim'.

During the late 1980s and much of the 1990s, the wearing of the *hijab* or the keeping of a beard was an act of assertion of Muslim identity that gave significance and confidence to young Muslims needing to challenge, but also to associate with, an identity that gave legitimacy and provided the uplifting experience of belonging to something greater than themselves (Layard and Dunn, 2009). These were, for some, symbols of rebellion against community and tradition but have instead, been appropriated by the 'community' as symbols of collective religious identity. Today, they are seen more as testaments of faith that have introduced for young people a new language in the way some describe themselves as 'practising Muslims'. I am not sure whether Tim Winter (2003) wrote the following to express his concern about how 'being a Muslim' was being increasingly understood. It comes very close to an act of definition and judgement:

> The moderns, it seems, being more interested in religion than in God, define religion by listing all the things that it cannot be. Hence Islam, we are loudly told, is a list of prohibitions. Everywhere we turn there is something we must not believe, and certainly must not do. The list of ideas entailing *shirk* (polytheism) or *bid'ah* (innovation) grows ever longer . . . Islam, then, is about *not* being and doing things. (Winter, 2003, p. 8)

Winter goes onto describe how this approach impacts on localized practices in towns and cities across the Muslim world, which I have described here in the British context as 'aspects of acts of extraction'.

This defining of what a 'practising Muslim' is can be the reworking in the modern context of the struggle between the literal and interpretative, or between essence and form, presented as an 'either/or' choice. For instance, does wearing a scarf or beard mean that you are not a practising Muslim? And if not, then what are you?

No choice but *to turn*

While religious identity is seen as a private or latent issue for young people in general, this is not the case for young Muslims, who not only live out the introspective development of their religious identity under the impact of 'headline Islam', but whose religious identity is the obsessive object of suspicion, surveillance, polls, surveys and interrogation (McRoy, 2005; Phillips, 2006).

Their *turning* to religion is not something that can be saved for a rainy day; rather it is something that is being forced upon young Muslims by a societal context that pathologizes them as individuals *and* their religion, which in turn is cited as the causal factor behind the mistrust, misinterpretation and mistreatment that they experience. Given this context, and the fact that young Muslims in Britain today are being subjected to sustained critical scrutiny, which many experience as a fundamental questioning of their identity and loyalty as British citizens, their ability to keep some sense of balance and proportion receives little regard from opinion makers. These extrinsic factors do have an impact on young people's religiosity. A recent Joseph Rowntree Foundation JRF report, 'Young people's experiences of transition to adulthood: a study of minority ethnic and white young people' (Cassidy et al., 2006), found that young Pakistanis identified a greater role for religion in their lives than their non-Muslim counterparts. This centrality of faith is an issue which those who work with young Muslims are little prepared for.

It is an often forgotten fact that young Muslims are tackling the core tasks of adolescent transitions within a faith community where 34 per cent of the community's population is under 16 years of age and 18 per cent is between the ages of 16 and 24 (www. statistics.gov.uk). Therefore, the youth marginalization highlighted in the work of Fahmy (2006), MacDonald (2008) and Cusworth et al. (2009), disproportionately affects the Muslim community when compared to the wider population with figures at 20 and 11 per cent, respectively. Attacks on Islam, and on young people's 'Muslimness', from a range of sectors such as the media, government and wider society are often felt as personal attacks on the young people's Muslim identity, which connects them to their family and the wider Muslim community. For young Muslims, their Muslim identity provides a moral compass, access to networks and activities, a routine while growing up, a source and guide on manners, etiquette, individual and social expectations and rites and rituals. Their Islam and British identities provide a commonality with a Muslim community in Britain whose members speak at least 70 different languages and originate from 56 different nationalities (Choudhury, Open Society Institute, 2005). It provides a frame of reference that legitimatizes or makes sense of the 'other'. Nevertheless, the focus on young Muslims solely as 'young Muslims' can be a disservice, especially when ignoring socio-economic marginalization and the challenges faced in the transition to adulthood (Cassidy et al., 2006) which are faced by all young people. According to Edelman (1996), this is also a society that has never before:

Exposed children so early and relentlessly to cultural messages glamorizing violence, sex, material possessions and the use of alcohol and tobacco with so few mediating influences from responsible adults. Never have we experienced such numbing and reckless reliance on violence to solve problems, feel powerful, or be entertained. Never have so many children been permitted to rely on guns and gangs for protection rather than on parents, neighbours, religious congregations (Edelman, 1996, p. ix, cited in John, 2003, p.164).

It is therefore unfortunate for young Muslims that youth work is particularly prone to internalizing Islamophobic sentiments embedded in a discourse of securing and protecting values, principles and human rights, that is, the positive and inclusive values and principles that lie at its foundation (Khan, 2006), but advocates instead a discourse that seems to actively marginalize family and faith in much the same way that Carby (1999) described schools in the 1980s and 1990s as 'civilising sites' for black children outside the influence family and community. Idealist intentions and the desire to 'make a difference' and 'be of service' attracted many individuals to youth work long before David Cameron's 'Big Society', but it can conceal a certain 'missionary zeal' that may have religious roots in the way that Davies (1999), in his history of the development of youth work in England, notes was very often pursued by those believing youth work to be an expression of their Christian faith and part of a process of instilling middle-class values.

Muslim identity has increasingly become a positive and yet a very painful terrain for young Muslim people to negotiate, yet youth work in general remains suspicious of confessional approaches that are understood to create little space for a critical relationship between the young person, their religion, or society. In the case of Muslim youth work, there is a specific need to comfort and reassure young people, and to shore up their identities in the face of such sustained hostility. However, this support process can be viewed as an indoctrination or manipulation of young Muslims; a learning process that is confessional and without choice. This often forces young people into what Hazel Blears (then Minister for the Department of Communities and Local Government) referred to as 'ungoverned spaces' at a Preventing Violent Extremism Conference (October 31, 2007). The spaces she was drawing attention to were the virtual and actual spaces, such as internet forums, gyms and coffee shops, that she believed facilitated religious extremism among young Muslims. In youth work practice this means that challenge needs to be held back until young people feel secure enough to be challenged.

In Britain, mediation between communities and the government is predicated on an organizational presence and this, by and large, has been the preserve of the middle classes and at the service of middle-class interests. Muslim communities and Muslim young people are not exempt from these class dynamics, which operate in ways similar to those studied by Janine Clark (2004) in the Middle East. Her research on various Islamic charitable institutions suggests that relationships between constituents and organizations served the interests of the middle classes, and not the poorer socio-economic classes. Young Muslims are therefore marginalized due to their age as far as Muslim organizations are concerned and, as a result of their 'Muslimness', where generic service organizations are concerned. Interestingly, in 2009, the Department for Children, Schools and Families (DCSF) awarded nearly £30 million – the largest government investment since the 1960s – to YMCAs for the implementation and delivery of new youth centres, to implement '*myspace*' projects across the UK (YMCA, 2009).

It seems that just as the presence of the YMCA has been strengthened by this funding, so the absence of Muslim organizations has been compounded.

This is the gap filled by organizations such as Hizb ut-Tahrir (HT), who give some credence to the angst, passion and idealism which are some of outcomes from this turn by young people, providing what David Clark (1973), in his conceptualizations of community, terms the 'three S's' – 'significance', 'security' and 'solidarity'. Within a Muslim youth context, the three S's can mean the following:

Significance – through acceptance; demonstrating trust through giving responsibility and leadership. Connecting the struggles encountered by Muslim youth to a wider political and historical struggle.

Security – this is achieved through appealing to the conservatism of young Muslim people through a very literal approach to the Qur'an, which connects to an aspirational community (the *Ummah*). Security is also found through numbers; that is, physical, but also mental, security through clear messages about what is acceptable and unacceptable, leaving little room for doubt.

Solidarity – connecting young people to peer groups, networks and activities that provide a sense of solidarity, common cause and routine. There is also the understanding of solidarity that emerges out of a sense of responsibility and significance of role and cause.

The emphasis on solidarity allows an outlet for shared anger and pain, something that Maajid Nawaz – Director of the Quilliam Foundation and a former leader in Hizb-ut-Tahrir HT (2008) – spoke about when describing his early attraction to religious extremism to the US Senate Committee on Homeland Security and Government Affairs hearing:

> Here was a man who could speak my language, who felt my pain and who most importantly of all could answer my questions concerning identity and faith in a radically different way. (Nawaz, 2008, p. 50)

This sense of significance, solidarity and security is a role fulfilled by an age-old phenomenon that has, according to Deuchar (2009), generated considerable contemporary activity and concern. Deuchar identifies gangs as performing roles that are similar to those of the family or school, especially for young people that have withdrawn from such influences. Similarly, Beckford (2004), in discussing 'peer gangs' among young black youth, highlights how these, in contrast to violent and major crime-based gangs, are based loosely on peer networks united by kinship, friendships or locale, and engage in more acts of nuisance than crime.

This sense of community among youth can be viewed in direct contrast to the ways in which some mosque bodies assume an inability on the part of young people to assert their own agency, instead 'believing' the youth to be somehow incomplete and viewed as works 'in progress'. This type of attitude results in a disincentivized and oppressive context in which young people are asked to participate. Lindner (2004) argues that a strong theological capacity exists among young people to articulate ontological concepts, piety and appreciate ritual, but that this often contradicts the widespread belief that young people are not capable of articulating their religious or spiritual needs.

Thus, the causes of the *turning to* religion on the part of the young people may have very little relationship to those understood by the Imams and elders running Muslim organizations and may well be as divided as the following story suggests. A group of young people and pastors were asked what events drew the young to the church. The pastors listed items such as:

> Day of baptism; First day of school; Day of first communion or confirmation; Day of departure for college or armed forces; Wedding; Death of parents or grandparents.
> (Linder, 2004, p. 60)

The young people listed the following:

> The day your best friend moves away; When you get left back in school or aren't selected for a team; When parents divorce; When your dog/cat/pet dies; When a kid you know dies; When parents or grandparents die. (ibid)

While this may not be the case in the Muslim context, even though making comparisons may be a useful inter-faith exercise, it would be misleading to simply assume that similar causes and issues exist between young people from differing faith groups. One could say that Muslim young people are the same as all young people, some young people or no other group of young people. What these commonalities and differences are is beyond the scope of this chapter, but this exercise is hampered by a comparative absence of investment in these important conversations. The UK's 'new' age of austerity, accompanied by the widely reported cuts to youth services across the country, will stunt further the development of narratives that can work these differences out to inform practice. Clark (2004) asserts that the relationship that Muslim organizations mediate is one between the individual and their religious community. This gives some credence to Tariq Ramadan's (2004) assertion that mediating organizations can reinforce Muslims and with it, young Muslims, as members of a community rather than citizens of a country. The voices of young people can jar the ears of institutions because they speak as citizens of a country rather than as members of community, with a voice that carries this inflection. This is a cognitive shift that at times is still to be made by those listening. The dialogue is about accountability and rights, in which the aggrieved is present rather than represented.

This is not to say that young Muslims have all the answers. If they had, then the lens would have its limitations and its advantages. Young people can be the most conservative in their religiosity, but this is typical of many young people from all faith backgrounds when they turn to religion. However, young people can provide the raw detail behind the policy jargon – such as 'community cohesion', or 'children as carers' – that anaesthetize the reality they are trying to describe.

The voice of the young people in this policy context is a complex issue. The policy of successive British governments has been to choose organizations that mediate a relationship with 'the Muslim community', but these organizations often end up becoming the sources that have the answers (or, preferably, *the* answer) to, 'what needs to be done.' Today, there is an expectation that young Muslims have all the answers to issues around radicalization, in the same way that the Muslim Council of Britain (MCB), the British Muslim Forum (BMF), the Sufi Muslim Council, the Radical Middle Way, or the Quilliam Foundation were assumed to have all the answers. Whether they inform policy or become seen as advocates and advisors of policy, there are serious ethical dimensions where young people are concerned. As young people, they are still forming their political viewpoints, testing the boundaries, being extreme but slowly locating the networks and relationships that can support them. The unequal power dimension between the State and an individual or group can lead to the imposition of a political position that becomes beyond the capacity of an individual or a small organization to challenge and counteract. An example of an act of engagement beginning as a consultation and then being converted into advocacy was the way in which New Labour established the 'Young Muslims Advisory Group' (YMAG). This started life conceptually as the 'Young Muslims Consultative Group' in 2008, and highlights the way a political party such as New Labour saw young people as 'advisors', as being politically more expedient than young people as 'consultants'.

The political imperative to demonstrate a direct relationship with young Muslims that was informing government policy compromised the potential safety of the young Muslims selected to the Group. While it is difficult to find details of the members of the Children's and Young People's Board, which was set up to advise government ministers directly on issues that affect them, the details of YMAG members are comparatively easy to find, including places of study, politics and areas in which they live. This led to one member, a young woman, finding herself featured in the national newspapers.

Nevertheless, many young Muslims are, as young people, interested in and responsive to invitations for engagement and service. However, there is a danger that they achieve little other than to reify a discourse that constructs them as latent terrorists with a greater propensity for acts of terror and extremism than other groups, and that this occurs in a context where the use of Islam by extremist far right groups is publicly and confidently advocated as 'the threat within' – a community with no innocents. Therefore, there may also be a vulnerability to exploitation as this *turn* may also influence a re-engagement with society, a belief that a difference can be made possible rather than living with the disempowering impact of conspiracy theories.

A useful comparison here is the experience of young Rastas and the use of the idea of 'Babylon' in the 1980s, and young Muslims' use of the term '*Kuffar*' (meaning, 'unbelievers'). Both describe a system normally described as 'the West'/'capitalism', or simply as 'the system', to capture its amorphous presence. (Interestingly, examples of capitalism's purest manifestations can be found in the Arab world, for example in Dubai, the UAE and Saudi Arabia for their employment of indentured labour.) 'Babylon', as a concept, was employed by young Rastas whose reality was being shaped by a generic western racism determined by colour and colonialism (Beckford, 2000), just as the notion of '*Kuffar*' has emerged as young Muslim lives are being affected by an increasingly confident and assertive Islamophobia (Allen, 2010; Vakil and Sayyid, 2010). Cashmore (1985) explains Rastafarianism as a coherent package providing young black people with new models of comprehending the workings of the world around them. It not only explained the present position, but the past and the future in an educational and social milieu that was pejorative and ignorant of black people and 'blackness'. While the music of Bob Marley and the anti-racist struggle provided a means by which non-blacks could demonstrate allegiance, the platform seemingly being used by Muslim organizations is that of inter-faith dialogue.

This inter-faith activity serves a number of purposes; while being a political necessity it is also an act of 'Abrahamic fidelity', since most inter-faith activity is across this tradition. However, as a cultural expression, this *turning to* is sometimes fashioned by individuals with an international appeal and with local and religious resonance. For example, the Pakistani singer Aa'shiq-al-Rasul, based in Birmingham, provides new anthems from old musical favourites, regardless of whether the source comes from the historic songs of the Middle East or Bollywood. Nasheed (Islamically oriented songs) singers, artists, Qur'an reciters, and television sheikhs are all contributing to this new cultural vibrancy, forming an emergent celebrity community that may act as role models to Muslim youth, but is definitely informing a new cultural landscape and industry in which the conversation does not always have to be explained. If we return to Sayyid's (2010) statement that 'being Muslim' means different things in different places, we can see that he asks for an engagement that can articulate the uniqueness of the context and the expression of the Muslimness formed in this *turning*. It is an engagement that requires resources and as such there is an industry emerging; whether it serves itself or facilitates further articulations of young Muslim identities, or both, is yet to be seen.

References

Allen, C. (2010) *Islamophobia*. London: Ashgate.

Anwar, M. (1998), *Between Cultures: Continuity and Change in the lives of young Asians*. London: Routledge.

BBC website (2011), 'State multiculturalism has failed, says David Cameron', 5 February 2011, http://www.bbc.co.uk/news/uk-politics-12371994, accessed 29 May 2011.

Beckford, R. (2000), *Dread and Pentecostal: A Political Theology for the Black Church in Britain*. London: S. P. C. K.

— (2004), *God and the Gangs. An Urban Toolkit for Those Who Won't Be Bought Out, Sold Out or Scared Out*. London: DLT.

Cantle, T (2001), 'Community Cohesion – A Report of the Independent Review Team'. London: Home Office.

Carby, H. (1999), *Cultures in Babylon: Black Britain and African America*. New York: Verso Books.

Cashmore, E. (1985), *Rastaman: The rastafarian movement in England*. (2nd edn), London: Unwin Paperbacks.

Cassidy, C., O'Connor, R., and Dorrer, N. (2006), *Young people's experiences of transition to adulthood: A study of minority ethnic and white young people*. York: Joseph Rowntree Foundation.

Clark, D. B. (1973), 'The concept of community: A re-examination', *Sociological Review*, 21, pp. 398–416.

Clark, J. A. (2004), *Islam, Charity, and Activism: Middle-Class Networks and Social Welfare in Egypt, Jordan, and Yemen*. Bloomington: Indiana University Press.

Coleman, J. C. & Hendry, L. B. (1999). The nature of adolescence (3rd edn). London: Routledge.

Collins-Mayo, S., Mayo, B., Nash, S., and Cocksworth, C. (2010), *The Faith of Generation Y*. Church House Publishing, London.

Cooke, M., and Lawrence, B. (eds) (2005), *Muslim Networks: From Hajj to Hip-hop*. Chapel Hill: The University of North Carolina Press.

Cusworth, L., Bradshaw, J., Coles, B., Keung, A., and Chzhen, Y. (2009), *Understanding the Risks of Social Exclusion across the Life Course: Youth and Young Adulthood*. London: Social Exclusion Task Force, Cabinet Office.

Choudhury, T.A. (ed.) (2005), *Muslims in the UK Policies for Engaged Citizens*. Budapest: Open Society Institute.

Davies, B. (1999), *A History of the Youth Service in England, Vol. 1 and 2*. Leicester: National Youth Agency.

Deuchar, R. (2009), *Gangs, Marginalised Youth and Social Capital*. Stoke-on-Trent: Trentham Books.

Edelman, M. W. (1996), 'Foreword', in L. Lantieri and J. Patti (eds), *Waging Peace in our Schools*. Boston: Beacon Press.

Fahmy, E. (2006), 'Youth, Poverty and Social Exclusion', in D. Gordon, R. Levitas, R and C. Pantazis (eds), *Poverty and Social Exclusion in Britain: The Millennium Survey*. Bristol: Policy Press, pp. 347–73.

Gilroy, P. (1987), *There Ain't No Black In the Union Jack: The Cultural Politics of Race and Nation*. London: Hutchinson.

Ignatieff, M. (1997) *The Warrior's Honour: Ethnic War and the Modern Conscience*. Oxford: Blackwell.

John, M. (2003), *Children's Rights and Power: Charging up for a New Century*. London: Jessica Kingsley Publishers.

Khan, M. G. (2006), 'Introduction: Responding to Lives, not Events', *Youth & Policy, Special issue: Muslim Youth Work*, 92.

Kymlicka, W. (2007), *Multicultural Odysseys: Navigating the New International Politics of Diversity*. Oxford: Oxford University Press.

Lewis, P. (1994), *Islamic Britain*. London: I. B. Taurus.

Lindner, E. W. (2004), 'Children as theologians', in P. B. Pufall and R. P. Unsworth (eds), *Rethinking Childhood*. New Brunswick: Rutgers University Press, pp. 54–69.

MacDonald, R. (2008), 'Disconnected Youth? Social Exclusion, the "Underclass" & Economic Marginality', *Social Work & Society*, *Special Issue: Marginalized Youth*, 6, 2.

McRoy, A. (2005), *From Rushdie to 7/7: The Radicalisation of Islam in Britain*. London: Social Affairs Unit.

Modood, T. (2007), *Multiculturalism: A Civic Idea*. Cambridge: Polity

Nawaz, M. (2008), (testimonial), 'The Roots of Violent Islamist Extremism and Efforts to Counter It', *Hearing before the Committee on Homeland Security and Governmental Affairs*, United States Senate, One Hundred Tenth Congress, Second Session, July 10, http://www.saneworks.us/uploads/application/87.pdf. Accessed 29 May 2011.

Ouseley, H. (2001), Community pride not prejudice – making diversity work in Bradford, Sir Herman Ouseley – The Ouseley Report.

Phillips, A. (2006), '"Really" equal: opportunities and autonomy', *Journal of political philosophy*, 14, (1), pp. 18–32.

Ramadan, T. (2004), *Western Muslims and the future of Islam*. Oxford: Oxford University Press.

Samad, Y. (1996), 'The Politics of Islamic Identity among Bangladeshis and Pakistanis in Britain' in T. Ranger, Y. Samad, and O. Stuart (eds), *Culture Identity and Politics: Ethnic Minorities in Britain*. Avebury: Aldershot, pp. 90–8.

Sardar, Z., and Masood, M. (2006), 'Ziauddin Sardar: paradise lost, a future found', 15 May, http://www.opendemocracy.net/globalization/sardar_3547.jsp., accessed 29 May 2011.

Sayyid, S. (2010), 'Thinking through Islamophobia', in *Thinking through Islamophobia: global perspectives*, eds, S.Sayyid and A. Vakil. London: Hurst Publications.

Vakil, A., and Sayyid, S. (eds) (2010), *Thinking through Islamophobia: global perspectives*. London: Hurst.

Winter, T. (2003), 'Some Reflections on the Psychosocial Background', in M. S. Seddon, D. Hussain and N. Malik (eds), *British Muslims: Loyalty and Belonging*. Leicester: Islamic Foundation: London.

YMCA (2009), 'YMCA Movement to Play Key Role in Delivery of *myplace* Projects', http://www.ymca.org.uk/pooled/articles/BF_NEWSART/view.asp?Q = BF_NEWSART_310609. Accessed 29 May 2011.

Young, K. (2006), *The Art of Youth Work* (2nd edn), Lyme Regis: Russell House Publishing Ltd.

Zuckerman, P. (2007), 'Atheism: Contemporary Numbers and Patterns', in M. Martin (ed.), *The Cambridge Companion to Atheism*. Cambridge: Cambridge University Press, pp. 47–65.

PART THREE

Education and New Media

7

'Growing up under lockdown' or 'educational pioneers'? Challenging stereotypes of British Muslim women in higher education

FAUZIA AHMAD

Introduction

One of the aims of this chapter is to highlight the under-researched area of young British Muslim women as educational achievers, and in many instances, as educational 'pioneers' , through examining their routes into higher education and the impact of educational success on their families. In doing so, this chapter also aims to question stereotypes that portray young South Asian Muslim women in Britain as 'victims' and recipients of oppression in patriarchal family relations, as women with fixed religious and cultural identities or as rebels and 'tearaways' from their families, cultures and religion. As higher education becomes an increasingly obtainable reality for growing numbers of Muslim women, this arena becomes all the more significant particularly as Muslim women's lives have become even more contested and objectified in media and policy discourses.[1] I have argued elsewhere (Ahmad, 2006, 2007, 2009) that the absence of research in this area may be due, in part, to at least three main reasons:

(i)   An emphasis on statistical realities that aim to explore disparities in the rates of employment and higher education participation among women of Pakistani and Bangladeshi backgrounds compared to other minority groups.[2] While earlier research attributed these disparities to 'cultural factors' (i.e., Islam and notions of 'purdah' as barriers to employment and higher education), more recent studies suggest instead that a combination of factors such as racism and discrimination, social deprivation and poverty, timing of migration and localized dynamics are more relevant and also point towards evidence of social change[3] and the production and reproduction of inequalities that are linked to gendered and racialized Muslim identities (Archer, 2002).

(ii) A tendency to frame Muslim women's presence in universities through discourses of Muslim student extremism on campus and Muslim male student criminality.[4] This can be evidenced in the near hysterical media headlines around Muslim faith schools and high-profile controversies around school uniforms for Muslim school girls, such as Shabina Begum's two-year high court battle against her school to allow her to wear the *jilbab* (2004–6)[5]; the subsequent banning of the *niqab* on some university campuses after they were deemed a 'security risk' following the London bombings of 7 July 2005; the now infamous comments made by the erstwhile Leader of the House of Commons, Jack Straw, questioning the 'integration' of young Muslim women wearing the *niqab*; reports that some Muslim women medical students were refusing to remove their arm coverings in theatre and were thereby posing a hygiene risk (Henry and Donnelly,2008); and more recently, following the stabbing of British MP Steven Timms in 2010 by 21-year-old student Roshonara Choudhry in an attempt to 'punish' him for his support of the Iraq war (Gemmel, 2010) after allegedly being 'radicalized' by the *YouTube* sermons of Anwar al-Awlaki, believed to be an al-Qaeda cleric.

(iii)   An emphasis on portraying South Asian family structures, cultures and religions as 'oppressive', 'excessively patriarchal' and restrictive of daughters education and career success, thus invoking discourses of 'degradation and despair',[6] and of Muslim women who have 'escaped' from strict 'cultural traditions' that involved 'growing up under lockdown', with strict 'moral directives' and 'pressures to safeguard familial honour'. Representations of Muslim women at university under this set of discourses are sensationalized and fetishized as women experiencing secret 'double lives' and the inevitable 'culture clash'.[7] Such representations claim to show that Muslim women, once 'liberated' from their oppressive families and religion by the secular freedoms of university life, enjoy these freedoms to excess by drinking, sleeping around, going to raves, taking drugs, wearing what they want and so on. These realities, or caricatures, feed into popular racist stereotypes about the alleged backwardness of Muslim communities and the incoherence of Muslim identities (Tyrer and Ahmad, 2005).[8]

Apart from feeding into anxieties that parents might have regarding the potential negative influences university may have on their daughters, such portrayals suggest that a university environment, in the face of difference, is an alienating rather than an empowering social milieu. It also suggests that Muslim women students lack a sense of their own agency and ability to create alternative subjectivities and spaces for the articulation of their identities.

Both (ii) and (iii) highlight how Muslim women's bodies, their apparent 'victimhood' and, ironically, their perceived threat to 'British values', continue to remain a source of fascination within the media- and government-led agendas. This 'victim focused' and pathological discourse is one that repeats simplistic 'modern/Western' versus 'traditional/Muslim' dichotomous frameworks. As a result, serious attention has not been paid to qualitative work examining whether higher education structures are accommodating of gendered faith-based needs and ways participation might be improved (Tyrer and Ahmad, 2006), or Muslim women's routes into and experiences of higher education and the impact that their experiences have on their identities. The fact that Muslim women are present in universities, and in some regions, such as Tower Hamlets in London, in steadily increasing numbers, is a significant indication of a rapidly changing social profile. It indicates a 'drive for qualifications' that is worthy of further study and acknowledgement (Modood, 1998) and presents a challenge for educational policies to address.

Broader debates on widening participation and inclusion and exclusion for 'non-traditional' entrants (which have included Muslim women), based on social class and (to a lesser extent) ethnicity (Reay et al., 2001; Ball et al., 2002; Archer et al., 2003; Read et al., 2003), have noted student experiences of feeling 'othered' or not 'fitting in' with the campus culture while at university.[9] These link into larger surveys of Muslim students' experiences on university campuses that have reported perceptions of racism on courses, concerns that lecture and exam times had not taken account of prayer times, and, for Muslim women students, assumptions that their presence within the university was likely to have been without the support of their parents. For instance, Christine Asmar's (2005) survey of Muslim students' experiences in Australian universities represents how Muslims as a student group are displaying strong commitments towards academic achievement and, in the case of women especially, towards their faith. Significantly though, this work (with Proude and Inge, 2004) noted how some Muslim students, especially Muslim women wearing hijab, felt excluded and alienated from the campus 'drinking culture' and by some discriminatory attitudes. Some of Asmar et al.'s findings resonate strongly with my own research (see Ahmad, 2007; Tyrer and Ahmad, 2006) and make for an interesting comparison with other surveys exploring Muslim students' experiences of racism and anti-Muslim discrimination in universities following the London bombings (OPM, 2009; Federation of Student Islamic Societies, 2005; Islamic Human Rights Commission , 2006, and reported in this volume).

In an earlier paper on British Muslim women and their motivations into higher education (Ahmad, 2001), I highlighted how the high educational aspirations among young British Muslim women and their parents noted in Basit's work (1995, 1996, 1997) had translated into realities for many of the Muslim women I interviewed. Their educational ambitions were also shared by their parents, regardless of social class, with many women stating the positive role played by *fathers* in encouraging their education, along with other family members, peer groups and Muslim and non-Muslim role models (Ahmad, 2001). These findings have since been backed up by other research on Muslim women's experiences of higher education and their educational aspirations (Ahmad, 2006, 2007; Tyrer and Ahmad, 2006; Equal Opportunities Commission, 2006; Hussain and Baguley, 2007; Ijaz and Abbas, 2010), including studies attempting to link young British Pakistanis' higher educational aspirations to theories of social capital (Dwyer et al., 2006; Dwyer and Shah, 2009). However, as these studies and the work discussed here show, these aspirations have not always been acknowledged or supported by schools, colleges, teachers or lecturers.

This chapter, then, develops the themes raised in my previous work on British Muslim women's educational motivations (Ahmad, 2001) by illustrating their educational journeys. In focusing on an under-researched area of social change in young Muslim women's lives, the research discussed here sheds light on Muslim women's achievements and their families' attitudes and interest in higher education. As I go on to show, Muslim women who experience educational success and have thus 'demystified the higher education experience' are, in many instances, placed in the role of educational 'pioneers' with many 'paving the way' forward into higher education for other female family and community members. It further highlights how Muslim women and their families increasingly view higher education as a personal and social commodity and means for upward social mobility. Even though 'class issues' are not stated as an explicit feature of this paper, they remain an embedded feature of the theoretical perspective adopted, but are also grounded in the empirical data through women's own emphasis on increasing social mobility and status as a result of their higher education.

The value that Muslim women attribute to their higher education experiences offers new challenges to stereotyped representations of South Asian Muslim women's identities and their families, and will serve to interrogate the legitimacy of deterministic and racist binarized discursive formations. Through a detailed exploration

of Muslim women's personal journeys into university, including
the barriers encountered, I argue for the need to remain cautious
against conflating barriers to higher education, which some Muslim
women can experience through stereotyped representations of
Muslim women and patriarchy.[10]

Methodology

I conducted detailed semi-structured interviews with 35 British
Muslim women of South Asian origin (14 Pakistanis, 7 Indians
and 14 Bangladeshis) who were either studying at 'old' or 'new'[11]
(post-1992) universities as undergraduates or postgraduates within
London, or had graduated and were in employment. Thirteen
were undergraduates, 4 were postgraduate students and 18 were
graduates mostly in professional employment. Most described their
backgrounds as 'working class' (21); a smaller number identified
their background as 'middle class' (14) and cited at least one
of their parents' professional employment and/or degree-level
qualifications.[12] The majority, in keeping with the general profile
of the Muslim population in Britain, were Sunni Muslims. Two
women identified as Shi'ah Muslims and one woman hailed from
the Ahmediyya sect (revealed once the interview had begun).

Although this sample was not representative, it was diverse in
terms of ethnicity, class and levels of religiosity – including two
participants who, despite volunteering for the interview, were
hesitant to identify themselves as 'Muslim'. In recruiting candidates
for participation in the study, I did not consciously make distinctions
between women who wore the headscarf or other manifestations of
'Islamic clothing' (definitions on what this represents vary); as a
Muslim woman myself, I did not wish to over-emphasize the hijab
as a key defining feature.

Interviewees were recruited via a mixture of direct approaches,
through student unions such as Islamic Societies (ISOCs), Pakistan
Societies (PakSocs) and Asian Societies, but the most effective method
proved to be snowballing. Research participants were between the
ages of 19 and 30 years, or were in their second year of degree study
as I wanted students who could reflect on their university experiences
without these being confused with the novelty of the first year of

university life, or of leaving home, for example. Interviews lasted between one-and-a-half to two hours (approximately) and covered women's motivations and reasons for wanting to pursue degree-level study, their points of entry, school experiences and routes into education, whether there were any particular preferences in degree and subject choice and higher education institution, their parents' views on their higher education choices and the impact of higher education on their religious and cultural identities, family relationships and obligations (Ahmad, 2006, 2007). The research was long term and charted periods before and after the 9/11 terror attacks.

Routes into University

The majority of women in my sample attended comprehensive single sex schools. Experiences at school were varied. Women who attended schools in areas where there were large Asian populations, such as women of Bangladeshi origin who lived in socially deprived areas in London (e.g. Tower Hamlets in the east end), felt less supported by their schools and teachers to pursue higher education. They were less likely to enter university through the A-level route (see below) but, rather, pursued alternative, vocational routes into university such as BTECH diplomas, Ordinary National Diplomas (OND) and Higher National Diplomas (HND), depending on their GSCE and A-level performances. They were also more likely to enter the 'new' universities and to live at home – a feature in keeping with data that shows show a concentration of people from Pakistani and Bangladeshi backgrounds in the post-1992 universities (Modood, 1998; Shiner and Modood, 2002; Connor et al., 2004; Modood, 2006).

Only a handful of women in my sample attended private, fee-paying schools (3). The rest attended either voluntary-aided former grammar schools (8) or local comprehensives (24). Experiences and encouragement to enter higher education were mixed, and I was unable from my sample to draw any distinct co-relations between the type of school attended, locality and encouragement to study. Some women in comprehensives, for example, were able to iden-tify inspiring and encouraging teachers, while others in ex-grammar schools – which were better equipped to prepare students academically and socially for higher education – felt stereotyped or ignored.

For instance, Shabnum, a recent graduate in maths, statistics and computing, felt 'let down' by her tutors at her local sixth-form college in Tower Hamlets for not having the necessary experience to support and prepare her for university entry. Despite gaining good grades at A-levels for Maths, she was advised to complete a HND instead. After passing this, she then proceeded on to the degree course and compared how the support and encouragement of her tutors on her HND course contributed to her gaining confidence in her abilities and achieving a 'good result' in her final degree, while the lack of interest from her school and college caused her to question her abilities. She believed her experience was common to other students of Bangladeshi origin, including her own younger siblings.

However, it was not just women from areas such as Tower Hamlets who felt inadequately supported by their former schools. Examples of racism experienced while at school included teachers ignoring women in class or ignoring instances of racist bullying; not taking an interest in, or being supportive of, women's career aspirations; through to rather more pernicious comments about 'arranged marriages' and 'pity' towards student's mothers who were housewives. One woman spoke of how one of her teachers only appeared to take an interest in the Asian girls in class when she wanted to talk about Asian clothes and food, locating Asian women in the class firmly within the domestic sphere. Another woman recounted how at the end of a physical exercise class, she resisted taking a communal shower with the rest of the class and brought a note from her mother, explaining that her modesty was a reflection of her faith, only to hear the teacher reply with disparaging remarks in front of the other students. Some more general comments included awkward feelings around Christian prayers and singing hymns (quite a few women said they felt teachers paid them particular attention to check they were singing) and feeling isolated from other students and teachers when being withdrawn from sex education classes. In short, the examples cited here served to undermine some women's confidence and ability to view themselves as achievers and future contributors to society. One woman, Shamim, described her school experiences as leaving her, 'not feeling part of British society or a British citizen'.

Given some of these significant barriers, there are some striking examples of women achieving 'against the odds'. For instance, Shamim, who eventually studied pharmacy, left school with a handful of CSEs, which she re-took at Further Education (FE) college, before going on to take A-levels and enter university. Another student, Aswa, left school with just two GCSEs, but after studying for an OND ended up with two first-class honours degrees in the biomedical sciences, and held aspirations towards studying for a master's degree. Tahira, with little encouragement from her parents and no substantive educational or career ambitions herself, left school with one GSCE in English and began working for a council in administration. She was sent by her employers to study part-time for a BTECH in business and finance. Following this, she then took further evening classes to study for a degree in social sciences, changed jobs, took an IT course, and after performing the Hajj (Islamic religious pilgrimage), took up a place with a bursary to study for an MSc in an IT-related subject. At the time of the interview she held a position as an 'Organizational Learning Consultant' for a large international IT company.

Other women decided to re-take their A-levels, or modify their initial course preferences and university choices in order to maximize their chances of gaining university entry at the first A-level sitting, or to gain entry into a specific institution or course, such as medicine. For example, Kishwer, re-took her A-levels in an attempt to gain entry into medical school but, having not made the required grades, took a place on a chemistry degree. After graduating (during which time she had also joined the Territorial Army), she entered medical school through the Medical Corps and served in Bosnia as part of its team. Saima, a genetics student at the time of the interview, also harboured hopes of entering medical school after graduating in her first degree and not gaining a place after her first application. We remained in contact and she now works as a qualified doctor. As noted elsewhere (Ahmad et al., 2003), the varying strategies that women utilized in order to enter higher education or study in the area of their choice indicates the high value associated with degree-level study.

Four of the women I interviewed were mothers; three of these were of Bangladeshi origin (Sara, Rezia and Fareena), and the other was of Pakistani origin (Arifa). Fareena and Rezia were both postgraduate students. An earlier study on South Asian women and employment (Ahmad et al., 2003) found that early marriage and associated child-care responsibilities were among the key barriers preventing young Bangladeshi women from entering university. The study also found, however, that once children could be adequately cared for, either by extended family members or in a nursery, women were encouraged to enter university. However, their choice of university was often limited to locally based post-1992 universities. This represents an interesting dimension to the routes that Muslim women take into higher education, but also indicates how their experiences of university are likely to be qualitatively different from other students without child-care responsibilities.

For instance, Sara, a final-year student in social policy and management, was 22 and had a three-year old daughter after marrying at the age of 18. Her early marriage or motherhood may not have significantly delayed her entry into higher education, but her account illustrates some of the struggles Muslim women experienced in order to achieve their academic goals and maintain familial responsibilities. After re-taking her A-levels, she began her degree and later worked part-time as a benefits advisor for the NHS. In thinking about her own experiences of higher education, she also reflected on its potential benefits for her own daughter and her future prospects:

> Well further education has actually given me a lot you know, I've gained a lot in terms of understanding society and understanding people and other things. Also, I think it helps me towards being a better mother as well now because I think of the importance of my daughter's education and what kind of school would be appropriate for her and everything. So I think it has helped make me [think] and – given my parental responsibility and everything, the whole experience has been very difficult, because I started soon after I had the baby in July and I went to university in September. So it's been very difficult to do the work in time, to actually attend the lectures and everything, so I think I am quite happy about how it has all gone. Because if I didn't have other responsibilities, you know, not just being a mother, but also being responsible for my family, because I don't have a brother, I had to do a lot of stuff for my Mum and sisters . . . I think of how I went and I'm very happy with it. (Sara, 22, BSc social policy and management student, Bangladeshi)

Her choice of university was limited to one close to her home in Tower Hamlets, and she felt that her personal circumstances hampered her ability to 'do better':

> A lot of the time it wasn't possible to do a lot of things that I wanted to do . . . or do better or something because I had other things and problems. So, every time I went in I had to rush in and rush out. So, I think I could have a lot better . . . if I was just concentrating on my education.

The early marriages of some women of Bangladeshi origin should not, however, be assumed to be reflective of a lack of importance on education by women or their families. In fact, their parents were just as keen to see their daughters succeed academically, but they believed that their daughters could pursue higher education once they were secure in terms of marriage and parenthood.

Arifa's trajectory into university also exemplifies women's determination to gain a degree, despite difficult earlier school experiences, lack of A-levels or child-care responsibilities. As an unmarried mother, however, Arifa's personal experiences and views diverged in ways that I have described elsewhere (Ahmad, 2003). Arifa suffered the loss of her father at the age of 17 following a long illness. The caring responsibilities she shared with her family contributed to her poor exam results (one O-level and three CSEs), which her teachers initially interpreted as 'laziness' rather than appreciating the responsibilities children from Asian families were expected to shoulder, especially during times of hardship, as Arifa explained:

> Well, all through my teenage years, from 13 onwards my father was really ill, he had motor neurone disease, where the brain is really active but all your muscles start wasting away so you can't do anything about it, so I had to look after him a lot. So, people at school (I was due to do 10 O-levels but in the end I only got one O-level and three CSEs. They thought I wasn't doing my work. They thought I was being lazy and eventually they got out of me that, you know, I had to look after my dad because he was really ill and stuff and so, academically I didn't do as well as I should have done. They didn't understand that in Asian families

everybody (there's no demarcation (if you're a child (so what (if you're a child you look after your parents and we had to do loads of that stuff. I got my exams and I did my first year of my A-levels, but on the second year, in August – we go back in September to enrol again for the second year – my dad died in August and I had to go to Pakistan to take his body back and we never came back until three months later. When I did come back they said I couldn't continue with my course, that I'd missed one year, missed too much work and my mother was in debt, so I had to get work, so I just applied for jobs and I just went for the first job that I could, which was in a bank. So I worked for three years and supported my mum, my brother and my older sister who has mental health problems. (Arifa, 26, BA Social Anthropology student, Pakistani)

By the time she reached 21, having left home at 19, Arifa wanted to go on to university and so she completed an Access Course in social science. Her entry to university was further delayed by another year by the arrival of her daughter, who was ill at birth and in need of medical attention for some months. She eventually entered university aged 23.

This brief profile indicates the ways in which women's school and college experiences were both racialized and gendered in class-specific ways. This was evidenced in the quality of support, guidance or information they received about higher education, and the ways in which perceived expectations, obligations and material circumstances as Asian and Muslim women impacted on their educational trajectories and identities. Their achievements, therefore, in light of their struggles, need to be understood holistically and in terms of the personal significance that they attached to these. Brah (1996) draws attention to similar processes affecting Muslim women's relationships to labour markets. The varying routes Muslim women adopted in order to gain entry into university can be compared to Mirza's (1995) work with African Caribbean women who adopted a strategy of 'resistance' to racist discourses by negotiating entry into further and higher education through 'the back door'. Shain's (2003) work with Asian schoolgirls also discusses young women's various survival and resistance strategies in response to racism. Each response or strategy highlights the contingent, discursive and dynamic nature of Asian women's identities, which actively challenge stereotypes of passivity, cultural pathology and 'arranged marriages'.

None of the women in my sample believed that higher education was an unattainable goal, or associated going to university with class-based notions of 'risk'. Instead, gaining a degree was an expectation from an early age, and increased social mobility and prestige were often cited as motivating factors. In this respect then, they differ from many of the respondents in some of the class-focused analyses of other studies on widening participation for 'non-traditional' students.

Pioneers paving the way – role models

Apart from receiving encouragement from their parents, a number of women also pointed towards the presence of other positive role models such as siblings, cousins, other extended family members (either in the UK, their country of origin or elsewhere), peer groups, parental social circles and teachers. These were representative of the ways in which growing expectations and trends towards higher education were reflected in women's social environments. For example:

> I have quite a few relatives in Pakistan – a couple of the girls are medics and the rest are teachers. They've all got degrees I don't know if it's just my family or what [sic] but generally, the girls are brainy and the guys are just layabouts really. I don't know if that's a family thing, or if that's a typical thing. (Saima, 20, BSc genetics student, Pakistani)

Having mothers, older sisters or aunts who worked was a conducive factor in women's education choices, and I found little difference (apart from the few mothers cited who showed limited interest) in the nature and strength of encouragement from families where mothers were housewives with those who were employed. For those women who were the first in their families to enter higher education – and this sample contained a number of 'pioneers' – what were their experiences? Did they encounter any additional difficulties in the pursuit of their aspirations and, if so, how were these overcome? How did other members of their families and communities regard them? What impact, if any, did their educational success have on the aspirations of other Muslim women in their families and peer groups? Were women generally encouraged in their ambitions, or were they discouraged? Or, were their achievements met with indifference? Here I focus on two examples – Jahanara[13] and Rehana, both hijab wearers and both from working-class families – to illustrate these very differing familial attitudes towards pioneer daughters studying and leaving home to live on campus.

Unlike other women in her local Bangladeshi community, Jahanara, a schoolteacher, had always been encouraged to study by her parents. Her father was particularly keen after his own educational opportunities were limited by the political situation prior to the formation of Bangladesh in 1971, and his own father had been a local headmaster and so instilled the importance of education from an early age. Apart from some initial questioning of Jahanara's choice of degree (which was psychology) and why she did not want to study 'one of the more popular subjects like law, accountancy, or medicine' – attitudes that are common across my sample – her family were supportive. She chose to study at a high-prestige university just outside London, but was also attracted by the prospect of leaving home to study, which her family also supported. Her success, as the first woman in her family to attain a degree, acted as an incentive to younger women in her family:

What about your cousins, how do they view you now?

They just think we're very educated and they are very proud. They do use us [her siblings and herself] as examples with their own children. My younger cousin, who's 16, she's all set to go to university, her father's for it because of the fact that I went to university as a girl and that my sister's going to university – they don't see anything wrong with it now I think, whereas before it was 'girls should stay at home'.

Why is that?

I think it's more 'cos [sic] of the culture they're brought up in, the environment where girls stay at home, help parents, mothers and so they brought the same values here, that the girls should stay at home. (Jahanara, 24, BSc Psychology, Primary School Teacher, Bangladeshi)

Jahanara's higher education is indicative of the social change that is becoming marked, particularly in communities such as the Bangladeshis in Tower Hamlets (Ahmad et al., 2003; Modood, 2006). Her own education may have acted to challenge patriarchal attitudes towards women in her community or family, though she had not consciously sought to influence others. In fact, she remained oblivious to the fact that she may have been the first woman in her family to achieve a degree until I pointed it out to her during the interview. Her experience can be contrasted with that of Rehana, whose experience illustrated some of the tensions and anxieties some women faced when announcing their desire to enter university. Rehana met with opposition to her plans, not from her parents but from her extended family in the shape of her father's older brothers. She was the first female in her family – either in Britain or in her parents' country of origin, Pakistan – to enter higher education, and as we can see from the quotes below, was determined to go despite their opposition. Her entry to university though, was further compounded by her wish to live in student accommodation for her first year. Her uncles were initially suspicious of her intentions to study, and even more so about her intentions to move out. They feared that her motivations stemmed from a certain 'looseness' of morality and were concerned that she would damage the family reputation, especially as female members of the family observed 'purdah' (literally, 'curtain', but usually taken to mean gender segregation), though this was practised in a fairly relaxed manner. She explained:

> 'Cos [sic] I'm the first girl in my family to go into "HE", to go to university, to live out for the first year, when my uncles found out, they're very conservative, my dad's brothers, my dad's younger brother's 'cos [sic] they're quite young, they were ok about it, but my dad's two elder brothers, they were really against the idea. And they were like [sic], "why do you want to study? You can't go". And I was like, "hang on a sec, I can go"

What were your uncles concerns for you?

That … I have no idea to tell the truth. Sometimes I thought they were just being a big pain and they couldn't stand the fact that I was going to university – it was "why does she have to go to university when she's gonna get married at the end of the day?" I thought initially. But they were also scared that I was gonna [sic] bring down the family name, and also the fact that I was the first girl that was gonna go and I made such a big fuss saying I was going and stood up against them. "I don't care what you're saying." So I think the reason why I did end up going to university was "cos [sic] so many people put so much objection, so I thought," "right, that's it, I'm gonna do this now, even if its to prove all of you wrong".

(Rehana, 21, BA English and History student, Pakistani)

Like the Punjabi women interviewed by Bradby (1999), notions of family 'honour' were strongly held values within Rehana's extended family. Her uncles perceived her higher education ambitions to have the potential to compromise these principles. She argued her case successfully, with much support from other female members of her extended family, most notably, from her mother and her aunts. What is also interesting here is that the opposition she met from her uncles, rather than cause her to question her plans, acted to cement her determination to achieve her degree. She also negotiated a semester living on campus, which was initially another source of tension between her and her uncles. Two years on, Rehana was still wearing her headscarf and was just as committed as before (if not more so) to her religion and cultural background, believing firmly that her university experiences had helped to rationalize her cultural and religious affiliations and beliefs. Her uncles' initial reservations had been proven wrong and, since she had not 'brought the family name into disrepute', the educational ambitions of other female members of her family were met with less opposition or suspicion:

How have they [uncles] been with your cousins since?

Well 'cos [sic] I've been to university and I haven't done anything, like I haven't dyed my hair or shaved my head or anything, or stopped wearing a scarf, or I haven't got tattoo or something [laughs], I think that because of that fact, they're letting their daughters go on now. One daughter is doing A-levels and plans to go to uni. Its not just 'cos [sic] of me, its 'cos they've seen that I've been here for two years, and thank God, I haven't done anything outrageous. I'm having my Nikah [Islamic marriage] done by the end of the year, so – because of the fact that I'm

gonna [sic] come out good at the end of this, they've got used to
the idea and its not such an objection for daughters now. Or my
sister for that matter, 'cos I had to go through it so it's easier for
them now.

So they've got a positive example?

They've got a positive example and they won't face the same
opposition, as I like to call it. It will be so easy for them to
go now ... It [suspicion from her uncles] was irritating but it
showed they took an interest and cared, but on the other side,
there were ulterior motives – are their daughters gonna [sic] do
this next? So at the end of the day, it was OK but it was to prove
them wrong. My uncles are OK now – they ask how I'm doing
and everything. It was a storm in a teacup.

(Rehana, 21, BA English and History student, Pakistani)

Both Jahanara's and Rehana's 'safe passage' through the higher
education system and their positive experiences have helped, in
part, to 'de-mystify' preconceived assumptions about the potentially
'secularizing' affects of university life and reassure family members
that it was possible to study and live within that environment
while remaining loyal to cultural and religious sensibilities. For
younger members, especially female relatives, their achievements
and experiences also signalled the attainability of a degree and
the opportunity to experience university life. In Rehana's case, the
support she received from her aunts, which from her descriptions,
was not 'openly' in defiance of her uncles, but was expressed as
personal support for her ambitions, was also significant. As she was
the only woman also within her family's social circle to enter higher
education, and in defiance of the elder male members of the family,
her struggles not only influenced other women and their families into
following her example, but also caused a shift in attitudes of her uncles.

It is difficult to assess from my data the extent and nature of parental
reservations and concerns about their daughters' higher education
studies as I was relying on daughters' accounts. The two examples
above, although illustrative of pioneer Muslim women and their
experiences, are also specific in that family dynamics and personal
relationships between daughters, their parents and extended family
members were certainly significant. The very different reactions that

both of the women in the examples experienced to their educational ambitions – that of encouragement or discouragement – are also highly significant and are indicative of diversity of expression among Muslim families in general. In the case of Rehana and Jahanara, both of whom were hijab-wearing, religiously observant, and from working-class families, the very differing reactions of their families to their higher education is also evidence of the variety of ways in which notions of 'izzat' ('honour'), 'purdah' and Muslim identities are negotiated, positioned, observed and understood.

However, there were women pioneers whose experiences are not represented in the above categorizations, and may be indicative of a third response from parents – that of neither actively encouraging nor discouraging but merely tolerating a daughter's higher education. Here, women's aspirations and achievements were neither supported nor acknowledged by either parents, but were instead met with indifference. Shamim, who was a pharmacist, spoke of how her father, in contradiction to many of those in this study and her other family members, was unsupportive of, and uninterested in, her educational and career aims:

> Well it wasn't so much my mother or brothers and sisters, they were just supportive of anything that I wanted to do, but my Father didn't want me to go to university. Didn't want me to study, didn't want me to go away out of London, didn't really want me to do anything except go back to Pakistan, get married and have loads of children and live off the council, and that is what he wanted me to do. (Shamim, 28, Pharmacist, Pakistani)

Despite successfully gaining a place at one of the established universities to study pharmacy – a degree that many women had cited as one of the key high-prestige professions for their parents – her father remained unsupportive and instead expressed disappointment that she was not studying for a career in medicine: My Father always did say to me why did you do pharmacy, why didn't you just be a doctor? He doesn't recognize the value of pharmacy at all, he thinks it is just pill-pushing basically, he doesn't understand, especially different areas of expertise in hospitals as well, it is just quite diverse.

His ambivalence towards her career aspirations acted instead to further provoke Shamim into pursuing her educational aims and gaining a degree of financial independence. In the extract below, Shamim interprets her father's lack of interest in her education (although she says elsewhere that he would encourage her brothers) as reflective of his own experiences as a self-employed builder and carpenter and former shopkeeper:

> I mean my father is not too keen on education full stop [sic], he thinks that you leave school and just go to work because that is what he did. He has never been one where he stayed at college and pursued and gone and got a degree or anything like that. He is a very hands-on type of person and this is what he wants to do so he didn't see the value of education or anything like that. Yet I felt at a very young age that if I wanted to get ahead quite quickly as a woman, as an Asian woman as well, I wanted a degree. I wanted a profession and I felt that, you know, I personally felt that I couldn't get ahead unless I had a degree, otherwise I would be stuck in a dead-end job where it would take me ages [sic] to get anywhere. (Shamim, 28, Pharmacist, Pakistani)

This last point by Shamim on her father's lack of interest in her education brings into play considerations of social class and allows us to further deconstruct some more stereotypical and racist notions of paternal lack of support for young Muslim women's higher education. Instead of attributing her father's lack of interest in her career to 'cultural' constraints, Shamim instead highlights her father's lack of interest in academic achievement because he was a 'hands-on type of person'. Shamim offered little further information on the overall relationship between her father and her, but his lack of interest in her achievements was obviously a source of sadness for her. She was very much a self-motivator, as indicated by the quote, and was well aware of some of the other potential barriers she could face as an Asian and Muslim woman. Her father's response can be compared to the attitudes of other working-class parents in my sample, such as Lubanna's father who wanted his children to gain the education that was denied to him. For instance:

> They genuinely do want us to get degrees, and I still haven't figured out why properly. I think its 'cos [sic] my Dad didn't do a degree and he's always telling us this by the way, that if he had done even A-levels, he would have been much cleverer than we

are! I think it's just that he wants us to do what he never could.
(Lubanna, 20, LLB law student, Bangladeshi)

Several women in my sample reflected this experience. The instilling
of a chosen profession for their children by many Asian parents
may appear to be stifling and controlling, but it is, nonetheless, a
reality demonstrative of high parental aspirations. The preference
of 'safe' educational routes may also mark a response to a relative
lack of dominant cultural capital and racism (Archer and Francis,
2006). Again, it highlights the significance attributed to higher
education by many parents, and the ways in which education was
viewed as an 'investment', symbolizing that a daughter's value as a
woman, both within the family and to those outside it, went beyond
patriarchal ideologies of women as 'homemakers'. By encouraging
their daughters into higher education, parents were not only able
to rest assured by their daughter's future economic potential as
individuals, but they were also able to attain and maintain social
status and prestige within their social circles.

Conclusion

Many of the women described in this chapter were educational 'pioneers'
not just within their families, but also among their parental social
circles. Although the majority I spoke to cited strong parental support
and encouragement, for some, entering university represented an initial
phase of struggle as parents' anxieties about the 'Westernizing' influences
of higher education surfaced. Their personal stories of negotiation with
their families in order to enter university, and subsequent 'safe passage'
and success, acted to 'demystify' the higher education experience and,
in many instances, paved the way for sisters or other women – either
within their own families or local communities – to also consider higher
education as a viable and empowering option.

A careful reading of the Muslim women's educational journeys
reveals that, far from clichéd representations of authoritative
and excessively patriarchal parental restrictions on Muslim
women's higher education aspirations, it was in fact the attitudes
of some school teachers and those working in further and higher
education that undermined Muslim women's educational and
career ambitions. That is not to deny some of the very real barriers

Muslim women can experience both personally and structurally in these arenas. However, if the interviews highlight anything, it is that women's abilities to achieve – and equally, the barriers they may encounter – are as much a reflection of their own levels of potential, personal experiences, familial and social relationships as they are of structural, local, temporal and global forces.

The qualitative value associated with the achievement of the degree, the sense of parental pride conveyed by most women and the various personal and social benefits women identified as a result of higher education show that for this cohort at least, the attainment of a degree represented far more than the academic qualification; it symbolized a personal achievement and the creation of opportunities for upward social mobility, sometimes in the face of negative stereotypes from teachers and other educational professionals. This, in itself, brings into question the deterministic and racist binary discursive formations which frequently situate Muslim families as being oppressive and restrictive of their daughters' educations, and which assume that Muslim women are 'victims' and recipients of oppression in patriarchal family relations, as women with fixed religious and cultural identities or as rebels and 'tearaways' from their families, cultures and religion.

Therefore, as I hope to have shown in this chapter, the barriers that Muslim women can experience in their educational journeys should not be viewed solely through statistical realities or rigid stereotyped assumptions that situate patriarchy, for example, as an overarching structure in Muslim women's lives. They certainly do not explain the complexities illustrated in the narratives of women's accounts of their educational journeys documented here; instead, they point to calls for more to be done in order to ensure that those responsible for the recruitment of students into higher education and careers guidance recognize the diverse backgrounds of Muslim women and support them as potential achievers.

References

Ahmad, F. (2001), 'Modern Traditions? British Muslim women and academic achievement', *Gender and Education*, 13, (2), pp. 137–52.
— (2003), 'Still "in progress?" – methodological dilemmas, tensions and contradictions in theorizing South Asian Muslim women', in N. Puwar

and P. Ranghuram (eds), *South Asian Women in the Diaspora*. Oxford: Berg, pp. 43–65.

— (2006), 'Modern Traditions? British Muslim Women, Higher Education and Identities'. Unpublished PhD thesis, University of Bristol, UK.

— (2007), 'Muslim women's experiences of higher education in Britain', *American Journal of Islamic Social Sciences: Special Issue on Higher Education*, 24, (3), pp. 46–69.

— (2009), '"We always knew from the year dot that university was the place to go": Muslim women and higher education experiences in the UK', in F. N. Seggie and R. O. Mabokela (eds), *Islam and Higher Education in Transitional Societies*. Rotterdam: Sense Publishers, pp. 65–82.

Ahmad, F., Modood, T. and Lissenburgh, S. (2003), *South Asian Women and Employment in Britain: the Interaction of Gender and Ethnicity*. London: PSI.

Alexander, C. (2000), *The Asian Gang*. Oxford: Berg.

—(2006), 'Imagining the politics of BrAsian youth', in N. Ali, V. S. Kalra and S. Sayyid (eds), *Postcolonial People, South Asians in Britain*. London: Hurst and Company, pp. 258–71.

Archer, L. (2002), 'Change, culture and tradition: British Muslim pupils talk about Muslim girls' post-16 "choices"', *Race Ethnicity and Education*, 5, (4), pp. 359–76.

Archer, L., and Francis, B. (2006), *Understanding Minority Ethnic Achievement: 'Race', Class, Gender and 'Success'*. London: Routledge.

Archer, L., Hutchings, M., and Ross, A. (2003), *Higher Education and Social Class, Issues of Exclusion and Inclusion*. London: Routledge Falmer.

Asmar, C. (2005), 'Internationalising students: reassessing diasporic and local student difference' *Studies in Higher Education*, 30, (3), pp. 291–309.

Asmar, C., Proude, E., and Inge, L. (2004) '"Unwelcome sisters"? An analysis of findings from a study of how Muslim women (and Muslim men) experience university', *Australian Journal of Education*, 48, (1), pp. 47–63.

Ball, S., Reay, D., and David, M. (2002), '"Ethnic choosing": minority ethnic students, social class and higher education choice', *Race, Ethnicity and Education*, 5, (4), pp. 333–57.

Basit, T. N. (1995), '"I want to go to college": British Muslim girls and the academic dimension of schooling', *Muslim Education Quarterly*, 12, pp. 36–54.

— (1996), '"I'd hate to be just a housewife": career aspirations of British Muslim girls', *British Journal of Guidance and Counselling*, 24, pp. 227–42.

— (1997), *Eastern Values; Western Milieu: Identities and Aspirations of Adolescent British Muslim Girls*. Aldershot: Ashgate.

BBC News, 'School wins Muslim dress appeal', Wednesday 26 March, 2006, http://news.bbc.co.uk/1/hi/education/4832072.stm (accessed 20 November 2010).

Bhopal, K. (1997a), *Gender, 'Race' and Patriarchy, A Study of South Asian Women*. Aldershot: Ashgate.

— (1997b), 'South Asian women within households: dowries, degradation and despair', *Women's Studies International Forum*, 20, pp. 483–92.

Bradby, H. (1999), 'Negotiating marriage: young Punjabi women's assessment of their individual and family interests', in R. Barot, H. Bradley, and S. Fenton, (eds) *Ethnicity, Gender and Social Change*. Hampshire: Macmillan Press.

Brah, A. (1996), *Cartographies of Diaspora, Contesting Identities*. London: Routledge.

Brah, A., and Shaw, S. (1992), *Working Choices: South Asian Young Muslim Women and the Labour Market*, Research Paper No. 91, London: Department of Employment.

Carby, H (1982), 'White Woman Listen! Black feminism and the boundaries of sisterhood', reproduced in HS Mirza (ed.) (1997), *Black British Feminism, A Reader*. London: Routledge.

Coleman, C. (2005), 'Amazing double life a growing trend among Muslim girls', the *Daily Mail*, April 11.

Connor, H., Tyers, C., Modood, T., and Hillage, J. (2004), *Why the Difference? A Closer Look at Higher Education Minority Ethnic Students and Graduates*, Research Report 552, Institute for Employment Studies, Department for Education and Skills.

Dale, A., Shaheen, N., Fieldhouse, E. and Kalra, V. (2002a), 'Labour market prospects for Pakistani and Bangladeshi women', *Work, Employment and Society*, 16, (1), pp. 5–26.

— (2002b), 'Routes into education and employment for young Pakistani and Bangladeshi women in the UK', *Ethnic and Racial Studies*, 25, (6), pp. 942–68.

Dwyer, C., Modood, T., Sanghera, G., Shah, B., and Thaper-Bjorkert, S. (2006), 'Ethnicity as social capital? Explaining the differential educational achievements of young British Pakistani men and women', Paper presented at the Mobility, Ethnicity and Society Conference, Thursday 16 and Friday 17 March 2006, University of Bristol.

Dwyer, C., and Shah, B. (2009), 'Rethinking the identities of young British Muslim Women', in P. Hopkins and R. Gale (eds), *Muslims in Britain: Race, Place and Identities*. Edinburgh: Edinburgh University Press.

Equal Opportunities Commission (2006), *Moving on Up? Bangladeshi, Pakistani and Black Caribbean Women and Work*. Manchester: EOC.

Federation of Student Islamic Societies (2005) *The Voice of Muslim Students, FOSIS Muslim Student Survey*. London: FOSIS.

Gemmell, C. (2010), 'Stephen Timms' knife attack: CCTV shows moment Muslim woman stabs MP', the *Telegraph*, 02 Nov. http://www.telegraph.co.uk/news/uknews/crime/8105085/Stephen-Timms-knife-attack-CCTV-shows-moment-Muslim-woman-stabs-MP.html (accessed 11 November 2010).

Henry, J., and Donnelly, L. (2008) 'Female Muslim medics "disobey hygiene rules"', the *Telegraph*, 03 Feb. http://www.telegraph.co.uk/news/uknews/1577426/Female-Muslim-medics-disobey-hygiene-rules.html (accessed 11 November 2010).

Hussain, Y., and Bagguley, P. (2007), *Moving On Up: South Asian Women and Higher Education*. Stoke-on-Trent: Trentham Books.

Ijaz, A., and Abbas, T. (2010), 'The impact of inter-generational change on the attitudes of working-class South Asian Muslim parents on the education of their daughters', *Gender and Education*, 22, (3), pp. 313–26.

Islamic Human Rights Commission (2006) 'You Only have the Right to Silence: A Review of Concerns Regarding Security Discourse on Muslims on Campus in Britain', IHRC: London.

Malik, S. (2005), 'Girls just wanna have fun', *Q-News*, March, Issue 361.

Mirza, H. S. (1995), 'Black women in higher education: defining a space/finding a place', in, L. Morley and V. Walsh (eds), *Feminist Academics: Creative Agents for Change*, London, Taylor & Francis.

Modood, T. (1998), 'Ethnic minorities' drive for qualifications', in T. Modood and T. Acland (eds), *Race and Higher Education: Experiences, Challenges and Policy Implications*. London: Policy Studies Institute.

— (2003), 'Ethnic149 differences in educational performance', in D. Mason (ed.), *Explaining Ethnic Differences*. Bristol: The Policy Press.

— (2006), 'Ethnicity, Muslims and higher education entry in Britain', *Teaching in Higher Education*, 11, (2), pp. 247–50.

Modood, T., and Acland, T. (eds) (1998), *Race and Higher Education: Experiences, Challenges and Policy Implications*. London: Policy Studies Institute.

Office for Public Management, (2009) *The Experiences of Muslim Students in Further and Higher Education*. Greater London Authority.

Read, B., Archer, L., and Leathwood, C. (2003), 'Challenging cultures? Student conceptions of 'belonging' and 'isolation' at a post-1992 university', *Studies in Higher Education*, 28, (3), pp. 261–77.

Reay, D., Davies, J., David, M., and Ball, S. J. (2001), 'Choices of degree or degrees of choice? Class, "race" and the higher education choice process', *Sociology*, 35, (4), pp. 855–74.

Shain, F. (2003), *The Schooling and Identity of Asian Girls*. Stoke on Trent: Trentham Books.

Shiner, M., and Modood, T. (2002), 'Help or hindrance? Higher education and the route to ethnic equality', *British Journal of Sociology of Education*, 23, (2): pp. 209–32.

Tyrer, D., and Ahmad, F. (2005), 'Those Muslim women are at it again!' *Q-News*, November 2005, Issue 364.

— (2006), *Muslim Women, Identities, Experiences, Diversity and Prospects in Higher Education*. Oxford: Liverpool John Moores University and European Social Fund.

8

Muslim youth at university: a critical examination of the British higher education experience

Introduction

This paper aims to reflect the experience of Muslim youth in the British higher education system and the challenges that they face as members of a faith community in campuses. The first part of the paper examines common understandings of 'race' and 'secularism' in British society and how this popular view affects the situation of the Muslim community in general. The chapter argues that there are of two chief obstacles for understanding the British Muslim community and creating a harmonious society wherein every component of the multicultural society is represented, accommodated and valued on equal terms.

The first obstacle is the current understanding of 'race' and 'anti-racism' that approaches the issue from a biological perspective and fails to recognize its cultural aspect. The second is a robustly implemented secularism which promotes the idea that religion should be restricted only to the private domain. The result is the non-recognition of the religious component of British Muslim identities.

In the second part of the chapter, I will be analyzing the findings of the Islamic Human Rights Commission's (IHRC) qualitative research on the experiences and expectations of Muslim higher education students. The research illustrates the general situation of Muslim students in the British higher education system and the problems stemming from the secular and racist structure of universities. It will also consider how the aftermath of the 9/11 and 7/7 terrorist attacks have affected Muslim students and exacerbated existing trends of racism and discrimination.

The 2001 census revealed a gloomy picture of the living standards of Muslims in Britain. They performed worse than the general population in education and employment, and they are three times less likely to be employed. Muslims are also more likely to live in deprived areas (Masood, 2006).

From 1990 onwards, multiculturalism has been given due attention in the context of American and British cultural studies (Hesse, 2001). Prior to the 1990s, interest on the subject was limited; the concept was largely considered to be a 'vaguely western political ideal' (Hesse, 2001, p. 1). The earliest definition of multiculturalism came about during the 1960s and 1970s. During this period the dominant sense of multiculturalism was 'harmonious cultural difference in the social, particularly where this meant the decontestation of "race" and "ethnicity" and their conflation with the individualist ethos of nationalist liberal-democracies' (Hesse, 2001, p. 1). Furthermore, from 1980 onwards, multiculturalism began to be considered as a frame of reference for ideas about cohesion in Western civil societies that are facing issues concerning national and ethnic identity.

The idea of multiculturalism emerged in Britain with the arrival of new migrants in the 1960s and 1970s. These migrations led to debates among the British public and politicians about the status and future of these migrants. The public was concerned about the economic and social consequences of accepting these newcomers into the society. These debates led to a British perception of multiculturalism that was defined as: 'a flattening process of uniformity, but, cultural diversity, coupled with equal opportunity in an atmosphere of mutual tolerance' (Hussain, 2004, pp.116–17).

This definition was very idealistic and failed to be realized by the practices of the British government. According to Abbas (2007), the hostility that the British Muslims were receiving since their arrival diminished the opportunities of Muslim groups to fully integrate into, and subsequently thrive within, the dominant economy and society. South Asian Muslims in areas such as Birmingham, therefore, found themselves restricted within the close boundaries of their community, which rendered them suspicious and alien in the eyes of their host society, and led to their loyalty being put into question (ibid).

The negative perceptions prompted a reaction from Muslims, especially 'Islamists' who constructed a British Muslim identity that grew from a 'culture of resistance' and 'unbelonging' to a colonial identity (Ansari, 2002, p. 9), albeit simultaneously feeling a great sense of belonging to Britain (Ameli and Merali, 2004, pp. 42–5).

As Tariq Modood (1992) has argued, one of the key issues that British Muslims face is the tendency of British social policy to limit definitions of racism to biological origin only, without acknowledging racism against members of cultural groups, such as groups who prefer to be defined by faith as their primary marker of identity, as in the case of Muslims. For example, he points out the emergence of a racial identity among British Jews, arguing that their 'otherness' helped to turn a religious identity into a separate racial identity so that Jews are now universally regarded (and regard themselves) as a racial rather than simply as a religious group (Modood, 2005).

In Britain, until the 2001 Census, estimates of Muslim populations relied on statistics relating to Pakistanis and Bangladeshis. This was due to the fact that their countries of origin are predominantly Muslim countries. Other Muslim communities had been rendered technically invisible, which resulted in difficulties estimating the size and socio-economic position of Muslims in Britain (Aspinall, 2000, p. 591). Through the inclusion of an optional question on religion in the 2001 Census, some reliable figures about the numbers of Muslims in Britain came to light.

An earlier study by the Policy Studies Institute (PSI) incorporated the notion of faith as a marker of identity and revealed that 80–83 per cent of the members of the South Asian Muslim community considered their Muslim identity as an important aspect of their identity (Modood et al., 1997). Furthermore, the Home Office

Citizenship Survey in 2001 documented that religion was more important than ethnicity in defining Muslims' identity among the Muslim minority of Britain (Open Society Institute Report, 2005, p. 22).

There is no doubt that the 9/11 attacks (Ameli et al., 2004) and, later, the July 2005 bombings ('7/7'), further exacerbated the situation for the whole British Muslim community. Immediately after the attacks there was a rapid increase in racist and xenophobic incidents (Masood, 2006), coupled with increased calls by secularists for the separation of religion from government policy.

Due to rapid developments and changes in British society during the 1960s, the secular thesis gained prominence over British society, thus circumscribing religion merely to the private sphere. This did not create much trouble for most of British society but has caused tensions for many minority groups where religion is an essential part of their identity. For Muslims, faith plays a significant role in their day-to-day lives and does not allow for the same separation of 'public and private spheres' (Modood, 1997). Thus, the failure to recognize faith-based identities is a direct consequence of a secular understanding that religion is a matter of private life.

Modood (1997) points out the distinction between the 'public' and 'private' space in the debate about multiculturalism, citing the ideas of John Rex (1985, 1986), who maintains that 'the fundamental distinction between a pluralist society without equality and the multiculturalism ideal is that the latter restricts cultural diversity to a private sphere so that all enjoy equality of opportunity and uniform treatment in the public domain' (p. 16). According to Modood (1997) there are two different approaches to the definition of equality based on the interpretation of 'public' and 'private' spaces. The first approach requires 'the right to assimilate to the majority/ dominant culture in the public sphere; and toleration of difference in the private sphere' (p. 20). The second approach is based on 'the right to have one's difference recognized and supported in both the public and the private sphere' (p. 20). Modood believes in the success of the second approach to equality, which would create a more sustainable multiculturalism in a given society.

In terms of defining the role of a state, Modood asserts that the state 'should protect religious freedoms but be neutral between religions' (2005, p. 19). In this regard, Modood (2005) is critical of secular bias against manifestations of religion in the public sphere.

He believes that the present understanding of secularism is a serious obstacle in the way of understanding Muslims:

> Part of the political culture and policy assumptions [. . .] make it difficult for Western societies to be just to Muslims. It is an obstacle to seeing the problems of Muslims and sympathizing with them, to seeing aspects of the oppression of Muslims, to recognizing Muslims, and offering solutions to them similar to those given to other oppressed and disadvantaged groups. (p. 20)

Finally, Modood (2005) asserts that there is an incompatibility between multiculturalism and 'radical secularism' which he believes is connected to political culture and prejudices of British politicians and society (p. 20).

Discrimination in the British higher education system

Since 1990, admissions to higher education began to be monitored ethnically. Studies of these figures established that there is institutionalized discrimination, exposing racism in selection processes, particularly in some of the older universities (Modood and Shiner, 2002; Modood, 2004). Even when ethnic minority students are admitted, it is very likely that minority students will have obtained better results than their white peers in order to secure a place (Modood, 2004). The Higher Education Statistics Agency (HESA) report published in 2003–4, documented the extent of the discrimination that ethnic minorities are facing in British universities, most prominently in Russell universities (BBC Education, 2005). Various other studies have also highlighted existing discrimination in higher education against minority students. The Runneymede Trust, through its 'Commission on the Future of Multi-Ethnic Britain' (2001), chaired by Bhikhu Parekh, examined the effects of discrimination on ethnic minorities across a whole variety of areas such as criminal justice and policing, arts, media and sport, access to health, employment, asylum and immigration, religion and belief and education. In terms of higher education, the Commission found that common problems that Asian and black students experienced in higher education were:

> isolation; the possibility of indirect discrimination in assessment procedures ... curricula and programs of study that do not reflect Asian and black experience and perceptions; assessment regimes that are not appropriate for mature students; timetabling arrangements that are culturally insensitive, lack of sensitive pastoral support for students experiencing difficulties associated with colour or cultural racism; and a lack of Asian and black lecturers and tutors. (p. 148)

Given the existing problems, the report recommended that 'courses and syllabi be reviewed with a view to making them culturally more inclusive wherever appropriate' (p. 148). The report also drew attention to the fact that 'there are at present no Asian or black vice-chancellors or pro-vice-chancellors, and few senior administrators, such as deans or registrars. It further recommended that *'all institutions of higher education review and improve their arrangements for the recruitment and retention of academic staff, particularly at the most senior levels'* (italics from original text; ibid).

Another report (2005) by the Higher Education Funding Council for England (HEFCE) suggested that applicants from ethnic minorities may experience discrimination when applying to university. For instance, applicants of Bangladeshi origin were seven per cent less likely to be offered a place to study law than white applicants. In order to redress the potential for discrimination, as ethnicity could sometimes be ascertained based on applicants names, HEFCE recommended that the University and College Admissions Service withhold students' names and pressed for the Committee of Heads of Law Schools to investigate application processes for students wishing to study law.

Despite the general perception that blacks are more discriminated than Asians, surveys indicate otherwise: the PSI survey cited above (carried out in 1994), found that the majority of people singled out Asians, especially Asian Muslims to be the greatest victims of ethnic, racial and religious hatred (op.cit). There is a great possibility that this has further increased after 9/11 (Modood, 2004, p. 94) in the US and the 7/7 terrorist attacks targeting passengers of London transport.

These have an impact on Muslim students in various direct and indirect ways (Federation of Student Islamic Societies (FOSIS), 2005). Below is a compilation of some recent major discriminatory incidents that have affected Muslims in higher education:

- On 25 October 2004, 14 students from Birmingham University were elected to represent the university students at the NUS Annual Conference in April 2005. All the elected delegates were of Muslim origin. The Birmingham Guild of Students, supported by the university, annulled the elections, and 10 days later produced a report that made various allegations regarding these elections. They were accused of fraud, intimidation and breaching the guild's anti-slate rules, according to which candidates cannot stand as a group and thus cannot support one another. As all of the 14 delegates were Muslims, the Guild must have considered them to be a 'group'. The University's Registrar passed the final ruling on 30 November 2004, which annulled the election and a new election was held in February 2005 (Islamic Human Rights Commission, 2006, p. 12)

- Nasser Amin, a Muslim student at School of Oriental and African Studies SOAS, wrote an article for the student magazine *Spirit* in March 2005. In his article, Amin discussed the morality of Palestinian resistance against Israeli occupation. Thereafter, national newspapers launched a frenzied attack against Amin's article accusing him of being anti-Semitic and supportive of terrorism. Even though Amin had not breached any laws in the article, SOAS publicly reprimanded him without any formal disciplinary hearing or legal procedure (Islamic Human Rights Commission, 2006, pp. 16–17).

- In May 2005, Special Branch, the unit of the UK Metropolitan police force responsible for overseeing security matters, asked the University Registrar and Secretary at Birmingham University for a list of all the members of the university Islamic Society. However, the Guild of Students turned down the request after seeking legal advice (Islamic Human Rights Commission, 2006, p. 21).

- In September 2005, the Social Affairs Unit, a right wing think-tank, published a report entitled 'When Students Turn to Terror: Terrorist and Extremist'. The authors of the report (Glees and Pope) alleged that British universities have become 'safe havens' for terrorist groups. The authors went so far as to allude that most of the British terrorists have been recruited at British universities. However, it was later revealed that the accusations were false as most of the names that the report labelled as 'terrorist' had either been acquitted or the charges had been dropped against them (Jafar, 2006). A similar report, from another right wing think-tank, the Centre for Social Cohesion, also made various allegations about book collections of the Islamic societies and Friday sermons delivered at campus prayer-rooms. It accused them of promoting 'political' Islam and 'intolerance', thus portraying a very negative image of Muslim students (Thorne and Stuart, 2008). Both reports have been heavily criticized for flawed methodologies and exaggerated claims (see Renton, 2008; Kundnani, 2008).

- London University's Imperial College issued a ban on staff and students wearing face veils and hooded garments in November 2005. The university claimed that the ban was part of an effort to 'improve campus security' after the July bombings in London earlier that year. The university had earlier taken away a room that was allocated for the staff and students to perform their weekly Friday prayers (Islamic Human Rights Commission, 2006, p. 14).

- Wakkas Khan, the President of the Federation of Student Islamic Societies (FOSIS), was detained at LA International Airport on 18 December 2005. Khan was to give a speech at a conference on combating extremism. He was considered to be a 'moderate' Muslim who had been selected by Tony Blair to be part of a 'taskforce' to counter extremism in the wake of the London bombings (Islamic Human Rights Commission, 2006, pp. 16–17).

- In May 2008, Rizwaan Sabir, a 22-year-old Muslim Masters student from the University of Nottingham, was arrested along with a member of staff under the Terrorism Act under suspicion of possessing extremist material. It was later revealed that he was studying radical Islamic groups for his dissertation. Prior to his arrest, Sabir had downloaded an edited version of the al-Qaeda handbook from a US government website and sent it to the staff member to be printed (Newman, 2008).

Moreover, students in the IHRC survey revealed how the terrorist attacks of 9/11 and the London 7/7 bombings had negatively impacted upon their experiences. For instance, a 22-year-old female studying Middle Eastern and Islamic Studies mentioned that after these events there was tremendous pressure on Muslim families to watch their children, which consequently made them overprotective and mounted increased pressure on Muslim youth. An 18-year-old female studying English literature added that, due to these pressures, some families forced their daughters to remove their headscarves. She further mentioned that their families subconsciously felt that they were second-class citizens and thus always advised their children not to become involved in anything, especially political activities, but to just 'go to school and come back'.

Lack of recognition of religious identity

Since Muslims have not been considered in the category of race in British law, it is very difficult to detect the exact nature of discrimination against Muslim students. The current picture of Muslims in higher education is largely based on what we can derive from figures about recognized ethnic origin categories that Muslims may fall into. This category is mostly indicated by South Asian ethnic background. Hence, it may be suggested that the foremost challenge that Muslim students face is the unfeasibility of assessing the depth of their discrimination through the conventional ethnicity-based categories of race. The lack of a given race status to Muslims also hinders any possible remedies for the present situation.

Another obstacle is the secular atmosphere of the universities. This, without doubt, negatively affects members of other faith groups; however, they are better equipped to deal these issues. Christians enjoy the long and deep-rooted religious traditions in British universities, especially in the old universities. Additionally, the Church of England is well resourced to deal with malicious media portrayal and support their followers (Muir and Stone,

2004). As for Jews and Sikhs, the Race Relations Act gives legal protection against discrimination.

Due to their visible attire, Muslim female students who wear the *hijab*, *jilbab* or *niqab* have been particularly prone to direct discrimination. The secular atmosphere found at many British universities, and the lack of protection against religiously motivated harassment, have left many Muslim female students feeling deeply alienated and, in some cases, subjected to racist incidents and institutional discrimination while at university (Tyrer and Ahmad, 2006).

Tyrer and Ahmad (2006), in their study of Muslim women in higher education, noted a perceived unwillingness on the part of universities to acknowledge Islamophobia in contrast to their readiness to tackle racism. The Muslim women in their sample highlighted, among other things, ways in which they had been excluded from consultations in the development of university equal opportunities policies. Women were also critical of the emphasis on ethnic origin rather than their religious identities on university equal opportunities monitoring forms. The research also touched upon important issues in terms of defining the identity of Muslim women. It indicated that female Muslim students 'rejected notions of essential, authentic primordial ethnic identity which they should adhere to and instead, stressed the dynamic, contingent and fluctuating nature of their identities' (p. 25). However, they also stressed the positive effects of the university environment and the ways it helped them in becoming more conscious about their gender, ethnic and religious identities. They stressed the significance of Islam in their lives and considered it an essential component of their identity.

Gilliat-Ray (2000) draws parallels between the lack of recognition of Muslim students and the increase in religious awareness among Muslims in higher education. Gilliat-Ray, in commenting on the findings of a survey carried out by Adia et al. (1996), which found that 60 per cent of students agreed that they have become more aware of their identities after their experiences in higher education, concludes that:

> It seems possible that the lack of recognition of religious identity by the institution could be one reason for students becoming more aware of the aspects of their own identity that are significant to them. By virtue of the fact that their institutions fail to recognize

different collective religious identities, identity becomes even more sharply defined. (Gilliat-Ray, 2000, p. 55)

Gilliat-Ray highlights increasing expectations among many young-generation Muslims and other faith communities for recognition of their religious identities in the public sphere. However, this expectation has not been met due to the present secular perception that considers religion merely a matter of private life (Gilliat-Ray, 2000, p. 55).

The IHRC conducted the research in 2009 on British Muslims in higher education as part of a wider project to examine the issue of British Muslim citizenship as a concept, which involved ascertaining the views of various sectors of the Muslim community. Students in higher education represent an aspirational stratum of the community, as well as being the focus of much government attention. The research followed a sociological approach based on 45 qualitative questionnaires that were administered across 45 universities in the UK. The total number of quantitative responses came to 1125. The majority of the respondents were male (64 per cent), with female respondents making up just over a third (36 per cent). All the respondents were from diverse ethnic backgrounds and the level of their religiosity and identification with Islam was also diverse, ranging from devout practitioners to cultural and secular Muslims. The respondents were questioned about their relations with fellow students and academic staff, equal opportunities and service provisions. Respondents were reached through an email alert, posting on the IHRC website, Islamic societies and various umbrella organizations, visits to some universities and word of mouth. The age, gender, location and universities attended by students were recorded (if provided); however, university names will not be disclosed here in order to retain anonymity.

Interaction with fellow students

Respondents were asked about possible problems regarding their interactions with the fellow students. There were a number of negative experiences expressed. Most of these revolved around the consumption of alcohol and relations between opposite sexes, both of which were the focus of many social activities. Alcohol, being a crucial component in many university and student union meetings and activities, left many Muslim students feeling isolated in these environments and unable to participate in such events.

Due to the difficulties faced by Muslim students in interacting with non-Muslim students and university staff in such environments, they often create their own social environment through student unions, prayer-rooms and friendship circles (Kukhareva et al., 2007). It seems that although this provides them the support they need, it also further isolates them from other social activities. For instance:

> As for the university environment, the predominant culture encourages partying and drinking, and this may deter Muslims from their religious obligations. Mixing is also an issue, especially when Muslims are seeking to build relationships. The problem of mixing is also present within halls of residence, where Muslims are compelled to make compromises in their religion due to liberal interactions. (Male)

Some students complained about the negative perceptions of Muslims, which became an obstacle in the way of their interaction with fellow students:

> The main issue would be that fellow students may be wary of Muslim students due to all the negative portrayal of their faith. (Female)

For female students, wearing headscarves and avoiding physical contact with the opposite sex stand as the two most important issues. Their accounts indicate that popular perceptions of Muslim women as being oppressed and forced to wear a headscarf, led to other students treating *hijab*-wearing Muslim women differently and keeping them at a distance.

> Many people tend to assume girls with *hijabs* are incapable of doing some jobs, however, they should try to look beyond their physical appearance and judge them by their minds and intellect rather than how they look. (Female)

> It is simply not understood; a lot of the reaction comes from misconceptions and ignorance rather than people having a problem with it. (Female, 21)

> *Hijab* is still very much a mystery to peers and tutors and few pluck up the courage to ask the questions they want to ask. It is not understood and can be seen as oppressive and foreign. (Female, 21)

Relations with academic staff

As for relations with university staff, some students believed that staff working within universities were just as likely to reflect the attitudes of wider society. For instance, several students complained about the Islamophobic attitudes of some academic staff. Examples cited included the inflexible approach of some university staff towards prayer times, though this was by no means universal and there are indeed good examples available. These were mostly concentrated in London universities, perhaps owing to their more diverse multicultural and multi-religious student population.

> Some staff, I feel, have an Islamophobic attitude towards the Muslims. You can see it in their behaviour towards the students. But not all really. (Male)

> I personally haven't had bad experiences, but one issue that affects Muslim students in [X University] is that tutor meetings at [X University] often involve alcohol – there are twice-termly meetings called 'drinks with tutors' where tutors give a drinks reception to their students, and this may be problematic for some Muslim students, and means they miss out on potentially useful time with their tutors. (Female)

One respondent mentioned the strict policy of university administration regarding exam times and dates, which completely disregards religious and cultural obligations. For one Muslim student, this inflexibility cost him a year of study. Some female students also complained about the biased approach of the academic staff towards their headscarves and their discomfort around the centrality of alcohol in student-staff interactions was raised:

> As a Muslim female medical student in clinical practice, some consultants can be awkward about allowing us to wear *hijab* in theatre or even surgical gowns to cover our arms as they see it as a 'waste of resources'. (Female)

> There was one teacher I had, who gave a snide [sic] remark. Directly looking at myself and a friend, he said, 'it's so hot; I don't know how some people can wear hats'. I felt he used the word 'hat' as a reference to our *hijab*. There were only girls in his class and, being a law teacher, he used every opportunity to

make us feel out of place. For example he would say, 'If we went back 100 years, you wouldn't own this book, because you are a woman'. (Female)

Another female medical student mentioned how some Muslim women felt uncomfortable shaking hands or being alone with male staff or patients, but also that:

> Social events with staff are held in pubs/alcohol-providing restaurants, which makes it difficult and uncomfortable to refuse on one hand, and to attend on the other. (Female)

One student suggested that Muslim students should put extra effort into improving their relations with university staff and fellow students. This may be an over-compensating suggestion resulting from the extra pressure that stems from a negative or hostile environment – in this case, a perceived Islamophobic atmosphere. However, not all accounts were negative; some of the respondents maintained that the attitude of the academic staff was quite fair towards Muslim students.

Equal opportunities

When asked whether, compared to non-Muslims, Muslim identity negatively affected opportunities in academia or not, the feelings were mixed. Some stated that there was no such problem at all in campuses and they felt that they had similar opportunities as non-Muslim students:

> I have a positive interaction with lecturers and other students at university. I have the same opportunities as non-Muslims. (Female)

However, other some students felt that they or some of their peers believe that their Muslim identities had somehow negatively affected their opportunities in academia. Some of the examples that were given revolved around ignorance about Islam and Muslims, and explicit hostility that manifested itself as the perceived downgrading of exam papers, or difficulties in administration.

These people seemed totally ignorant to our existence. They lacked cultural awareness – they were almost, without exception, surprised to see any black person. It was embarrassing. For them and for me. (Male, 26)

It's generally good, I try to be friendly to other students and I've had no problems with lecturers or staff. But I know of other Muslim students who've had bad experiences with professors – for example, one of my sister's professors treated her very badly, gave her consistently bad grades while all the other professors agreed her work was excellent, and gave her a terrible reference. She [the professor] made it clear she had a very bad view of Islam, and this affected the way she treated Muslim students. This adversely affects Muslim students' opportunities. But I personally have had no problems. (Female)

In another example, the reference to alcohol consumption at university social events was again mentioned as having an effect on Muslim students' access to equal opportunities through the emphasis on events geared towards fostering good relations between students and staff.

Availability of service provision for Muslim students on campus

Some students highlighted the availability of chaplaincy services and of *halal* food provisions for Muslims.

There are a large number of chapels and Christian prayer spaces – pretty much in every college. There is some provision for kosher food. There is, however, a Muslim 'chaplain' which was taken for *juma namaaz* (Friday prayer) and offers support. (Male)

Only a few students suggested that there were no such services available in their university campuses. However, many students did report problems with class timetables and prayer times, especially during winter when daylight hours are shorter and students experienced difficulties offering their daily and their weekly Friday prayers. One student stated that their lecturers did not understand religious requirements and consequently denied requests for prayers and taking time off on religious holidays. However, not all students felt this to be the case; some stated that if they talked to their lecturers and explained the situation, their lecturers were quite helpful and allowed them to perform their religious duties.

Thus, it appears that overall it is not a case of systematic discrimination in terms of not allowing Muslim students to perform their religious obligations, but rather an issue of not understanding the religious rituals and duties of Muslim students. Left up to individual judgment, this may cause problems for those who encountered unsympathetic lecturers and staff. In order, therefore, to avoid unpleasant situations it would be crucial for university administrations to make it university policy to be flexible for prayer timetables and major religious occasions.

Conclusion

The above findings demonstrate the effects of the dominant secular culture on Muslim higher education students. They show that an overtly secular culture can dramatically restrict Muslim students' participation in the social and academic life of universities, causing frustration among the Muslim youth and forcing them to form close-knit groups, which in turn, increase the isolation and alienation felt in the university environment. The current understanding of 'race' and 'anti-racism' is not useful as it fails to acknowledge the religious and cultural identities of Muslim students and fails to provide protection against discriminatory practices. The terrorist attacks of 9/11 and 7/7 created an atmosphere in which Islamic student societies and Muslim students have been targeted and stereotyped as potential terrorists. This has created further tensions for some Muslim students, especially in terms of their perceived acceptance as members of the university. It is important to conclude this chapter with Muslim students' expectations of higher education in Britain. There are four major expectations from Muslim students that are intricately connected to the issues of 'race'/'anti-racism' and 'secularism':

1   Tackling Islamophobia and discrimination. This could be achieved through introducing laws and regulations that consider Muslims in the status of a race, as is the case with

Jews and Sikhs. The necessity of extending the Race Relations Act to include religions has also been stressed by Muir and Stone (2004).

2 To raise awareness about Islam within British universities and respect Islamic values.

3 To provide better religious facilities and food that meets Islamic dietary requirements (Siddiqui, 2007).

4 To allow for the rearranging of timetables for Muslim prayer times and religious festivals.

This chapter has aimed to illustrate how Muslim youth can face certain challenges and tensions due to the racism and Islamophobia they sometimes face within the higher education environment. Adopting a purely race relations or secular approach to the concerns of Muslim students, highlighted in this research and others, is failing to bring forward any tangible solutions to the concerns of Muslim students. The only way forward is to give audience to the young Muslims who are expecting to be heard.

References

Abbas, T. (2007), 'Muslim Minorities in Britain: Integration, Multiculturalism and Radicalism in the Post-7/7 Period,' *Journal of Intercultural Studies*, 28, (3), pp. 287–300.

Ahmad, F. (2001), 'Modern Traditions? British Muslim Women and Academic Achievement', *Gender and Education*, 13, (2), pp. 137–52.

—(2007), 'Muslim Women's Experiences of Higher Education in Britain', *American Journal of Islamic Social Sciences*, 24, (3), pp. 46–69.

Ameli, S., Elahi, E., and Merali, A. (2004), *British Muslims' Expectations of the Government: Social Discrimination across the Muslim Divide*. London: Islamic Human Rights Commission.

Ameli S. R. and Merali, A. (2004), *Dual Citizenship: British, Islamic or Both? — Obligation, Recognition, Respect and Belonging*. London: Islamic Human Rights Commission.

Ansari, H. (2002), *Muslims in Britain*. UK: Minority Rights Group International.

Aspinall, P. (2000), 'Should a question on "Religion" be asked in 2001 British Census? A public policy case in favour', *Social Policy & Administration*, 34, (5), pp. 584–600.

BBC Education, (2005), 'Plans to Erase University Bias', BBC News: http://news.bbc.co.uk/1/hi/education/4484540.stm. [Accessed 05 January 2009.]

FOSIS, (2005), *The Voice of Muslim Students: A report into the attitude and perceptions of British Muslim Students following the July 7th London attacks.* United Kingdom: Federation of Student Islamic Societies (FOSIS).

Gilliat-Ray, S. (2000), *Religion in Higher Education: The Politics of the Multi-Faith Campus.* Wiltshire: Ashgate.

HESA, (2004), *Higher Education Statistics for the UK.* Cheltenham: Higher Education Statistic Agency.

Hesse, B. (2001), *Un/Settled Multiculturalisms: Diasporas, Entanglement, Transruptions.* London: Zed Books.

Hussain, D. (2004), 'The Impact of 9/11 on British Muslim Identity', in R. Geaves, T. Gabriel, Y. Haddad, J. Idleman Smith (eds), *Islam & The West: Post 9/11.* Aldershot and Burlington, VA: Ashgate, pp. 115–29.

Islamic Human Rights Commission, (2006), 'You only have the Right to Silence: A Briefing on the Concerns Regarding Muslims on Campus in Britain'. Available at: www.ihrc.org.uk/file/ YouONLYhavetheRighttoSilence.doc. [Accessed 23 August 2010.]

Jafar, A. (2006), 'Promoting good campus relations: dealing with hate crimes and intolerance' Issues affecting Freedom of Expression, in *A Response to the Ebdon Report*, Parliamentary University Group.

Kukhareva, M., Eames, J., Sinclair, T., Kendall, S., Chakravorty, M., and Watts, M. (2007), *Ethnic Minority Participation in Higher Education in the East of England*, Association of Universities in the East of England, Cambridge.

Kundnani, A. (2008), 'How are think tanks shaping the political agenda on Muslims in Britain?' 2 September 2008, Institute for Race Relations, http://www.irr.org.uk/2008/september/ak000003.html. [Accessed 6 May 2011.]

Mansfield, E., and Kehoe, K. (1994), 'A critical examination of anti-racist education', *Canadian Journal of Education*, 19, (4), pp. 418–30.

Masood, E. (2006), *British Muslims Media Guide.* UK: British Council.

Modood, T. (1992), 'British Muslims and The Rushdie Affair', in J. D. Rattansi (ed.) *'Race', Culture & Difference.* London: Sage Publications, pp. 260–77.

— (1997), 'The Politics of Multiculturalism in the New Europe', in T. M. Werbner (ed.) *The Politics of Multiculturalism in the New Europe.* London: Zed Books Ltd, pp. 1–25.

— (2004), 'Capitals, ethnic identity and educational qualifications', *Cultural Trends*, 13, (2), pp. 87–105.

— (2005), *Multicultural Politics: Racism, Ethnicity and Muslims in Britain*. Edinburgh: University Press.

Modood, T. et al. (1997), *Ethnic Minorities in Britain: Disadvantage and Diversity*. London: Policy Studies Institute.

Modood, T., and Shiner, M. (2002), 'Favourite colours,' the *Guardian*: http://www.guardian.co.uk/world/2002/jun/25/race.newuniversities19922012. [Accessed 3 January 2009.]

Muir, H. and Stone, R. (2004), *Islamophobia: Issues, Challenges and Action*. UK and US: The Commission on British Muslims and Islamophobia.

Newman, M. (2008), 'Research into Islamic terrorism led to police response' in *The Times Higher Education*: http://www.timeshighereducation.co.uk/story.asp?sectioncode = 26&storycode = 402125&c = 2. [Accessed 01 March 2009.]

Open Society Institute, (2005), *Muslims in the UK: Policies for Engaged Citizens*. Budapest: Open Society Institute.

Siddiqui, A. (2007), 'Islam at Universities in England: Meeting The Needs and Investing in the Future', Report submitted to Bill Rammell MP Minister of State for Lifelong Learning, Further and Higher Education.

Thorne, J., and Stuart, H. (2008), *Islam on Campus: A Survey of UK Student Opinions*. Great Britain: The Centre for Social Cohesion.

Tyrer, D., and Ahmad, F. (2006), *Muslim Women and Higher Education: Identities, Experiences and Prospects*. Oxford: ESF and Liverpool John Moores University.

9

Muslim youth and citizenship education: idealism, Islam and prospects for successful citizenship education

NADER AL-REFAI & CHRISTOPHER BAGLEY

Introduction

According to the literature we have reviewed (Al-Refai and Bagley, 2008), in British schools today, having a religious faith – any faith – can make a positive contribution to identity, citizenship and the common good. Our conclusions in the monograph on which this paper is based suggest that the role of citizenship education is not only to serve a political function by addressing levels of political apathy, but also to try and deal with certain aspects of injustice and social discontent in British society today. For Muslim youth who have settled in Europe, the challenges to their traditional religious identity are strong. They seek empowerment, but at the same time many wish to retain a traditional set of Muslim values (Malik, 2006).

Particularly during the last 15 years, Muslims in Britain have become more involved in a number of spheres of social action and organization. Politically, socially and culturally, their presence has become increasingly apparent. There are a number of important factors central to the presence of Muslims in Britain, within the context of Muslim social and political mobilization, and subsequent state responses (Anwar and Bakhsh, 2003). Over the last decade, there has been increasing debate on a number of issues concerning Muslims in Britain and the national schooling system. Today, Muslims comprise the the third-largest practising religious group in Britain (after Anglicans and Catholics). Many Muslims who are growing up in Britain are having to face the prospect of defining their identity in peaceable, productive and law-abiding ways in a society that is increasingly Islamophobic (Sheridan, 2006), This question of identity affects second- and third-generation Muslims, who have to balance their religious upbringing and traditions with the demands of the culture surrounding them (Gilliat-Roy, 2010).

The ongoing faith schools debate has opened up into various discussions which focus on the implications and effectiveness of single-faith and multi-faith schools; the differences between single-faith schools and state schools; and the importance and general effectiveness of independent Muslim schools. Thus, with an increasing number of independent Muslim schools being established in Britain, this chapter aims to discuss the ways that the subject of citizenship is taught in these schools, as compared with state schools, and to assess the adequacy of citizenship teaching in preparing young Muslims for a productive and moral existence in a society in which religious groups recognize one another's differences and strengths, and are able to live together harmoniously.

Possibly the biggest issue for Muslims in Britain, and one that concerns both national and local groups, is education. Muslims have felt discomforted in the British school system (Anwar and Bakhsh, 2003), and have also struggled to gain funding for their own faith schools. In the 1960s, the British school system was significantly restructured. Reforms included the removal of most single-sex schools, just when Muslim parents were beginning to look into them with interest. In the 1970s, England began to contemplate some practical concessions to make Muslims more comfortable with British education. They believed that a multi-faith approach to religious education (RE) would encourage Muslims to enrol (Anwar and Bakhsh, 2003). It is estimated that there is an approximate population of 450,000–500,000 Muslim pupils in Britain of compulsory school age (5–16), and that figure is likely to increase substantially (Peach, 2006) – the large majority of these children of Muslim parents are enrolled in state schools, including many nominally designated as 'Church of England' schools.

Although Muslims generally accept the British view regarding the basic purpose of education, for Muslims the idea of 'good citizenship' is also synonymous with being a 'good Muslim'. Muslims have pressed for many changes in state schools, including prayer-rooms in schools with a large Muslim population, excused absence for children attending Friday prayers and major religious festivals, segregated swimming and PE lessons and *halal* provisions in meals. It is argued that although these changes are specific to Muslim pupils, they are not intended to be divisive with other faith groups and, generally, implementing them bears little impact upon the rest of the school organization.

Reflecting these concerns, three types of Islamic educational institutions have developed: first, there are the mosque schools; second, there are schools that are run in private homes or in separate places; and, third are full-time primary or secondary schools, such as Al-Isra Islamic College in Malvern, Worcestershire and the Islamic College in East London (Anwar, 1993).

Muslim Education Systems, Citizenship Education and Religious Schooling

Many Muslim families in Britain have a dual system of schooling – supplementary schools represented by weekend and evening schools; and independent full-time schools. In the 1980s, the Muslim community in Britain began to set up Muslim schools. The first was in London, and now there are some 140 schools educating more than 12,000 pupils. Muslim schools have now joined the maintained sector, but most are still making efforts to become 'maintained Muslim schools' as part of a drive to raise standards and increase diversity. The Association of Muslims Schools (AMS) estimated in 1997 that approximately two per cent of the total number of Muslim children attend full-time Muslim schools though this figure at the time of writing was unverifiable. Full-time, or day-time independent schools are divided into two types in terms of the curriculum. The first are religious schools which do not teach anything other than Islamic education. The second are schools that teach national curriculum (NC) subjects alongside other religious and cultural subjects such as Urdu, Arabic, Islamic studies and Qur'anic science.

The importance of teaching citizenship in parallel to, or in conjunction with, religious education are promoting spirituality; encouraging pupils to play a helpful part in everyday life; teaching pupils about the economy and democratic institutions and values; encouraging respect for different national, religious and ethnic identities and developing pupils' abilities to reflect on issues and take part in discussions.

By the early 1990s it was estimated that there were about 60 state and Anglican schools with a Muslim intake of 90–100 per cent, and over 200 schools with over 75 per cent Muslim intake (Parker-Jenkins, 1995, p. 86). There are also now a significant number of Muslim independent schools, founded by individuals and groups, which aim to incorporate Islamic ideals into the education system, thereby fulfilling many religious and cultural requirements for Muslim children.

Development of the National Curriculum, and Citizenship Education

David Blunkett, the then Secretary of State for Education, set up an Advisory Group on citizenship which reported in 1998 (Osler and Starkey, 2001). The Advisory Group proposed the national programme of citizenship education for English schools in its final report (the Crick Report, 1998), which consisted of an outline programme of study and preliminary guidance (Qualification and Curriculum Authority [QCA], 2000). The Crick Report has three main strands: (1) social and moral responsibility – children learning, from the very beginning, self-confidence and socially and morally responsible behaviour both in and beyond the classroom, both towards those in authority and towards one another (this is an essential pre-condition for citizenship); (2) community involvement – pupils learning about and becoming helpfully involved in the life and concerns of their communities, including learning through community involvement and service to the community; (3) political literacy – pupils learning about, and how to make themselves effective in, public life through knowledge, skills and values (QCA, 1998, 2000).

These developments have caused individuals and groups to consider how citizenship is related to national and regional identities, and have encouraged the debate about the meaning of nationality, national identity and citizenship, and the extent to which individuals and groups from both majority and minority communities feel a sense of belonging to the nation and the state (Osler and Starkey, 2001).

Citizenship education as a new subject was introduced for the reasons outlined in the Crick Report, and as an attempt to deal with institutional racism, which became a serious concern of government and public sector workers after the publication of a report and other research on the survival or racist attitudes and actions in Britain (Home Office, 1999; Lawton et al., 2000). The government has highlighted citizenship education as a key means by which education for racial equality can be achieved (Osler and Vincent(2002). Racism has been identified as serving to undermine democracy in Europe, and needs to be addressed through programmes in schools and in teacher education (Verma, 1989, 2007). Citizenship education in England is therefore seen as a means of strengthening democracy and of challenging racism as an anti-democratic force. The government sees citizenship education as a key means through which race equality initiatives will be developed in the curriculum (Osler and Vincent, 2002).

In 2000, the national curriculum (NC) underwent considerable revision. The introduction of citizenship was the most significant new development. From 2002, 'citizenship' became a statutory subject in secondary schools (years 7–11: ages 11–16). On the other hand, although citizenship is taught in many primary schools as part of the statutory requirement to deliver personal, social and health education (PSHE), it has no status as a subject in its own right. At both primary and secondary levels, the provision of citizenship education is to be monitored through the School Inspection System. The QCA has published guidance for schools on the citizenship curriculum. In spring 2002, the QCA launched guidelines and an interactive website for teachers to demonstrate how schools might value diversity and challenge racism within the framework of the national curriculum, which can be found at: www.qca.org.uk (Osler and Vincent, 2002).

Education for citizenship has become a leading concern for educational policy and debate in the advanced economies of the English-speaking world, where education systems and agencies have produced reports on curriculum guidelines and school programmes in surprising number. The following discussion traces the factors that influenced the concept of citizenship in the modern state, such as the political, social and educational factors. The Department for Education and Skills (DfES) made it clear that teaching citizenship is a whole-school issue by declaring that the ethos, organization, structures and daily practices of schools have a considerable impact on the effectiveness of citizenship education. Adopting a whole-school approach to provision will ensure that citizenship runs through everything schools do. According to the National Curriculum Handbook for teachers, schools have a crucial role in providing opportunities for all pupils to learn and achieve, and in promoting children's spiritual, moral, social and cultural development; as well as preparing them for the opportunities, responsibilities and experiences of life.

The citizenship education (CE) curriculum has been divided into the Foundation Stage, where the curriculum for primary school children is meant to make a positive contribution to children's early development and learning which are critical to their perception of themselves and their relationships to others; and Key Stages One and Two, which aim to promote pupils' personal and social development, including health and well-being. The programme of study described in the non-statutory guidance manual for PSHE and citizenship covers the knowledge, understanding and skills that prepare pupils to play an active role as citizens. This aims to promote pupils' personal and social development, including health and well-being.

In Key Stages Three and Four (middle and final stages of secondary schooling), statutory requirements are set out in the NC programme of study. Planning of provision should reflect the need to ensure that pupils have a clear understanding of their roles, rights and responsibilities in relation to their local, national and international communities. The three strands in the programmes of study which are to be taught are: (1) knowledge and understanding about becoming an informed citizen; (2) developing skills of enquiry and communication; and (3) developing skills of participation and responsible action.

The QCA has provided schemes of work for citizenship which provide guidance for teachers on how to plan provision for citizenship and expand on teaching, learning and assessment outcomes. The schemes of work reflect the flexible nature of the curriculum, allowing schools to build on what they may already be doing, varying the depth of coverage of aspects of knowledge and understanding, being innovative and developing their own approaches to citizenship, and promoting a continuity and progression that builds on previous learning (DfES, 2005).

In the early years, pupils are engaged in activities which contain such topics as: graffiti, friendship, looking after people and friends, wanting things that cost money, fairness, helping and litter. Between the ages of 7 and 11, students are expected to know their rights and responsibilities, and they need to be able to link these to other ideas such as notions of right and wrong, fairness and unfairness. They also should be able to recognize rules and laws; explain how the country is run; be able to relate to other people and the community they belong to and be able to make their views heard. In this way they may learn to influence what is happening around them in the school and wider community, both nationally and internationally.

Between the ages of 11 and 14 the curriculum covers three areas of learning: (1) political literacy, (2) social and moral responsibility, and (3) community involvement. Pupils learn about legal and human rights and responsibilities; key aspects of parliamentary government, including elections and voting; local and central government; the diversity of national, regional, religious and ethnic identities in the UK; the need for mutual respect and understanding; the significance of the media; and the world as a global community and the implications of this, including the role of the European Union, the Commonwealth and the United Nations.

In the final two years of compulsory schooling, citizenship should assist pupils to discover the things they need to know and comprehend in playing an effective role in the community at local, national and international levels. They learn about how legal and human rights relate to citizens; the origins and implications of the diverse national, regional, religious and ethnic identities in the UK, and the need for mutual respect and understanding; the work of parliament, government and the courts; the opportunities for individuals and voluntary groups to effect change; the importance of a free press and the role of the media; how the economy functions, including the rights and responsibilities of consumers, employers and employees; and the UK's relations within Europe, the Commonwealth and the United Nations; and the wider issues of global interdependence and responsibility, including sustainable development (DfES, 2005).

Education for both Muslims and non-Muslims is seen as a critical requirement through which pupils can not only learn about various responsibilities and obligations of citizenship, but also what it means to exist in a multi-faith and multicultural society. The QCA document provided a starting point for schools to discuss the links between citizenship at Key Stage Three and in religious education (RE). The QCA provides a leaflet that maps the areas where the two subjects are compatible. It also suggests some opportunities for teaching citizenship through RE referring, where appropriate, to relevant units in the RE scheme of work.

From the QCA perspective, RE can contribute to citizenship education by:

- providing opportunities for pupils to see how individual, group and political choices, policies and actions (e.g. human rights), are inextricably linked with, and influenced by, religious and moral beliefs, practices and values
- providing opportunities for pupils to understand and deal with local, national, European and global issues through knowledge and understanding of their religious dimensions and contexts
- enabling pupils to understand and exercise the meaning of personal, social and moral responsibility
- enabling pupils to see how human beings across the world treat one another and their environments and why they treat them as they do
- enabling pupils to develop active citizenship by involvement with voluntary religious and charitable activities. (DfES, 2004)

There is no other subject on the school curriculum which offers this type of opportunity for reflection in such depth or content. It is suggested, therefore, that RE should have that opportunity to provide pupils with vital knowledge in understanding and contributing in a major way to developing value-based, positive attitudes and reflections on the diverse and plural country that Britain has become.

The scope of Citizenship Education

In September 2006, the Office for Standards in Education OFSTED published a major review of the teaching of CE in secondary schools (OFSTED, 2006). The report was based on the inspection of a large number of schools and observed that, despite 'significant progress', there was not yet a strong consensus about the aims of CE, or about how to incorporate it into the curriculum: 'In a quarter of schools surveyed, provision is still inadequate reflecting weak leadership and lack of specialized teaching.' However, in another quarter of schools, it was judged that satisfactory progress in the understanding, organization and delivery of citizenship education had been made. The report implies that the 'failing' schools were probably those experiencing stress for a variety of reasons. Profiles of such failing schools have been presented by Bagley (2008).

The OFSTED report found that schools had responded to the goals of CE in very different ways: 'Some, a minority, have embraced it with enthusiasm and have worked hard to establish it as part of their curriculum. Others, also a minority, have done very little.' The inspection report found contrasted methods of delivering CE, though most offered it as part of PSHE classes. Many teachers were unclear about the standards by which CE should be assessed, and written work in CE was poorer than that produced by the same pupils in other subjects. Standards were best when CE was included in GCSE subject teaching. However, in 2006, only 53,600 pupils were entered for GCSE examinations in citizenship. The OFSTED report found that many teachers had not been adequately prepared for instructing their students in CE, and recommended that teachers should be seconded on to the growing number of short courses in CE instruction. It was also suggested by OFSTED that schools should use the recommended reference manual on CE by Huddleston and

Kerr (2006). A valuable overview of key issues such as citizenship education and moral values is provided by Halstead and Pike (2006).

Background and objectives of the present research

The key aim is to investigate the differences between Muslim and state schools, contrasting ways of delivering CE in Muslim schools and examining the role of Muslim schools in preparing pupils for a role in British society by focusing on both Islamic education and education for being a good citizen.

The study further aimed to explore ways of delivering citizenship in Muslim schools in terms of the national curriculum (NC) guidelines, the differences in teaching citizenship between Muslim and state schools, the attitude of pupils in Muslim schools towards the teaching of citizenship, the attitude of educational professionals, parents and community leaders towards the teaching of citizenship; examining the role of Muslim schools in preparing pupils for a role in British society; investigating the relationship between Islam and citizenship; and demonstrating the possible contribution of Islamic studies to the teaching of citizenship. A full account of the resulting research and discussion of the issues can be found in Al-Refai and Bagley (2008).

The present study aims to shed some light on the citizenship curriculum in order to explore the ways in which citizenship is being taught in Muslim and state schools within the same geographical areas. Interviews and questionnaires were completed with 364 respondents (including 25 teachers) in the areas of curriculum, pedagogy, assessment and teacher training. The informants in this research included Muslim and state schools' head teachers, CE teachers in Muslim and state schools, CE teachers in state schools, Islamic studies teachers in Muslim schools and Muslim community leaders and opinion formers.

The present study is not only a sample of pupils, but is also a case-study of Muslim schools, which were accessed because of their willingness to participate and their geographical location in northern England. The final selection of Muslim schools for study is biased in that it reflects our perception of what is 'best practice', in terms of the ways in which CE was delivered. In policy terms, we are seeking to describe what appear to be models of best practice, in which religious principles inform CE, and vice versa.

The number of Muslim secondary schools in England that are available for study as determined by the Association of Muslim Schools (AMS), was fifty-seven – thirty-three for girls and twenty-four for boys. Within the area of research (North-West England) there were thirteen Muslim secondary schools, eight of them for girls and five for boys. This number represented some 23 per cent of the total number of Muslim secondary schools in England; the principal researcher contacted them individually to arrange the fieldwork visit.

The final sample chosen for intensive study included five Muslim secondary schools which were confident and active in their delivery of CE from different regions in the North of England. Three were girls' schools and two were for boys. Information about the numbers of pupils, together with their teachers, was obtained from the head teachers of each participating school. These were schools that felt confident or satisfied with how they were delivering CE, and thus the researchers were unlikely to have accessed the 25 per cent of schools which OFSTED (2006) judged to be failing in their delivery of citizenship education. The principal researcher, of course, unlike the OFSTED inspectors, had no right of access to a random sample of schools.

Furthermore, pupils in the schools had the right to decline the completion of the questionnaire or the interview, since this often took time from other activities. The final samples then, are likely to be biased in favour of the most confident schools and those pupils who found CE particularly interesting or important – it is interesting in this context to note that 88 per cent of pupils in Muslim schools agreed to complete a questionnaire or interview, compared with less than 60 per cent of those in state schools, and the one faith school (Anglican, which resembled state schools in terms of ethos and curriculum). The state schools and the Anglican faith school were selected because the head teachers were enthusiastic about their CE programmes, which they felt to be successful; because these schools had a significant number of Muslim pupils; and because they were situated within the catchment areas of the Muslim secondary schools.

In Muslim schools, 176 pupils (90 females and 86 males) responded to the questionnaire which was administered in the five schools, and 23 pupils (11 females and 12 males) responded to the extended interviews. There is a slight gender bias in the samples, with more females completing questionnaires in the Muslim schools than in the state schools. This is because three of the Muslim schools contained only girls, while the remaining two Muslim schools contained only boys. There is also a slight age bias, with more respondents from Year 10 (around age 14) in the Muslim schools. However, results did not differ between Muslim and state schools when separate analyses by gender and year of study were undertaken for both questionnaire and interviewee respondents, and therefore results in the following tables and discussions have not been presented separately by gender, age or year of study.

The sample from the state schools included 111 pupils who responded to the questionnaire, and 29 pupils who were interviewed personally, answering not only the topics covered in the questionnaire, but also giving their opinions on a range of relevant topics. As with the Muslim schools sample, the ages, genders and other demographic profiles of those interviewed personally were similar to those completing questionnaires (Al-Refai and Bagley, 2008).

Citizenship Education and Best Practice

The findings of this study of 'best practice' secondary schools revealed that pupils from both types of school, Muslim and non-Muslim, are aware of their rights and responsibilities to the wider society they live in. They would also like to contribute towards improving society when they become adults, through many different routes. The responses of the young people are, for the most part, refreshing in their enthusiasm.

The majority of Muslim pupils for example, saw CE as interesting and important. They saw such education as helping them understand and live in the wider society: 'it teaches us how to live in a multi-ethnic, multi-faith society'. Many pupils thought that CE could help them to relate to the wider community in harmonious ways, and had taught them good values, in terms of right and wrong. It had taught them to respect others not only in school, but also in the wider society. CE was seen by many pupils as a factor in self-development – for Muslim pupils in particular it was a way of acquiring a meaningful social identity in a complex and sometimes hostile culture. Muslim pupils in particular said that their citizenship classes had helped them understand both their rights and their responsibilities, and had also enhanced their understanding of the moral directorates of their faith: 'We can now see the big picture.' In this 'big picture' many of the young Muslims interviewed or answering questionnaires, saw themselves both as striving to be good citizens and to be 'good Muslims', which were seen as interlinked tasks and goals.

Another theme identified in CE classes was assistance and understanding in career choice and employment applications. Pupils in several schools (both Muslim and secular) commented on how interesting their outside visits were, and the visiting speakers concerning CE.

An intriguing set of responses were elicited by questions about the nature of a 'good' and 'bad' citizen. Most Muslim and non-Muslim pupils who responded appeared to be both knowledgeable and enthusiastic about the characteristics identified. The 'good citizen' is seen as someone who is kind, helpful and altruistic not only in his or her school or local community, but in the larger society as well; it is someone who obeys and respects the law; someone who is tolerant and respectful towards fellow citizens from different cultures, ethnic backgrounds and religions; a productive member of the community; being loyal, and taking part in political life; participating in voting and electing and someone who cares for the environment. Pupils also observed that practising Muslims or Christians should aim to be good citizens because their respective religions have the potential for promoting the common good.

It is apparent that a large part of the sample in both Muslim and state schools, including pupils, teachers and religious and community leaders, believe that teaching citizenship in schools is important to pupils' education. Most of the pupils in the sample believed that studying citizenship helped them to become aware of their role in society and to become good citizens. Citizenship lessons seem to be enjoyable for the majority of pupils, although these views may be based to a certain degree on sample selection, which was biased both towards 'best practice' schools, and towards the most enthusiastic students who agreed to take part in the research.

Muslim pupils do appear to have a preference for instruction on citizenship to be given by a teacher who reflects Islamic values. In Muslim schools pupils are subject to religious influence in terms of pro-social behaviours and positive attitudes towards others, whatever their ethnicity or faith. These schools appear to be rather successful in building their pupils' value systems. Islamic studies and lessons in the Qur'an are often used to support the teaching of citizenship, and this too appears to be quite successful. Muslim schools are therefore judged to have the potential for the development and evolution of a new form of Muslim national identity within Britain, through citizenship education, in useful and meaningful ways. This is significant given the difficulties encountered in the delivery of citizenship education in schools of all types according to the OFSTED (2006) review.

Virtually all pupils from Muslim schools linked citizenship with Islamic studies, while most pupils from state schools compared it with RE. The following conclusions were drawn: most pupils in Muslim schools, but only a minority in state schools, found that studying a religion is akin to studying citizenship because they both teach similar things. Pupils referred to this relationship with respect to the content of both subjects, and the consideration that both subjects, in many cases, teach the same topics.

Many Muslim pupils observed that Islamic studies and citizenship both teach the concept of being a good citizen, and emphasized the moral aspect of their lives. Many pupils in state schools also said that they studied the same aspects of good or moral behaviour, but from different viewpoints.

Conclusion

One of the most significant aspects of this study has been to try and answer the question of whether Muslim schools and their teaching of citizenship could be a tool for inclusion, or conversely, whether such teaching serves to isolate Muslim pupils from the wider community. Muslims in Britain are keen to remain recognized and valued members of society. One of the main aims of Muslim schools is to foster an Islamic identity and to help transmit Islamic belief systems and values for future generations through the education system. Many Muslims feel that faith-based schools are the only way to achieve this aim.

While full-time Muslim secondary schools are valiantly trying to incorporate CE within their curriculum in various ways, they still face a number of problems. First, the amount of work required looking after not only the NC subjects, but also RE and the integration into wider society of pupils, is a major challenge. Secondly, financial problems minimize the ability of these schools to enact their plans, and can restrict them from the use of new and effective resources. The reason for this is that most of the Muslim schools are dependent on pupils' fees and contributed donations from the community. At present, few receive any funding from the government, despite the legal right to seek such funding under the Education Act of 1944. Currently, less than a dozen Muslim secondary schools in Britain are grant-aided in this way, compared with several thousand Anglican, Catholic and other religious schools in Britain.

When the findings of the present study are compared with those of OFSTED (2006), it appears that we have enlisted into the research confident and cooperative schools who are particularly likely to have been successful in their CE. The findings of the present study should be read in conjunction with the OFSTED report in gaining a fuller picture of the challenges that face the further development of CE in Muslim schools. Clearly, the curriculum and model of delivery of CE in Muslim schools is changing and evolving, and from this and other research new models of practice can be proposed.

Muslim secondary schools, as this study shows, can be very successful. Despite some problems, their citizenship curriculum can successfully educate young people in expressing confident and tolerant values concerning other religions, and the wider society. Many of the pupils that were studied also drew on Islamic values in presenting a multicultural identity that is optimistic and idealistic in the expression of a set of pro-social values.

Finally, we conclude that the present study has shown how valuable British Muslim secondary schools can be in enabling the roles of young people – whose attitudes to the wider society are magnanimous and enlightened, and who have used their Islamic education to take maximum advantage of their citizenship education.

References

Al-Refai, N., and Bagley, C. (2008), *Citizenship Education: The British Muslim Perspective*. Rotterdam: Sense Educational Books.

Anwar, M. (1993), *Muslim in Britain: 1991 Census and Other Statistical Sources*. Birmingham: Centre for the Study of Islam and Christian-Muslim Relations.

Anwar, M., and Bakhsh, Q. (2003), *British Muslims and State Policies*. Warwick: University of Warwick, Centre for Research in Ethnic Relations.

Bagley, C..(2008), "The education and social inclusion of disadvantaged children in Britain." G. Verma and C. Bagley(Eds) *Challenges for Inclusion: Educational and Social Studies from Britain and the Indian Sub-Continent*. Rotterdam: Sense Publications.

Department for Education and Skills (DfES) (2004), *Schemes of Work: Citizenship at Key Stage 3*. London: DfES Publications.

—(2005), *The National Curriculum for England*, [Online] Available at: http://www.dfes.gov.uk/citizenship/.

Gardner, R., Cairns, K., and Lawton, D. (eds) (2005), *Faith Schools: Consensus or Conflict?*. London: Routledge-Falmer.

Gilliat-Roy, S. (2010), *Muslims in Britain: An Introduction*. Cambridge: Cambridge University Press.

Haines, W. (2000), 'Identity and authority in citizenship education', *Muslim Educational Quarterly*, 18, pp. 1–7.

Halstead, J. M., and Pike, M. (2006), *Citizenship and Moral Education: Values in Action*. London: Routledge.

Home Office (1999), 'Stephen Lawrence Inquiry: Home Secretary's action plan'. London: Home Office.

Huddleston, T., and Kerr, D. (2006), *Making Sense of Citizenship: A Continuing Professional Development Handbook*. London: Hodder Murray Educational Books.

Lawton, D., Cairns, J., and Gardner, R. (eds) (2000), *Education for Citizenship*. London: Continuum Books.

Malik, R. (2006), 'British or Muslim: creating a context for dialogue', *Youth and Society*, 92, pp. 91–105.

OFSTED (2006), 'Towards consensus? Citizenship in secondary schools'. London: Office for Standards in Education.

Osler, A., and Starkey, H. (2001), 'Citizenship education and national identities in France and England: inclusive or exclusive?' *Oxford Review of Education*, 27, pp. 287–305.

Osler, A., and Vincent, V., (2002), *Citizenship and the Challenge of Global Education*. Stoke-on-Trent: Trentham Books.

Parker-Jenkins, M. (1995), *Children of Islam*. Stoke-on-Trent: Trentham Books.

—(2000), 'Citizenship at Key Stage 3 and 4: Initial guidance for schools'. London: QCA.

—(2002), 'Qualification and Curriculum Authority (1998), 'Education for citizenship and the teaching of democracy in schools. Final report of the Advisory Group on Citizenship (The Crick Report)'. London: QCA.

Sheridan, L. (2006), 'Islamophobia pre- and post-September 11th 2001', *Journal of Interpersonal Violence*, 21, pp. 317–36.

Verma, G. K. (1989), 'Education for all: a landmark in pluralism', in G. K. Verma (ed.) *Education for all: A Landmark in Pluralism*. London: The Falmer Press.

—(2007), 'Diversity and multicultural education: cross-cutting issues and concepts', in G. K. Verma and C. Bagley (eds), *International Perspectives on Educational Diversity and Inclusion*. London: Routledge.

PART FOUR

Methodologies of Engaging

10

Activity and alterity: youth work with Muslim 'girls'

GILL CRESSEY

Introduction

Young Muslim women in the UK are trapped in dominant narratives (Richards, 2009) that stereotype and diminish them as 'other' in European society. 'Alterity' means categorizing someone and thereby labelling and diminishing them. For many, this alterity is compounded with other ways in which they are treated as different. It acts as an essentializing tool, constructing a radical alterity — the 'other' (Caglar, 1997), whereas recognition involves being aware of issues of similarity and difference, individually and culturally, and being confident and respectful in the process. Drawing on constructivist theories, this chapter will critique the activity programmes designed by youth workers for Muslim young women. The object of such curricula will be explored against discourses that assign social positions to 'Muslim girls'. Drawing on detailed case-studies, the chapter analyses these activity programmes with a view to proposing a tentative model of youth work with young Muslim women. This will lead to a discussion of what could constitute an approach that affords positive recognition and personal development to young Muslim women.

It seems to be common to view youth work with Muslim young women as separate and different from other youth work practice. According to this view, youth work with young Muslim women is always single sex, always chaperoned, always about 'safe spaces', always reliant on parental consent, always 'culturally appropriate' and always separate from other youth work provision. Policy-makers persist with their assumption that young people face a conflict between the values of their home background and the 'superior' freedoms offered by so-called Western culture (Bhattacharrya and Gabriel, 1997), particularly in relation to young Muslim women. Despite many people feeling more at ease with subjectivities that encompass plural and fluid cultural identities, and the critique since the 1980s challenging earlier theoretical constructions of culture as homogenized and bounded (Caglar, 1997), Muslim women continue to be construed as having a fixed and stable identity attached to one allegedly discrete Islamic culture. Therefore, taking youth work with Muslim young women as a point of exploration, this chapter uses case-studies to test 'common views' in relation to youth work activity programmes for young Muslim women in the UK.

This enquiry began during the first national conference on Muslim youth work in Birmingham in December 2005. One of the workshops at the event was entitled 'The Ultimate Separatist Cage?' and began a conversation between practitioners, academics and young women about the issue of whether or not targeted youth work with young Muslim women is separatist. At the follow-up event in Bradford in 2006, 'Muslim Youth Work: Conversations and Actions', there was an opportunity to continue the debate about youth work with young Muslim women. This led to a publication drawing together ten case-studies of youth work with young Muslim women. The approach adopted for that publication was collaborative with organizations producing their own accounts of the work they do, with contributions from youth workers and young women complementing academic commentary and analysis (Cressey, 2007). From these discussions and presentations of case-studies, it became clear that 'to try to understand the needs of young women in Britain today is to try to understand a complex embodiment of economic, political and cultural processes' (Cressey, 2007, p .2). To describe Muslim women as if they can be categorized simply, and to routinely portray them as if they are a homogeneous group in British society, when, in fact, they are very diverse, is the nature of stereotyping and alterity.

Therefore, this chapter focuses on manifestations of alterity supplemented with details of daily youth work practices and activities arising from the original case-study material documented earlier (ibid.), which has been re-examined through the lens of alterity.

Methodology

Following Billis (1991) in his work on the development of voluntary organizations and based on the social analysis approach developed by Ralph Rowbottom (1997) and his early work on the study of management and organizations, social analysis has been adopted as the methodological approach used in this research. Rowbottom (cited by Billis, 1991) has described social analysis as:

> an activity devoted to (1) gaining scientific understanding of, and thereby (2) facilitating enacted change in (3) social institutions, through (4) collaborative exploration by those actors immediately concerned in their working, and an independent analyst (p. 21).

Social analysis, being rooted in an action research perspective, is particularly useful in gaining a social scientific understanding of youth work with young Muslim women in the UK, especially when considering sociological themes such as gender and 'race'. The research described here is the result of a long-term collaborative exploration with youth workers, young women and myself as the researcher – or to use a term from the social analysis tradition, 'analyst'. As a research process, it is intended to inform practice directly so as to enact change and development in a range of social institutions, from mosques to uniformed youth organizations. Using data from the original ten case-studies of activity programmes with young Muslim women, I explore how these activities either frame young Muslim women as 'other' or challenge such essentialisms. David Billis (1984) contended that tentative models and theories for understanding the nature of voluntary organizations can be generated from the problems posed by those organizations. This chapter draws on issues posed by youth workers and young women in workshops, in conversations within their own organizations and through women's written articulations of their experiences. Some of the issues discussed include the lack of agency of young women

in relation to the design of youth services to meet their different
needs; the onslaught of media and political discourses about young
Muslim women in Britain and ongoing stereotyping, labelling and
alterity. In order to analyse activities designed by youth workers
for young Muslim women across the ten case-study organizations
(and documented in Cressey, 2007), the aims and objectives
named by each, the activities listed by them in their descriptions
of the programmes they offer and some of the considerations they
highlighted when working with young Muslim women, have been
amalgamated to form three lists. Rather than use the case-studies to
compare and contrast them with one another, I have focussed instead
on looking at how these youth work organizations stated aims and
objectives, the activities offered to young Muslim women and the
considerations made in their work, can signal differing approaches
and relationships to alterity. This chapter then, aims to present a
tentative model or theory for understanding the nature of activities
and alterity in relation to young Muslim women in the UK.

Alterity and youth work with young Muslim women

Amal Treacher (2006) writes about feeling bothered and undermined
by everyday reminders that she does not quite belong in England, as
someone who grew up in Cairo with a Muslim religious upbringing,
she writes that:

> None of us are immune from the erosive attacks that take place
> in seemingly innocent and ordinary connections. (p. 28)

This is a familiar experience for many young Muslim women in
Britain. Alterity is woven into the fabric of everyday interactions
and activities. It can be felt and recognized every time there is a
suggestion, intended or not, that one does not belong. Reactions
that show that someone considers a person to be different, 'other'
and 'outside', may be defiant and loud and violent, but they can
also be subtle and seemingly unintended, innocent and ordinary.
Nonetheless, they can erode a person's sense of acceptance, respect
and recognition. For instance, the Macpherson Report (1999) into

the response of emergency and police services to the death of the black teenager Stephen Lawrence in South-East London in 1993 described how institutional racism:

> can be seen or detected in processes, attitudes and behaviour which amount to discrimination through unwitting prejudice, ignorance, thoughtlessness and racist stereotyping which disadvantage minority ethnic people. (Macpherson, 1999: Para 6.34)

The key words linking Amal Treacher's comments and the Lawrence Enquiry are 'unwitting prejudice', 'ignorance', 'thoughtlessness' and 'racist stereotyping', all of which are evident when young Muslim women face alterity on grounds of racism or on other grounds such as gender, marital status, nationality or religion. They are a result of social constructions (Searle, 1995) that create categories or 'constructs' to describe social groups. The more this construct is adopted and imposed, the clearer and stronger is the boundary that marks one group out from another . Being Muslim, or assumed to be Muslim by association or name, has come to signify a collective identity of people previously identified by place of origin (Anthias and Yuval-Davis, 1993). Here, the construct used to describe a social group that has been adopted and imposed is 'Muslim'. Sara Ahmed (2000) uses the phrase 'stranger fetishism' to describe the production of the socially constructed 'stranger'. She argues that the agency of the Western self and nation is constructed, mobilized and legitimized through such fetishism (Ahmed, 2000). Alterity takes social constructs a stage further by attributing negative characteristics to whole categories of people and thereby constructing them as 'other', strangers and lesser than 'us'. The organizations, and their aims and objectives, activities and considerations made when working with young Muslim women, present an opportunity to examine social relationships that are concealed by social fetishism and alterity.

Analyzing youth work with young Muslim women

It is important to stress that all organizations that formed the original case-studies recognized 'difference'; however, what is significant for

the purposes of this chapter at least, are the differing responses
to dealing with difference and the ways these differing responses
impacted on work with young Muslim women. For instance, if we
look the list of collated aims and objectives in Table 10.1, they can
be grouped in at least three ways:

1 Aims and objectives that reinforce and encourage communal
   or 'traditional' roles. Women conforming to these roles are
   given a sense of belonging to the group. For some Muslim
   women, this approach can be reassuring.
2 Aims and objectives that encourage and support women to
   make individual choices.
3 Aims and objectives that emphasize working with other
   communities.

It is important to note that none of the three approaches above are
mutually exclusive, and there were overlapping themes across all
organizations.

Looking at the types of activities offered by the various youth
work organizations in Table 10.2, it is interesting to note that
'activities' often reflect an organizations aims and objectives. For
instance, organizations that encourage 'traditional' or communal roles often emphasized activities such as Islamic study circles,
Qur'an recitation, Arabic classes or *Nasheed* (Islamically oriented
singing) performances. However, as I go on to discuss below, it is
important to note that rather than reproduce static and simplistic
understandings of Islamic texts, this emphasis can, and often does,
result in varied interpretations of texts and practice.

'Activity' has been the focus of educational research with a view
to designing effective activities to maximize learning and to achieve
particular learning outcomes. Vygotsky (1978) pioneered some
of the most seminal work on activity theory setting a benchmark
for subsequent studies, particularly his work in Russia and North
America. Vygotsky focused on the connections between people and
the socio-cultural context in which they act and interact in shared
experiences (Crawford, 1996), while post-Vygotsky educational
psychology by North American socio-cultural researchers focuses
on the gradual transformation of a novice into a competent
participant in the shared activity of a community (Stetsenko and

Table 10.1 Aims and objectives cited in working with young Muslim women

Encouraging traditional/ communal roles	Encouraging individual choices	Emphasizing work with other communities
'To attain the pleasure of Allah (SWT), to bring people closer to Allah and help them to emulate the ways of the Messenger Muhammad.'	'Creating and sustaining supportive networks and opportunities for young women to explore thoughts and feelings.'	'Challenging religious hatred and intolerance by bringing communities together.'
'To support, not detract from, the traditional roles parents and elders see for girls and young women.'	'For young people to become critical and willing to examine, understand and possibly change their day to day experiences (Hooks, 2003; Hill-Collins, 1991).'	'Intercultural, faith and ethnic dialogue and interaction.'
'To grow, to bond and to learn spiritually and socially.'		'To allow women to interact with other women from different cultural and religious backgrounds.'
'To be a safe haven.'	'Challenging stereotypes.'	
'Friendship, a sense of community and cohesion.'	'To take the young girls out of the niche of traditional stereotypical outings such as museums and art galleries to the thrills of quad biking, horse riding, canoeing, skiing, biking and rock climbing [. . .] while still taking into account cultural sensitivities.'	'To create spaces where diverse groups of young women are able to come together.'
'Expressing ourselves and telling others about our feelings and thoughts.'		
'By Muslim women and for Muslim women: to support young women in a way that only someone who has been there themselves can do/self-help.'		
'Representing ourselves.'	'Self esteem and confidence.'	
'Muslim women working for the welfare of Muslim families.'		

Table 10.2   Activities cited in working with young Muslim women

Sporting/Health	Religious	Creative / Personal development
Sports: Basketball, girls' inter-mosque football tournament and sports day Archery – a sunnah/tradition of the prophet Muhammad (saw) Adventure scheme Health and fitness: boxercise, football, badminton, netball, rounders, wall climbing Healthy living and lifestyle choices Health issues workshops Women-only exercise space/gym	Study circles and Islamic studies courses Arabic classes Other language classes Qur'an recitation Shared *Iftar* (fast breaking) during Ramadhan *Eid* parties *Nasheed* performance Basic Arabic and *Tajweed* (the science of reciting the Qur'an) Ramadhan diary radio project Prayers (prayer-room is segregated)	Poetry writing and reading Accredited qualifications Drama, comedy and music Creative arts: drama, dance, creative writing, arts and crafts Media skills Day trips International visits and exchanges Talking about: self-esteem; sexual Health, sexuality; relationships and emotions; body image; peer pressure; home and school demands; caring responsibilities; motherhood; being a single parent; coping with bereavement, employment, volunteering and further education; the practices of Islam; their take on recent world events, identity of young British Muslim women in society, portrayals of Muslims in the media, problems at school and parental pressure and expectations to do housework and homework.

Arievitch, 2002). Post-Vygotsky scholars such as Harry Daniels (2007) criticize Vygotsky for his lack of an account of social positioning within discourse, as well as the social, cultural and historical production of discourse. Instead, Daniels links ethics and morality to the concept of identity tied to concrete practical activity and understands 'the discursive regulation of interpersonal relations in terms of processes of social, cultural and historical regulation' (Daniels, 2007). Case-studies then, are a useful entry point for discussion of these processes as they relate to specific activities.

The organizations and their activities discussed here, as seen in Tables 10.1 and 10.2, differ significantly in socio-cultural contexts but share a concern to foster connections between young women who might otherwise feel isolated from one another. Looking at the aims and objectives of the work with young women, much of the emphasis of some organizations and groups is on inducting young women into the life of the wider Muslim community. This begs the question of how the organizations gradually transform new members into competent participants in the shared activity of the Muslim community. Others are oriented outwards from the community to relationships with the wider society and to British institutions, and thus help young women to find strategies and skills for participating in public life in the UK. With this civic orientation to British society, how do these youth work projects organizations transform novice young Muslim women into competent citizens in British institutional life, such as students, workers and consumers? The organizations discussed in this chapter will be used to shed light on the function of activities organized by various organizations, but will also explore whether there is a link between activities and alterity.

I argue that the alterity experienced by Muslim young women in the UK can only be understood in the context of social, cultural and historical development of discourses about Islam and, more specifically, about young Muslim women's relationships with 'the West' (in the form of British institutions like schools and the youth service), with young men, with their extended families and with communities.

Sameness and alterity

From the case-studies documented in Cressey (2007) and the analysis of activities offered here, it can be seen that there is dedicated work going on to gather young women and to provide them with a wide range of opportunities to take part in activities and to make new friends. There are positive attempts to support them and to allow them to discuss issues that they may face, and to provide them with a 'safe space'. When faced with the question of what this has to do with alterity, three possible answers could be suggested:

- nothing at all
- the activities support existing alterity, or
- the activities challenge and counteract alterity

Taking alterity as an ongoing experience within young Muslim women's lives in Britain, what difference does youth work with Muslim young women make to their sense of being routinely denigrated? Through alterity a person is diminished by a lack of recognition and respect for difference, and thereby for them as an individual human being. How do youth workers respond to this when designing the curriculum of activities for their programmes? What does youth work offer to young Muslim women? How does that offer, in terms of activity programmes, relate to young women's needs for inclusion, recognition and individuality? Do the activities take young women towards particular combinations of sameness, difference, alterity or recognition? The model developed below in Figure 10.1 tries to explore the relationship between activities and alterity and to provide a tool for analysing and designing educational practices to suit different aims and objectives. This can be illustrated by Figure 10.1 where sameness and difference are thought of as a continuum and forces above or below this represent recognition, or not, of alterity.

Young women feeling recognized and part of a group of people whom they consider similar to themselves and who treat them as belonging – such as women calling one another 'sisters' within an Islamic society or a Muslim young women's project – have an identity that is communal. They identify themselves as part of a community and they are identified by others within and beyond that community as belonging to that community. This is the kind of 'safe space' that many projects for young Muslim women claim to be providing. This combination of sameness and recognition offers solidarity, belonging, integrity and collective identity. It is a comfortable, reassuring place to be for anyone who aspires to

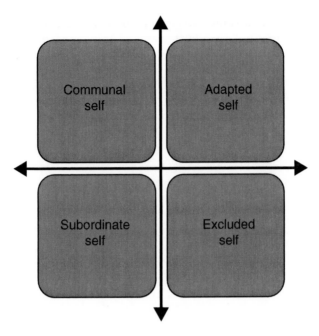

FIGURE 10.1 Individual responses to difference: from alterity to recognition

belong to a community and to participate fully within that. The price of belonging and of retaining recognition is participation and fitting in with 'the way things are done around here'. The aims of groups subscribing to this communal way of thinking refer young women to Islam, to the Muslim community and to families within that community. 'To attain the pleasure of Allah to bring people closer to Allah and help them to emulate the ways of the Messenger Muhammad', is a clear example of setting Islam as the reference point for the group and organizing a programme of activities to fit with this ethos. For example, the group with this aim had archery on their programme of activities for recreation and a collective activity and justified its inclusion in terms of the *sunnah* (exemplary way of life) of the Prophet Muhammad. Another organization, which was seeking to broaden its membership to include more Bangladeshi young women to reflect the local demographics, aims to 'support, not detract from, the traditional roles parents and elders see for girls and young women'. In doing so, they are making an interesting assumption that modifications will be needed to the activities and conduct of the organization in order to accommodate difference. The assumption is that there are specific roles that parents and elders agree are suitable for girls and young women; and that these traditional views are at variance with activities offered by other youth work and education institutions. While most people could hazard a guess as to which roles parents and elders would see for girls and young women, it is an unviable generalization to suggest blanket agreement about these roles. Furthermore, it is controversial for a youth work organization to promise not to detract from parents' wishes without considering whether these wishes may differ from young people's wishes and even best interests. This declaration fits within the intention to initiate novices into participation in a particular community with a specific social, historical and economic character. Another neighbourhood-based organization announced:

> We take the young girls out of the niche of traditional stereotypical outings such as museums and art galleries to the thrills of quad biking, horse riding, canoeing, skiing, biking and rock climbing . . . while still taking into account cultural sensitivities.

This sounds like it is taking young women beyond a specific community and 'niche' in society, whereas the closing phrase reassures anyone who may not approve of young women being drawn away from a particular culture, that there is nothing to worry about. Young women will be engaged in all of these thrilling activities, but there is a limit that will not be crossed which is 'sensitivities'. Again, the emphasis is on preparing young women to continue participation in a specific community and to reproduce cultural sensitivities despite breaking away from stereotypes about participation in adventurous commercially provided activities.

A group of young Muslim women who set up their own association described their aim as 'to grow, to bond and to learn spiritually and socially'. This could be taken to mean to bond in order to strengthen the Muslim community in particular or it could be taken to mean to bond with one another as young women with choices and differences to deal with individually and collectively. When the same group goes on to describe their meetings as 'a safe haven', what are they saying about safety? Is safety in similarity and understanding based on sameness or is it safety from criticism for being different and alternative to dominant expectations of young women? Creating and sustaining supportive networks and opportunities for young women to explore thoughts and feelings is a community-building exercise on one hand, and on the other it could be an opportunity for young women to choose to strike out on a new and unique life path. In the case of the organization that declared this aim, its strong links with a close-knit *Jama'aat* (Muslim congregation) make it likely that the idea is for young women to explore thoughts and feelings and support one another without radically challenging the organization or the culture of the *Jama'aat*. Another case explained their approach as: 'we create an atmosphere where girls and young women express themselves as they desire. This does not mean that we deliberately go against their religion, we just create space for their existence as girls and women alongside their faith.' The idea of self-expression and agency is counteracted with a promise not to 'go against their religion'. With such a multiplicity of possible ideas among Muslims about what would constitute 'going against religion', how can such a promise be made and kept? Who is this promise intended to please? Young women? Parents? Imams? Clearly this organization is committed to young women keeping 'their faith', and thereby continuing and reproducing the Muslim community. Expressing ourselves and telling others about our feelings and thoughts is sometimes the start of a departure from tradition, at other times it reinforces community and heightens a sense of membership and belonging. Friendships and a sense of community and cohesion are clearly fundamental for building and sustaining a community. In the current context, organizations such as those 'for Muslim women that are run by Muslim women' can support young women in ways that only those who have shared experiences and identities can do. It is an example of communal activity and support for intra-Muslim community building. Muslim women working for the welfare of Muslim families are engaged directly in sustaining a community. Activities such as study circles and Islamic studies courses, Arabic classes, Qur'an recitation, shared *Iftar* during Ramadhan, *Eid* parties, and basic Arabic and *Tajweed* (the science of reciting the Qur'an) classes, are all activities with a clear and unequivocal Muslim identity. Charity and aid work (e.g. raising money for orphans in Palestine and Chechnya) also draw young women towards an Islamic identity and gradually involves them as community participants with increasing levels of skill and responsibility. Activities like girls' inter-mosque football tournaments, sports days and Ramadhan diary radio projects teach participants to engage with 'the Muslim community' as though this is one undivided community. In reality, an inter-mosque competition could play out old divisions and rivalries; and the diary project could illustrate how different people's experiences are rather than how similar they are. However, the clear intention is to emphasize sameness. Prayers literally call the community together to remember Allah in a specifically Muslim way. Even this is less straightforward than it may first appear; some women may feel that it is inappropriate to take part at that time, and the global divisions between Shi'ahs and Sunnis, for example, mean that negotiation sometimes takes place about when, how and in what grouping to pray.

'Considerations' made in youth work programmes for young Muslim women tend to focus on providing safety and protection, and on deeming that activities are suitably 'appropriate' (see Table 10.3). Issues such as transport, timing, child-care, ensuring that activities are for women only, parental support and protection from 'harmful influences', could all be taken to apply to youth work with all young women, but they seem to be mentioned by youth workers in several case-study organizations as holding special significance for young Muslim women. They are all organized with a view to allowing participation without compromising *hijab* and without losing chaperones.

Some young women who are in groups that are treated as homogenous may feel constrained and obliged to subordinate

Table 10.3   Considerations cited in working with young Muslim women

Safety and protection	Appropriateness
'Transport'	'Unlike the brothers, who play football regularly on the Astroturf, the sisters have to play indoors and conform to the wisdom of the *hijab* rules'
'Timing'	
'Child-care'	
'Protection from "harmful influences"'	'Women only'
'Staffing'	'Parental support/leaders have worked to build the trust of parents'
	'Cultural differences'

their own aspirations and individual identity within the group or community and feel expected to play by the rules of the culture of that group or community, whether this is a family, a neighbourhood or a youth group with a particular set of expectations. They may have been placed in this group by people inside the group or outside it. Either way, individuals are subsumed within the group identity. One feature of alterity is diminishing people by labelling them as a homogenous group and disregarding their diversity. This combination of sameness and alterity can lead to disadvantage, domination and restrictions on individual opportunities. Sameness or difference could be formulated on various bases including religion, gender, class, age, marital status, sexuality disability, 'race', language or nationality. The current research lacks data for the analysis of many of these factors and is limited, for now, to commenting on gender, age and religion. Young women may be subordinated on grounds of being Muslim or on grounds of sex or age. For many young people a combination of all of these factors comes into play. They are grouped together and placed in a subordinate position in a social hierarchy. Challenging stereotypes becomes a priority for youth workers working with groups of young people that are excluded as a group and disadvantaged in relation to the economy, to education, employment, housing and services. Empowering women to break down negative stereotypes is a direct reaction to the ways in which young Muslim women are categorized as a subgroup in society, treated as if they are all the same and as if their identities can all be subsumed under one label. Hence, when a case-study describes how 'the project focussed on society's views of young women and what views they had of themselves', it is responding to a combination of being treated as the same as other young Muslim women, different from everyone else in society and as making less contribution to society than everyone else. Judith Butler describes this as a 'struggle for recognition':

> Bound to seek recognition of its own existence in categories, terms, and names that are not of its own making, the subject seeks the sign of its own existence outside itself, in a discourse that is at once dominant and indifferent. Social categories signify subordination and existence at once. In other words, within subjection the price of existence is subordination. (Butler, 1997, p. 20)

Thus, if the subject is a young Muslim woman, she may seek recognition in the category of being a 'young Muslim woman' even though that category is not of her own making. Discourses about young Muslim women are dominant and expressed regularly through the media, and while there may be occasional shifts, the nature of the discourse remains relatively fixed. Inclusion then, in the category of young Muslim women, offers a clear identity but, I argue, at the price of subordination.

Difference and alterity

Whenever young Muslim women are treated as different and less than others, they are being excluded and treated as inferior; they are being disrespected, oppressed and, in some instances, even subjected to violence. The excluded self has a clear sense of otherness and barriers to participation. This is a position lacking recognition, resources and opportunities. Many young Muslim women face this as their daily reality in workplaces, schools and colleges and struggle to overcome the discrimination they face. Youth work provision is not immune from making young Muslim women feel this way. When working with young women on the margins, youth workers need to challenge racism and ignorance. Taking an anti-discriminatory approach, particularly an anti-sexist and anti-racist stance, is one response to exclusion. Another is working to support individual young women, helping them to develop strategies for inclusion and recognition. One of the case-studies I looked at claims to help young women come to terms with a volatile and not always welcoming Britain. They did this by talking about issues such as:

> Self-esteem, sexual health, sexuality, relationships and emotions, body image, peer pressure, home and school demands, caring responsibilities, motherhood, being a single parent, coping with bereavement, employment, volunteering and further education; the practices of Islam; their take on recent world events, identity of young British Muslim women in society, portrayals of Muslims in the media, problems at school and parental pressure, expectations to do housework and homework.

Conversely, whenever young Muslim women are in a situation where they are treated as being different yet recognized and respected, able to contribute and to define their own lives and make choices, they are exercising agency. The price of this is risk taking and isolation, but the reward is opportunities in society for work, education and self-determination. Projects working with young women towards being 'adapted selves' stress helping and supporting women emotionally, socially and economically. They also claim to be aiming for integration, acceptance and understanding, and sometimes refer to aiming for closer relationships between Muslim communities and 'mainstream services'. One such project among the case-studies offers:

> "A neutral setting to welcome diversity"; and another is committed to "challenging religious hatred and intolerance" by bringing communities together.

'Intercultural, faith and ethnic dialogue and interaction' is given as an aim by more than one of the case-studies – this is partly a desire on the part of the organizations, but it is also partly a phrase used to please actual and potential patrons. The fact that groups feel a need to 'allow women to interact with other women from different cultural and religious backgrounds', implies that they agree that there is a problem of separatism or of exclusion that divides communities on cultural and religious grounds.

Some examples of activities that celebrate cultural and religious difference and give recognition to young Muslim women's contributions are *Nasheed* performances, or poetry writing and reading. For example, one of the case-study organizations developed a poetry and spoken word project with a local repertory theatre. The mixed audience at a venue like a famous city-centre theatre literally becomes a platform for representation. Another group developed an adventure scheme with other local community organizations and through this increased the range of activities that young Muslim women could participate in alongside young women from other cultural and religious communities, and alongside older women in the neighbourhood. Many of the weekly activities of young women's groups reflect the recreation facilities on offer to everyone living in specific areas, such as sports and creative arts and day trips. International visits and exchanges offer a very obvious opportunity for cross-cultural learning and expanding young people's horizons. Media skills provide a chance for self-expression and positively representing young Muslim women within wider society. Accredited qualifications increase access to education and employment for young Muslim women, and health promotion programmes help to inform their lifestyle choices and to be aware of health services and how to access these for themselves and others within their circle of relationships.

Ideally, young women should be able to live as 'undivided selves' (Richards, 2009), making their own choices about identity and participation, recognized and respected as individuals rather than representatives of an imagined category. A combination of all the selves in the model would be needed for young people to feel whole, to develop positive self-esteem and confidence. How then, can an educator such as a youth worker enable young women to articulate an undivided self (Richards, 2009) and become critical and willing to examine, understand and possibly change their day-to-day experiences (Hooks, 2003; Hill-Collins, 1991)? One young Muslim woman explained this succinctly when she described what she had gained from participation in one of the case-study organization's activities:

> It's given me the confidence not to allow myself to be
> swallowed by society but to live in it confidently.

For this to happen, the tentative model put forward here is that all four quadrants in Figure 10.1 need to be taken into account so that young people's needs are met and they are able to withstand and overcome alterity and exclusion, and to make their own choices about how and where and with whom to live their lives. Referring back to Tables 10.1 and 10.2 listing aims and objectives and activities, Figure 10.2 highlights the ways in which organizations respond to difference or alterity in the design of their activity programmes.

Community-oriented activities, such as *Nasheed* concerts, are needed for young women to develop a sense of belonging and to feel a part of the Muslim community in a positive sense, equipped with the knowledge required to become full and active members of

FIGURE 10.2 Organizations responses to difference: activities

that community. Support and self-help activities and groups, such as student support groups (one of the ten organizations was a Muslim women student group), or other forms of helping activities, such as direct interventions of various types, are needed to counteract alterity and to take an anti-discriminatory stance. Civic participation and inclusion activities, such as organizing charity events, are needed in order to give young Muslim women a better chance of equality of opportunity in education, employment, citizenship and accessing services.

According to Lila Abu-Lughod (1991), the notion of culture retains earlier tendencies of 'race' to 'freeze' difference. Ricoeur (1984) suggests that people become trapped in the stories available to them and are thus unable to develop their own identities, lives, and relationships. Communal activities without any other options may be rich in stories but may also restrict the stories available to young Muslim women about who they are and who they can be. Civic participation provides an opportunity to consider alternative stories. However, there are major narratives recounted, repeated and varied; formulae texts and ritualized sets of discourses (Foucault, 1984) about young Muslim women that trap them. Youth work with young Muslim women, therefore, needs to support them to move beyond the available stories (within and outside their communities) about who they should be, and to develop their own identities, lives and relationships.

Considering the activities using Bloom's (1956) taxonomy of learning – 'knowledge', 'comprehension', 'application', 'analysis', 'synthesis' and 'evaluation' – allows the tentative model to be further developed by considering the kinds of learning and knowledge which would enable this personal development to take place. In Bloom's taxonomy, knowledge that is memorized verbatim is portrayed as the lowest level of thinking. This is at odds with the status afforded to memorization and recitation by Muslims. Memorizing verbatim is a familiar practice for every young Muslim person who has attended classes to learn the Qu'ran. It commands a good deal of respect traditionally because of the religious status of recitation. In fact, the Qur'an can be translated literally as 'the recitation', and its significance can be seen in the foundational story of Islam where the Prophet Muhammad received the first verses of the Qur'an orally transmitted to him by the Angel *Jibril* (Gabriel) in the mountain cave of Hira. From the case-studies I looked at, activities relating to this tradition include Qur'an recitation, *Nasheed* performance, basic Arabic lessons and *Tajweed* (the science of reciting the Qur'an).

'Comprehension' consists of the thinking involved in paraphrasing, summarizing and translating. This is likely to be a familiar skill among young Muslim women in Britain due to the number of them who are bilingual or multilingual. Youth work settings with young Muslim women often use English as the common language, but in a very multilingual context. Arabic classes, other language classes and sports all require comprehension of the rules and purpose of the game. Both memorizing and comprehension are traditional methods and approaches to learning within Muslim communities. They are a means of transmission of values, cultural practices and languages. They are therefore, typical of the communal self and of community activities.

'Application' is another key facet to learning and involves using information to solve problems. Learning to transfer abstract ideas to practical situations is a key activity for Muslim youth work with young women as discussions about decision making and ethics require this level of thinking, especially when religious teachings are used as a reference point for debating morality and choice. 'Analysis', as in identifying components, determining logical sequences and understanding semantics is not widely cited as a feature by many of the organizations that I looked at, but it is evident in some of the activities mentioned by young women's projects, such as study circles. Another example is team sports, which tend to be strategic in nature but also involve analysis and logic, not just physical activity. Both 'application' and 'analysis' are necessary learning activities for young women as they negotiate their roles and contributions to society beyond their own families and immediate community, to those engaging in civic activities.

'Synthesis', combining information to form a unique product requires creativity and originality, and was evident in activities such as poetry writing and reading, drama, comedy and music. This is particularly significant for young Muslim women, helping them to draw on a diverse range of inspirations to find ways of expressing themselves authentically and uniquely. Finally, 'evaluation', making decisions and supporting views ,requires an understanding of values. Examples of activities that encourage the development of this kind of thinking among young Muslim women are charity and aid work activities, such as raising money for orphans in Palestine and Chechnya, and a Ramadhan diary radio project. Both synthesis and evaluation skills are important in helping young women to achieve a sense of integrity and develop a stable, healthy individual sense of positive identity, self-worth and confidence.

Conclusion

Although youth work with young Muslim women has undoubtedly continued to evolve and progress, there is room for further consideration of how to develop a curriculum of activities that enhances young women's ability to develop their own identities, lives and relationships with the confidence of a firm foundation and sense of belonging and recognition. A variety of activities is needed to address the circumstances of a wide range of young women. They have in common the need to be included rather than excluded or discriminated against, the need for supportive friendships and a range of life choices, the need to participate and to learn and to make a positive contribution that will be rewarded appropriately. A combination of community activities, help, support and civic participation activities is needed. Recreational activities can be used to meet a range of different aims, depending on how they are organized and by whom. A simple activity such as walking in the park could be a community activity if it is with a particular group of people; it could be a helping activity if it provides a chance to talk informally about issues the young women are facing; it could give young women a sense of support and comradeship to walk as a group and could assert their right to make use of public spaces; and if the young women themselves organize it as a charity walk, it could be an act of civic participation.

The analysis of data from case-studies of youth work practices in designing activity programmes with and for young Muslim women has led to devising a tentative model. The search for ways to develop possible alternative approaches to Muslim youth work with young women that move beyond alterity and are based on a new paradigm is ongoing. The contribution of this chapter is to suggest a model that can be tried and tested by youth workers and young people, and hopefully in the process can be revised and can lead to a better and more useful model. By 'othering' young women we reject the rich and powerful stories they bring us about who we have become as a community, about social structures that bar them access to significant resources (Wierenga, 2001) and we deny ourselves the chance to be part of a society in which they make a marked contribution. This underlines the necessity of recognition and relatedness (Treacher, 2006), conscious self-definitions and new articulations (Bhattacharyya and Gabriel, 1997) of 'undivided selves' (Richards, 2009).

References

Abu-Lughod, L. (1991), 'Writing against culture', in R. G. Fox (ed.), *Recapturing Anthropology: Working in the Present*. Santa Fe, NM: School of American Research, pp. 137–62.

Ahmed, S. (2000), *Strange Encounters: Embodied Others in Post-Coloniality*. London: Routledge.

Anthias, F., and Yuval-Davis, N. (1993), *Racialised Boundaries: Race, Nation, Gender, Colour and Class and the Anti-Racist Struggle*. London: Routledge.

Bhattacharrya, G., and Gabriel, J. (1997), 'Racial formations of youth in late twentieth century England', in J. Roche and S. Tucker (eds), *Youth in Society*. London: Sage, pp. 68–80.

Billis, D. (1984), *Welfare Bureaucracies*. London: Heinemann.

— (1991), 'The Roots of Voluntary Agencies', *Non Profit and Voluntary Sector Quarterly*, 20, (1), pp. 57–70.

Bloom, B. S. (1956), *Taxonomy of Educational Objectives, Handbook I: The Cognitive Domain*. New York: David McKay Co. Inc.

Butler, J. (1997), *The Psychic Life of Power: Theories of Subjection*, Stanford: Stanford University Press.

Caglar, A. (1997), 'Hyphenated identities and the limits of culture', in T. Modood and P. Werbner (eds), *The Politics of Multiculturalism in the New Europe*. London: Zed Books, pp. 169–85.

Crawford, K. (1996), 'Vygotskian approaches to human development in the information era', *Educational Studies in Mathematics*, 31, pp. 43–62.

Cressey, G. (2007), *The Ultimate Separatist Cage? Youth Work with Muslim young women*. Leicester: National Youth Agency.

Daniels, H. (2007), 'Discourse and identity in cultural-historical activity theory: A response.' *International Journal of Educational Research*, 46, (1–2), pp. 94–9.

Foucault, M. (1984), 'The order of discourse', in M. Shapiro (ed.), *Language and Politics*. Oxford: Blackwell, pp. 108–38.

Hill-Collins, P. (1991), *Black Feminist Thought: Knowledge, Consciousness and the Politics of Empowerment*. New York: Routledge.

Hooks, B. (2003), *Teaching Community: A Pedagogy of Hope*. New York: Routledge.

Macpherson, W. (1999), 'The Stephen Lawrence Inquiry Report'. Presented to Parliament by the Secretary of State for the Home Department by Command of Her Majesty. February 1999.

Richards, W. (2009), 'His master's voice', *A Journal of Youth Work*, (2), pp. 7–23.

Ricoeur, P. (1984) *Time and narrative: Volume 1*. Mclaughlin and Pellauer (trans.), Chicago: University of Chicago Press.

Rowbottom, R.W. (1977), *Social Analysis*. London: Heinemann Educational.

Searle, J. (1995), *The Construction of Social Reality*. London: Penguin.

Stetsenko, A., and Arievitch, I. M. (2002), 'Learning and development: contributions from post-Vygotskian research,' in G. Wells, and G. Cluxton, (eds) *Learning for Life in the 21st Century: Sociocultural*

Perspectives on the Future of Education. London: Blackwell,
    pp. 84–97.
Treacher, A. (2006), 'Something in the air: otherness, recognition and
    ethics', *Journal of Social Work Practice.* 20, (1), pp. 27–37.
Vygotsky. L. S. (1978), *Mind and Society: the Development of Higher
    Mental Processes.* Cambridge, MA: Harvard University Press.
Wierenga, A. (2001), 'Losing and Finding the Plot: the value of listening
    to young people'. Conference paper for 'Starting where they are;
    International conference on young people and informal education',
    University of Strathclyde. pp. 6–9 September 2001.

11

Youth work and Islam: a growing tradition

BRIAN BELTON

Introduction

The following chapter seeks to generate a sense of the development of youth work with young Muslims in North and East London over the last 40 years via autobiographical and narrative research. It seeks to demonstrate how an awareness of Islam and religious practice can enrich and enliven young Muslims and will include analysis of the experiences of Muslims who grew up in the area, their encounters with youth provision and how they developed to become youth workers. I believe their contribution not only exemplifies the influence of Muslims in youth work over the years, but also shows the relevance of Islam to the field in the contemporary period.

This chapter attempts to draw attention to the relatively long history Muslims have had with youth work provision in the above areas of London, and to provide a greater analysis of the impact this has had on those concerned. This is achieved by highlighting how Islam has influenced the sphere of practice of particular workers and the way in which insights drawn from Islamic teachings can inform current practice on a generic basis, while often proving more relevant and appropriate than some of the more outmoded or deficient philosophies and theories that can be found in the literature surrounding the practice of informal education and youth work.

I should say at the outset that I am not, by any stretch of imagination, a scholar of Islam. My Arabic is limited and mostly self-taught with the aid of one or two more learned and more linguistically aware friends. For these shortcomings I apologize in advance, but my first hope is that you can hear what I have to say in the spirit of seeking knowledge and understanding. For my part, I have been involved in youth work for more than 40 years, much of this working alongside Muslim colleagues and with Muslim clients. My second hope is that this will be seen as being worthy enough to serve as the foundation of my position.

Muslims and youth work

Any attempt to portray the general experience of an eclectic population such as Muslims is, perhaps, bound to fail to do little more than make the most of vague stereotypes in order to produce an image that has no real use and even less authenticity. However, for most of its history, the investigation of faith-based youth work has ignored the participation and contribution of individual Muslims and the general influence of Islam. In saying this I am aware that I might be met with – probably understandably – defensive responses. A few that I have experienced over the last few years, from both Muslims and non-Muslims, have been variations of:

> "Muslims haven't played much of a part in faith-based youth work until relatively recently."

> "There is no mainstream Islamic youth work."

> "Muslims don't have any time for anything other than formal education."

Such rejoinders come largely from people who believe they are able to speak for all Muslims across all times and places. However, at the same time, such views also espouse the idea that Muslims have been, and are, people who play no significant part in mainstream youth work and informal education, and are not youth workers. I believe this to be lazily myopic more than purposely untruthful – first, because there is no youth work 'mainstream' as such. The discipline continues to be what it has always been, an eclectic and evolving response to young people, delivered in an almost overwhelming range of forms, in an endless series of locations, deploying a continually growing array of techniques and approaches, all of which are motivated by a superfluity of motivations, policies and beliefs. Consequently, because youth work practice has taken place in such an array of situations, delivered under so many guises via a plethora of methods adhering to a shifting and fluctuating philosophy, the idea of a typical or archetypal form of youth work is fanciful. Secondly, Muslims have been part of youth work, both as participants and facilitators ever since its emergence in Britain as a national phenomenon in the 1960s. There was also a Muslim presence before this in some of the numerous activities of missionary, instructional, moral and disciplinary attention given to young people from the nineteenth century onwards, which some commentators mistakenly claim to be the direct progenitors of today's practice. For all this, it is probably enough to say that Muslims and their faith have been part of youth work in the UK for at least a couple of generations. The following section then, seeks, in a limited capacity, to add to the wider aims of the chapter, in an effort to generate a recognition and understanding of this social reality.

'ilm and youth work

The term used for knowledge in Arabic is *'ilm*, which has a much wider connotation than its synonyms in English and other Western languages. 'Knowledge' falls short of expressing all the aspects of *'ilm*. Knowledge in the West is often taken to mean information about something, divine or corporeal, while *'ilm* is an all-embracing term covering theory, action and education; it gives these activities a distinctive shape. It has been argued that this type of comprehension is of supreme value for Muslims and that indeed *'ilm* is Islam, in that Islam is the path of 'knowledge'. No other religion – and indeed, no ideology – puts so much emphasis on the importance of *'ilm*. Each of us, being the creations of Allah (as *al-Alim*, 'the source of all knowledge', and *al-Hadi*, 'the absolute guide of humanity'), no matter how humble or even ill-informed, has the potential to access and add to *'ilm* via attempting to understand and listen to our fellow humans (not necessarily agreeing with them). This can be understood as one of the basic precepts of *'ilm* and it is perhaps why *'ilm* is at least one of the pillars of youth work and, as such, necessary to the reflexive practice of the same.

In my experience, this perspective is one of the many treasures that Muslim youth workers have brought to the general practice of youth work. However, this kind of contribution has gone largely unacknowledged, partly because when we think of youth work and Islam we mistakenly understand it as an expression of a relatively recent aspect of the wider field of practice, and partly because it has been introduced into youth work as being something specifically associated with Muslim faith and culture as something that, in the main, has been delivered quite unconsciously. By this I mean that most effective youth workers bring facets of themselves to their practice and it is the heterogeneity this generates that makes youth work a uniquely responsive and eclectic discipline. At times, in certain places, *'ilm* has, as an aspect of Islamic identity and culture, been infused into youth work practice in a pleasingly informal way and much of what follows will relate to this phenomenon.

Islam, science and youth work

In the last few years there has been a growing awareness of the need to think about youth work and informal education in Muslim contexts. More recently, perhaps, there have been a few of us that have been working to bring attention to how the teachings and traditions of Islam can, and do, contribute to the work we do with young people from a range of backgrounds, regardless of religious and cultural affinities. However, in this chapter I want to highlight a sense of the development of youth work influenced by Islam, which has, I argue, a history of at least half a century, although the dynamics of what might be called the 'Islamic world-historic legacy' also underpin the nature and conduct of practice as British law, education, medicine and the foundation of the achievements of Occidental science all have significant roots in Islamic heritage.

Among the very first things that a trainee youth worker is taught, to varying degrees, are the skills of observation; how to look at and inspect things and people. This is usually followed by the recording of these observations, which are then used as forms of evidence that work has taken place, and that information has developed about the trajectory of particular pieces of practice and/or agency direction over time. However, observations can also prove to be a means of analysis of what has happened and/or been accomplished – what people do when things are done, how individuals and groups undertake tasks and why they might be motivated to act in certain ways. This process is first undertaken to demonstrate what happened, when and who was involved, but the 'why' question takes the procedure into the 'diagnostic' realm. It is at this juncture, where youth work meets with science, that an awareness of what has happened can be used to predict future events – if this thing happened, with these people involved, in this way, then it is likely that, given similar circumstances, much the same thing will happen the next time those people do those things, in that way. This modality provides the potential to either seek to replicate situations or change personnel or environments to alter outcomes. In short, this is doing what science seeks to do: manage or control what seemed to be (without observation, recording and analysis) random, unpredictable and uncontrollable events or circumstances – 'truth from proof' – not 'the' truth, but the pursuit of the same or, as the medieval Muslim philosopher Al-Kindi is attributed as saying, 'nothing should be dearer to the seeker of truth than the truth itself'. While science cannot be said to be solely the product of Muslim endeavour, the call of Islam to seek knowledge in the broadest sense of the word has had a profound effect on the development of scientific knowledge. According to the Prophet Muhammad, 'seeking knowledge is an obligation upon every Muslim'. (cited in Siddiqui, 1990, pp. 135–6).

The Muslim 'Golden Age' of Baghdad, Persia and the Iberian Peninsula from 632 to 1258 CE was the first of a sequence of 'golden ages' of Islamic thought, which ranged from Saffavid Iran to Mughal India, up to the eighteenth century. These intellectual waves represent great worldwide efforts on the part of Muslims to seek, collect and refine knowledge, and they led to new discoveries and innovations. This cultural flowering or 'gathering of knowledge' was later known as the Muslim 'Golden Age'. This was a protracted era of concentrated and multifaceted dialectic, under Islamic auspices that grew out of a consciousness that violent (violating) force can hardly ever positively resolve issues of the spirit or soul

– with regard to individuals, groups, communities or societies, and that the path to whatever we might achieve as human beings lies in honing knowledge and understanding through the commitment to dialectical relations between people. This dialectic (not merely the act of dialogue) is, for me, is the rock on which the practice of youth work stands, it is at the same time a product of Islamic culture, a means to acquire and comprehend *'ilm*. While many people are becoming ever more aware of the historical contribution of Islamic civilization to Western thought, there is a need to reiterate this fact in the context of this chapter because it is the sort of runway on which Muslim educationalists land on the British youth work scene; it is just a hint of the cultural foundation of the Islamic influence in education.

'Ummah' – The influence of Islam

Anecdotally, I cannot truly say that there was a moment in my own life when I first felt the influence of Islam on my direction in life. I was born and raised in Newham, in East London, which for my first dozen years or so was East and West Ham. I was an inhabitant of the latter, less prosperous of the two boroughs. At the age of eleven I was consigned to a secondary modern school, which was regarded as very much the dustbin of West Ham's low achievers and juvenile miscreants, for whom education was as much a joke as it was an imposition. At that time the borough languished in the depths of poor achievement in secondary education in Britain, during a period when the UK slithered around the bottom echelon of secondary educational attainment in Western Europe. Hence, I can boast that I attended, what was probably at the time, the worst school in Western Europe! My behaviour at primary school had led to my expulsion, so I never actually took the eleven-plus examinations that decided which part of the then tripartite system one would be 'sentenced to', but my former head teacher made that sure I was set nicely in the very lowest education stream at the secondary modern I attended.

On my first day in secondary education I found myself being one of only two English speakers in my class. That first day was less than 20 years after the Partition of India, at a point in time when the effects of the recent civil war in Cyprus were still being dealt with, and, as a consequence, although I had very little awareness of this at the time, the majority of my peers were Muslims. Our teacher was Mr Said, a gentle but firm Muslim from Pakistan. He was one of the many teachers who had come to my school from across the world. The school also boasted American, Canadian, Indian, South African, Ugandan, Kenyan and Russian teachers, most of whom had come to the East End to hone their skills in a challenging environment. Indeed, an American teacher, Mr Wilson, told me, 'if you can teach here you can teach anywhere!' Hence, we also attracted people from Oxbridge, who came as well-meaning but ill-prepared missionaries who put up with an awful lot from reluctant pupils, but they did make an impact. However, as my first teacher, none had the same influence as Mr Said. It was he who taught me his understanding of 'ummah' but, probably more importantly, a way to activate the spirit of this concept. Unlike 'community', which is often seen as its equivalent, ummah (the term 'ummatun wahidah', meaning 'a single community', in the Qur'an refers to the whole of the Islamic world unified) embodies a potentially all-embracing inclusiveness. The meaning of community embodies both sameness and difference; it defines some people as 'inside' and others as 'outside'. As such, community is effectively a means of discrimination; the tighter a community is, the less likely it is that it will interact with other communities. In such situations communities become isolated, introverted and inward looking; they tend to be arenas were little knowledge comes in or goes out; hence they are contrary to the ethos of Islam as they become pools of ignorance.

Contrary to the negative effects of community, the Qur'anic precepts concerning 'ilm (knowledge) embody a pragmatic means to avoid communities developing the prejudices that tend to arise out of the propagation/sharing/promotion of ignorance. Yet, just as ummah refers specifically to the community of Islam (Muslims), the concept does not preclude people by birth, creed, colour, education, race, ethnicity, culture, neighbourhood, wealth, poverty, intellectual leanings and so on in the way that the limited term 'community' might. On reflection, it is often quite difficult to either enter or extract oneself from a community. In fact, often when people leave communities they are seen to have 'sold out' or are viewed as 'traitors'. On the other hand, those attempting to enter communities usually have to deal with suspicions of being

'outsiders' and/or 'deserters' from another community. As a West
Ham football supporter, I would find it difficult to enter into the
'Arsenal' community (even though I'm married to a 'Gooner'). I
will never cease to be a former West Ham community member.
Likewise, all the other 'faithful' West Ham supporters will see me as
irredeemably a defector and turncoat. This process, I believe, is the
antithesis of the concept of *ummah*, in that we all have the capacity
to be accepted by everyone else within the concept of the *ummah*
– as a sacred destiny of humanity in oneness. Conversely, the limited
notion of community represents a purposeful carving up of people
into discreet categories and, as such, a form of difference and
division that can, at worst, result in violence. However, within the
framework of the *ummah* we are all football supporters, regardless
of our particular individual footballing loyalties.

Muslimun

Mr Said also taught me another retrospective lesson – the term
'Muslimun' (the plural form of Muslim), meaning 'those who have
peacefully submitted'; that is, the believers of Islam. This collective
submission might be thought of as part of the creation of the
connection or wholeness between those within the faith (potentially
all humanity). For me, this bond reflects something of the nature of
Islam, promoting as it does a concept that human beings are born
with the capacity to be integrated and become part of a collective
expression of being. Various aspects of our shared and individual life,
religious, political or educational, need not be regarded as separate
spheres in that they are expressions of the wholeness/connectivity
that we prospectively embody. To separate my education from my
faith or from the rest of who I am, rather than making room for,
or allowing, the same to coalesce, is symbolically or metaphorically
similar to cutting off a limb and examining it as if it had only a
tangential relationship to the rest of my body. At the same time,
this severance can create division between others and me. The
possibility to share our 'whole selves' is undermined as individuals
compartmentalize different aspects of themselves. Instead of the
whole 'me' connecting with the whole 'you', we will need to find the
bits of us that can meet, but in such a process we will perhaps only
identify that which cannot be accepted by the other. It is possible

that this violation of self-separation is exacerbated by the effort to dissect education into formal and informal elements as is also the habit in youth work training. A good teacher and enlightened youth worker, like Mr Said, will use what others might recognize as informal and formal methods interchangeably, but to him there would be no dichotomy as his efforts were integrated into an educational enterprise that is about the student's realization of their self as an integrated individual and as potentially part of *ummah*. As such, for myself, now more than 40 years on, I can recognize the influence and impact of *ummah* and *'ilm* on my practice both as a youth worker and lecturer, and would like to highlight the value of these concepts to the realms of Muslim youth work.

Models of good practice

Mr Said was a good educator, which encompassed being a teacher, but he did more than teaching; he was also prepared to be taught by those he worked with and among. He was, seemingly, endlessly interested in us, his pupils, and asked as many questions of us as we asked of him, if not more. Often bad behaviour was met with genuine curiosity; 'Why did you do that?' The answer was always met with another question. For example:

'Because I wanted to.'
'And why did you want to?'

The overall effect of his unusual approach was a wearing down of our bad behaviour because most of us couldn't be bothered to act up in his class and then have to suffer the third-degree consequences. Mr Said's approach obliged us to look at ourselves and our motivations, and often the consequences of the same: 'What effect do you think that had?' 'How do you feel about it now?' This was hard work as one thing most East Enders of my generation could not help doing, in common with my Indian, Cypriot, Turkish and Pakistani class-mates it seemed, was answer any question asked of us. I think Mr Said understood this; it was something he had learnt about us. Of course, when someone takes the trouble to learn about you, you find yourself learning about them; learning, if it is learning, is hardly ever a one way process. So, Mr Said was not just a teacher; he was a social educator, constantly involved in his own social education. I now understand that he was also a youth worker; a person who literally worked with, cared and learnt about, taught, talked and listened to youth.

Social kindness

Youth work practice is and has been carried out by Muslims in all sorts of contexts and ways. Over the years I have collected many examples of these as part of an effort to discern how Islam can benefit and broaden our response to young people. Mostly they are instances in practice where a socialization within Islam can be seen to have had an impact, but what makes them fascinating for me is how this influence is largely unselfconscious and, as such, quite gentle. I would suggest that the overall impact fosters an authority that manifests as a social kindness, in an atmosphere that has been given some very sharp edges by Western capitalism. In order to illustrate some of the concepts discussed in a Muslim youth work setting, I want to outline the case-studies of two youth workers and the ways Islam has influenced their work.

Muzaffer

Muzaffer arrived in Britain in the late 1950s from Turkey at the age of three. His parents were observant Sunni Muslims. He was brought up in Brighton, where his father worked in the catering industry. His mother found employment, first as a cleaner and then as an administrator, in a large hotel. The family came to London to live in the Green Lane's area of Haringey, and as a 17-year-old Muzaffer got a job, like his dad, working in the catering industry. He was married in 1977 to Aisha, a student who went on to become a primary school teacher. Her family had fled Uganda and the persecution of Idi Amin in 1972. The couple had two children and faith was an important part of family life. It was through the children's attendance at a youth club in Haringey that Muzaffer became involved in youth work. By 2000 he had almost 15 years' experience working with young people, first as a football coach and then, after achieving a string of part-time qualifications, as a detached youth worker. He told me he would certainly have done the work for nothing, although could not have devoted as much time to it as he did as a paid worker. His faith has been a constant source of inspiration and reflection in his youth work practice:

> At first I didn't have a clue how to work with young people. I just did what come naturally and did the best I could. It was not until I started to work with others that I became a little bit critical of what I saw. I had always seen kids as being basically good. When they were a naughty there was nearly always a reason and once you sorted that out things were generally ok. So when I first went to meetings with youth workers it felt slightly uncomfortable, because they seemed to all agree that the kids they were working with "had problems"; it was as if there was something wrong with them, like as individuals. They either were "unable to concentrate" or "lacked self-esteem" or were covered by an expression I never understood – they "had issues". But the Qur'an asks "Why do they not reflect on themselves?" It is too easy just to point out what someone else does, especially someone who is young, and say, "the reason they are bad is that they are bad". If I look to myself, what is it about me that is not helping this person to be good, then I think you tend to get a lot further with the person you are working with.

This attitude is in alignment with the position that Sufism (a mystical expression of Islam), which focuses primarily on spiritual self-reform rather than fault-finding in others.

Models of deficit

What Muzaffer has seen in operation was the 'deficit model' of young people that runs through much of youth work practice and related literature. This perspective depicts those we work with as lacking something in themselves; the attitude that lower achievement is due to a problem with the individual rather than considering the role of educational institutions, instructional practices, organizational structures and so on. Deficit is often ascribed to individuals using a lexicon of vague terms, mostly drawn from the overlap between psychotherapy and psychoanalysis, which include 'attention seeking'. Deficit also includes a 'lack of self-esteem' – although this category

hardly ever provides what this 'lack' is being compared to – people who
have 'just enough' self-esteem perhaps? Nor does the person making
such a statement tell us how or by what criteria they are measuring
self-esteem, or in what way they are qualified to undertake this
measurement. William Ayers and his cohorts (2005, 2006; with Ford,
2008; with Quinn and Stovall, 2009; and with Alexander-Tanner,
2010) are the latest in a long line of thinkers that have written about
the effects of young people's experience of being treated as somehow
'lacking', the consequences of the same and possible strategies to avoid
the blithe application of deficit labels (see for example Berg, 1972;
Holt, 1964; Kohl, 1991). Deficit theories apart, one can probably
think of many examples of this kind of amateur analysis based on the
premise of another's 'lack'. However, in the main, a prognosis of this
type suggests that the person being referred to is suffering from some
personal malady or pathology. It is in fact much less common to hear
youth and social workers look to political, economic, environmental
and/or situational influences on behaviour and it is even rarer to find
youth workers, as an initial response, looking at how they themselves
might have elicited or invited the seemingly negative, but perhaps
rational, response of a young person.

The 'right word'

From an Islamic perspective, these assumptions about young
people's psychological states, or 'uneducated' guesses about people's
dispositions, are not acceptable:

> O you who believe! Keep your duty to Allah and fear Him, and
> speak always the right word. [Qur'an, 33:70]

The 'right word' is not some handy expression that might be used
to fit a particular moment or response. To find the 'right word' we
need to, at the very least, look at a range of possible motivations.
If we fail to do this we are in danger of becoming prejudiced, pre-
judgmental and setting ourselves above others (i.e. young people)
based on what we believe to be our superior experience or insight.
At this point the youth worker begins to lose sight of the resource
of personal humility, and humility, from a Muslim perspective, is
acknowledged as a much-needed component of an individual's

character; it displays just how little we might actually know about the complex character of any individual, let alone those we might see for a few hours in one particular context in any given week.

Elena

From my earliest days as a youth worker I was involved with Gypsy, Traveller and Roma young people. This was chiefly related to my own background, but from the late 1960s through to the mid-1970s, I was involved in the lively and, at times, brutal politics arising out of what was nothing less than the persecution of the nomadic people of Britain. It was at this time that I met Elena, whose parents had come to London from Bulgaria just after the Second World War. Elena, a Sufi Muslim, had been involved with Travellers from the late 1940s, motivated in part by a response to the threat to her family who had been labelled as 'Pomaks' under Nazi and, later, Communist rule during and after World War Two. After losing touch with her religion for a few years in her twenties, and after becoming a single parent, politics did much to fill the vacuum. However, later Elena found a new vigour for her faith, and over the years she became something of a student of Islam. This, she told me, had worried her parents almost as much as her previous wandering away from with her beliefs. At the time I knew Elena she was studying for a degree in human rights. Her son, who she brought up in Islam, was very much the centre of her life, but she continued to have an active interest in social justice and minority rights. In a long conversation with Elena that went on through one cold January night, while observing police and bailiff behaviour at a prospective eviction (such a presence often meant that removals of caravans would be less brutal), Elena told me:

> In Britain, most institutions, be it legal, educational or whatever were formed during the time of British colonialism and it would be surprising if they did not operate showing that influence and history. So youth workers and social workers are sent out into communities just as missionaries were sent to India and Africa to bring 'civilization' and 'education' to the 'natives', which meant getting them to act according to the standards and values that were 'acceptable' to 'respectable' British people. The idea was to

make them 'good subjects' and useful to the Empire even if a lot of well-meaning people didn't see this. That is also the purpose of education and welfare in Britain. It is not really education; it is not about 'helping others' or 'learning to question' – why would the government sponsor that? It is a form of colonization that uses indoctrination and propaganda designed to produce relatively cheap, relatively flexible workers that are useful to capitalist enterprise. Of course not all teachers or social workers see this; else many of them would not want to do what it is they do. But we live in a capitalist state, what else could be the case?

Since this conversation, I have grown to understand that while seeing people in deficit has an obscure lineage, its origins in Britain are probably historically linked to the age of British colonialism. This was a particular time when the privileged class of the Empire sought to bring their culture, religion and education to what they took to be those in deficit; the 'natives' of the subjugated territories (see, Said, 1978; Fanon, 1967). In the process, British institutions, education, law, government and so on were formed, shaped and defined, and, as a consequence and to certain degrees, are still imbrued with the culture of colonialism. Many state and public institutions propagate a deficit perspective of those they encompass, both functionaries and clients. Through such procedures, the educator may often approach the pupil or student, not primarily with the motivation of learning about them, but with the misinformed view that they are more or less ignorant, that they lack knowledge/awareness/ understanding. For example, the moment one presents oneself to a medical practitioner, one is treated as someone who lacks health, who is sick, not as an individual with who is healthy, but as one who is experiencing a measure of discomfort or relative infirmity (see, Foucault, 1963, 1969). Likewise, the educator approaches those they seek to educate with the assumption that they are ignorant – and maybe they are in some respects, but they also have something valuable to teach the educator; this knowledge/information is the means to make the teacher a more effective educator.

Elena the *'Mujahidah'*

For me, at that time, Elena's stance was pretty radical and her outlook has continued to influence my thinking up to the present, but she did not adopt the usual anti-colonial rhetoric or propose reactive or revolutionary responses. Her articulation of her perspective provided an insight into how her faith guided her practice:

> Sufism has the something called *"mujahada"* [I later found out this is related to *jihad*] which is an intense determination to follow a spiritual life that the Prophet (peace be upon Him) exemplified. The hardest conflict is the struggle with your physical self, which is morally more demanding than protesting against or fighting others, but produces something in the individual that is more permanent than just turning the oppressors into the oppressed by what looks like victory but is in fact the continuation of injustice.

This position reflects the position of the fourteenth-century Persian Gnostic Sayyid Haydar Amuli that *jihad* (struggle), at the higher levels, becomes a struggle against the self and against the doubts and misgivings of the speculative intellect. However, this can also be taken as a profoundly anti-colonial attitude echoed by the likes of the South African anti-apartheid activist Steve Biko in his passionate assertion that as soon as one rejects the label of 'the oppressed' one is no longer oppressed. This change of perspective is not achieved primarily by a conflict with others, but by a struggle with self to overcome a perspective born out of persecution and domination and by transplanting a more rational and autonomous view of the self with, first and foremost, the glorious, complex and beautiful creation of God.

Elena's work was essentially built around learning about and being sensitive to the *jihad* (struggle) of others and being able to identify with the inner travail this involves for the individual. *Jihad* can be very informed and move on a solid trajectory, but for many of us, particularly the young, this inner striving can have a confused direction and/or be guided by a not altogether rationalized purpose or clear motivation. This sense of 'inner struggle' is not innate, it is something that needs to be nurtured and tempered over time and contexts. Like much of what makes us human, the spiritual, like the intellectual or the physical, is something in the process of growth and development (known in Arabic as '*tazkiyyah*', meaning 'self-purification'). Retrospectively, this is what I think Elena understood and had come to know how to work with. As she informed me:

Finding what we believe in is not about being told or even guided, although this might help. People need to go though their own struggles; they belong to them and they are for them. Allah does not take away our tribulation but he has given us the means to face and overcome obstacles, and perhaps make them something we learn from. If we didn't have these things, if we did not have the challenges of life, how could we become more than what we are? How could we develop?

For me this has become a driving force in my work with others. Blame or bemoaning personal misfortune is very much an easy exit and something that is profoundly 'anti-developmental'. As soon as I unload my situation, often caused by external forces, I have shed responsibility for my own actions and claimed that there is a force that shifts my destiny and in that shifting, it is greater than God. Social factors certainly have an influence on what I do and how I do it, but none of us are 'corks in a social sea'. We have our intellect and will, the sail and rudder, given to us by God. We also have the compass of his word and the teaching of his Prophets. We are not helpless or without the means to chart a route – we all have a course to steer in life. Like Muzaffer, Elena's work was about developing her own consciousness of these esoteric assets in herself and others.

What I am suggesting is that 'things cannot change unless you change'. As much as environments can dictate the responses of individuals, individuals can collectively change environments by their responses to them. However, people will not be able to alter environments via the insistence of professionals in propagating a view of the individual as 'pathological' or 'lacking' in some way. Cleaver (1968), Carmichael and Hamilton (1967), Fanon (1965, 1967) Steve Biko, through his political struggle, all essentially confirm the process of *jihad* – that people are capable of undertaking a disciplined and determined examination of themselves in order that they might work towards a world without colonizers or the colonized.

This emphasis has always appealed to me as a means and aim in my work with young people. Overall, it is very straightforward, and it insists on attempting to see those I work with in a positive light that reflects upon human beings as each having equal potential as the creation of God and working with them on projects, events and activities that might help them embark upon, continue and endure their own personal consistent and focused *jihad*. In doing that I maintain my own '*mujahada*'; and together we move towards an ever more liberated environment, as it is made up of ever more liberated individuals.

The offering of self

Both Muzaffer and Elena, from their different perspectives within Islam, had both developed an anti-deficit approach, but this appears to be a largely unselfconscious response which did not seem to be deliberately focused either for or against. If you like, it was something that became innate within them, long before they got into the realm of youth and community work. It would appear that their individual immersion in Islam made both of their responses a part of their nature (what is described in Islamic theology as '*fitrah*', meaning 'primordial disposition'); that is, a gentle emanation coming from the people they were. It is something quite difficult for people coming into generic training in youth work to understand that this faith-sensitive approach offers an alternative way of doing things that is neither absolutist nor seminal. That is to say, that the codes and commands of the books and websites devoted to informal education have a place, as must the policy and organizational demands placed on youth work. However, the richness of the practice is centred on the people who deliver the work and on those who participate in the same informal, educative methods of learning as our clients. The most effective youth workers then, are those who are able to bring a little of their unique selves to what they do and allow those we work with to teach us about them. In this proposed strategy we might be able to detect something of a peaceful submission in that it probably requires some humility and suspension of ego. Unless we do this, how will we know those we work with, build associations with them or engender trust? If we do not know them, and their wants or needs, how will we be able to work with them effectively? This is what Elena and Muzaffer taught me: how they, as individuals and as Muslims, learnt about those they worked with and how they saw them as a resource above and beyond whatever personal knowledge they had. This is how they personally, from within themselves, interpreted their practice

– it is precisely this facet that made their youth work distinctive, humane and effective.

Faith-based work

There has been a comparatively great deal of discussion and writing about 'faith-based practice' within youth work over the last decade or so but, I'm not sure there is a great deal of discernable commonality between or within faith-motivated practice. Some years ago I was discussing the issue with someone who worked for a Christian youth organization. He and his colleagues would wander around a midlands city centre wearing Parka jackets emblazoned with huge crosses on the back. He related his experience to me regarding how he approached a young man and without introduction or any preamble telling him, 'Jesus loves you'. He went on to claim that simply by making this statement to this young person it changed the hearer's life. I have found that such so-called 'faith-based work' is peppered with similar sorts of claims and anecdotes, leading us to believe or conclude that a few magic words can start a palliative process that in turn fires up a process of redemption. The above comments are not intended to prefer specific forms of Christian youth work over other forms, but rather to raise a cautionary note regarding simplistic, 'evangelical' approaches to youth work that focus more on proselytizing and missionizing than on the real and immediate needs of the youths themselves. Such faulted practices and approaches bring 'faith-based' youth practices and approaches into much disrepute.

The YMCA, integration and *jihad*

One of the biggest youth organizations in the world is the Young Men's Christian Association, (YMCA) a worldwide movement of more than 45 million members from 125 national federations affiliated through the World Alliance of YMCAs. Founded on 6 June 1844 in London, England, by George Williams, it is undoubtedly underpinned by a distinct Christian evangelicalism, but some of the specific methods employed have a usefulness and relevance for youth work that extend beyond particular 'faith-based' approaches and methodologies. The core of the movement has become the cultivation of mind, body and spirit, a kind of take on the 'three-in-one' notion recognizable as inherent in much of Christian doctrine. Within this culture, in ethos, somewhat comparable to the concept of *Muslimun* (singular form being Muslim, e.g. 'one who has submitted to God'), human beings are seen as being integrated entities in as much as it is taken as evident that;

- When you cultivate the spirit, it has an effect on mind and body.
- When you nourish the mind this enriches the spirit and this will have influence on the body.
- Nurture of the physical self will positively affect state of mind and the feeling of spiritual well-being.

No line that makes up the YMCA's symbolic triangle exists independently of the whole; if it did then there would be no triangle, just three separate lines. However, all this does not happen or even start with a youth worker making a statement. It begins with the commitment of the individual, the giving of oneself to (a 'peaceful submission'), which is premised on a particular and definite set of ideas, principles, beliefs and a faith. However, this faith is two-way; it is faith in God and in yourself as an expression of God. Such commitment requires constant effort and exercise of self-will. It is not something that happens once only. However, if it is practised as exemplified by Elena and Muzzaffer, what is produced in response to others becomes something unselfconscious and natural. As a result, every day faith is challenged and the will to continue in the faith is more or less strong or weak. In order to be realized, faith needs to be energized and renewed; just as doubt is part of modern human existence, it is then also an element of contemporary faith. This situation makes demands of those of us who take on faith as something that permeates our work and our lives. For those of us who have faith or a particular religious conviction, we may well believe that we have some answers, but there are ultimately more questions for us and our faith to answer. In such circumstances, faith itself raises a number of important questions and in response faith should require us to gain a better knowledge and understanding of the world and of others. As Mr Said hoped of my peers and myself many years back, I too hope that the reader might be able to draw some parallels here between the character and the practice of Muslim youth workers I have presented and perhaps a little of the spirit of Christianity and faith-based youth work in general.

Conclusion

This chapter has attempted to respond to some of the big issues that need to be addressed concerning faith-based, particularly Islamic, approaches in modern youth work. In doing so, I have tried to suggest, in a limited way, how Islam, as a religion that seeks to encompass a holistic approach to social problems and realities, can humanize some of the more mechanistic aspects of youth work practice. My discussion suggests that much of what we term 'youth work' has become overshadowed by what often seem like economic imperatives and rationalizing, and as such it has tended to transform contemporary youth work into something quite mechanistic, producing only instrumental outcomes that are in danger of dehumanizing the whole of youth work engagement. The possible impacts of such a mechanical engagement could seriously undermine the social reality that young people are not objects that need to be moulded or 'changed' by what we might deem to be more cost-effective and appropriate means of engaging. Instead, by overlooking the particularities of the Muslim communities and other similar communities, such a flawed approach will largely fail to relate to the particular needs and specific issues of a very religiously plural and multicultural contemporary Britain.

References

Ayers, W. (2005), *Teaching Toward Freedom: Moral Commitment and Ethical Action in the Classroom*. Boston: Beacon Press.
—(2006), *To Become a Teacher: Making a Difference in Children's Lives*. New York: Teachers' College Press.
Ayers, W., and Alexander-Tanner, R. (2010), *To Teach: The Journey, in Comics*. New York: Teachers' College Press.
Ayers, W., and Ford, P. (2008), *City Kids, City Teachers: Reports from the Front Row*. New York: The New Press.

Ayers, W., Quinn, T., and Stovall, D (eds), (2009), *Handbook of Social Justice in Education*. New York: Routledge.

Berg, L. (1972), *Look at Kids*. London: Penguin.

Carmichael, S., and Hamilton, C. V. (1967), *Black Power*. New York: Random House.

Cleaver, E. (1968), *Soul On Ice*. New York: Bantam Doubleday Day Publishing Group.

Fanon, F. (1965), *The Wretched of the Earth*. London: MacGibbon & Kee.

—(1967), *Black Skin White Masks*. New York: Grove Press.

Foucault, M. (1969), *The Archaeology of Knowledge*. London: Routledge.

—(1973), *The Birth of The Clinic*. London: Tavistock Publications Limited.

Holt, J. (1964), *How Children Fail*. New York: Pitman Publishing Corporation.

Kohl, H. (1991), *I Won't Learn From You*. New York: The New Press.

Said, E. (1978), *Orientalism*, Newyork: Vintage Books.

Siddiqui, A. H. (trans.) (1990), *Mishkat-ul-Masabih(Vol. 1)*. New Delhi: Kitab Bhavan.

12

Training Muslim youth to be 'Khateebs'[1]

ARIF FITZSIMON

Introduction

What do we mean when we speak of 'youth'? Definitions of youth vary in different societies. For instance, the National Youth Agency (NYA) in the UK defines the remit of youth workers as usually working with young people between the ages of 13 and 19 but can be broadened to cover the 11 to 25 age range,[2] while the National Youth Council of Singapore defines youth in the 15 to 35 age range[3].

In practice, British Muslim organizations tend to regard the upper limit of youth as 25, within which a youth is a child until the age of 18. Traditionally, for Muslims, there is no fixed starting age for a definition of 'youth', though at puberty (which varies across individuals) a youth is considered to be an adult. Muslims have also traditionally had a far higher upper age limit for youth. The Qur'an (46:15) says that that the age of 'full strength', that is, maturity, is 40. This implies that, from a Muslim perspective, the upper limit of youth is 39. Muslims are, however, required by their religion to abide by the law of the land they live in so they have to abide by legal implications of definitions of youth (e.g. the age of marriage).

This chapter, rooted firmly within a practitioner perspective, aims to highlight the work of the Muslim Youth Foundation (MYF). It begins with a brief outline of some of the challenges facing Muslim youth, before moving on to a summary of the MYF's guiding values and projects, focusing on the 'Khateeb Project' with the views of some existing and trainee Khateebs on their views of the challenges facing Muslim youth, and the role of both the Khateeb and Muslim organizations in addressing these issues.

Challenges facing Muslim youth – A Muslim practitioner's perspective

According to Census 2001, Muslims comprise around 3 per cent of the whole population. 34 per cent of the Muslim population are in the 0 to 16 age group and approximately the same percentage makes up the 16 to 34 age group, with 46 per cent of the British Muslim population being born in Britain. As many commentators have noted, this makes Britain's Muslim population relatively young (Gale and Hopkins, 2009; Lewis, 2007; Peach, 2005). In addition, Muslim communities in Britain are among the most socially and economically deprived, with high unemployment, poor health and disproportionate numbers of Muslims in prison compared to the general population. According to Prison Service (2004) statistics, Muslims represent around 10 per cent of all inmates – that is, three times as many Muslim inmates when compared to the size of the Muslim population. Two-thirds of Muslim inmates are young men between the ages of 18 and 30. Bangladeshi and Pakistani boys have tended to be the lowest achievers in schools, although there are indications that this is beginning to change (Ahmed, 2009).

As Muslim youth work practitioners, we see many challenges facing British Muslim youth. While some are common to British youth from various backgrounds, such as the impact of globalization, consumerism, drugs and gang culture and the generation gap, more specific issues facing Muslim youth centre on their religious identities and sense of belonging, and on Islamophobia and radicalization (though it should be remembered that non-Muslim white youth can also be subject to radicalization from extreme right-wing groups).

Globalization, for instance, impacts on Muslim youth and their sense of spirituality in various ways, whether it is through migration, consumerism or through technology such as satellite TV and the internet, exposing young British Muslims to alternative media ranging from *Al-Jazeera* to *YouTube*. Recent incidents involving British Muslim young people – such as the stabbing of MP Stephen Timms by student Roshonara Choudhry, who was influenced by the YouTube sermons of an Al-Qaeda preacher – have pointed towards the role of an unregulated internet in allowing young Muslims to be exposed to extremist websites.

Another challenge to the spirituality of Muslim youth lies in drug and gang cultures, which are often interlinked. Anecdotal evidence within Muslim communities points towards Muslim youth group violence such as territorial fights and glorification of gang culture due to the influence of hip hop and rap music. Claire Alexander (2008), for instance, talks of the ways the term 'gang' has been used to describe a variety of groups from youth groups to 'street' gangs and 'organized crime', and has become, in effect, a 'contemporary urban legend' (p. 7). She highlights the ways in which Hollywood stereotypes of the 'gang' have stigmatized black and Asian communities, including Muslims. A report by Hassan et al. (2009) on Somali youth in the UK highlighted how young Somalis felt stigmatized by the label of 'gang' even when only two youths were 'hanging around in the street' (p. 15), and cited the lack of targeted youth programmes, extracurricular activities, housing problems, Islamophobia and racism (especially with respect to police 'stop and search') as being significant issues that contributed to a 'feeling of exclusion' (p. 16). Similar perceptions were noted in Sughra Ahmed's (2009) report on young British Muslims. Here, young Muslim men spoke of how the closure of youth centres and the need for space away from the parental home where they could socialize with friends and smoke (to do so in front of parents was considered disrespectful) meant there was little alternative but to congregate in the streets and risk coming under suspicion by the police for alleged criminal activity.

Drugs are infesting the Muslim community with links between drug use and the high level of Muslim youth in prison (Ahmed, 2009). This is now recognized and acknowledged by some Muslim organizations who have established drug awareness projects such as the 'Substance Abuse Awareness Project' set up in 1999/2000 by the Lancashire Council of Mosques (based in Blackburn) in part-nership with Lancashire Constabulary and the local health author-ity, which aimed to raise drug awareness among the local Muslim mosque-schools (*Madrassas*). In another example, the negative effects of smoking weed are featured in the Muslim Youth magazine *the Revival* in an article called 'Eid not weed!' (Khan,September 2005). Here, the magazine recounts the phenomena of Muslim male youth going to Wilmslow Road[4], becoming drunk and getting high on weed, hassling women and fighting with police. Personal communication with police sources suggests that the major drug dealers in Blackburn are Muslims. This is not just an issue in Blackburn but is also present in other cities, such as Bradford. Research by the Joseph Roundtree Foundation on British Pakistani men in Bradford indicates that drug dealing is seen as a 'career option' by some of the Muslim youth there (Alam and Husband, 2006).[5]

Another area that practitioners often have to contend with are the difficulties Muslim young people face in communicating with the older generations, both within the family and in Muslim public spaces such as mosques. The generation gap between Muslim youth and the older generation impacts upon various aspects such as cultural and religious practices, lifestyles, career choices (Bari, 2005) and relationships (Ahmed, 2009). In addition, some young Muslims view their parent's culture as either 'outdated' or to contain elements of *bid'ah*[6] – innovations contrary to Islamic teachings (al-Lami, 2009, p. 5). Arguably, an understanding of youth that goes beyond the age of 25 may go some way towards alleviating this generation gap between British Muslim youth and older Muslims as youth work would not, for example, have the cut-off point of that age. The advantage of this is that the generation gap would be partially bridged as younger youth would still interact and learn from the experience of older youth, while the older youth would benefit from the younger youth in terms of their creativity and dynamism and would understand better their concerns. Hence, a number of our projects encourage older and younger youth to learn from each other's perspectives.

The development of an assertive Muslim identity among British Muslims has been apparent since the Rushdie Affair in 1989, with the younger generations of Muslims very often asserting their religious identity over their ethnicity, regardless of personal levels of religious practice (Hamid, 2006), as they 'expect to be treated as equal British citizens' (Anwar, 2003, p. 60). Tariq Modood (2009) has likened the public assertion of a Muslim identity in Britain as similar to the Black Pride equality movements in the US. A recent report by Gallop and the Coexist Foundation (2009) found that while only 55 per cent of the general public identified themselves as British, 77 per cent of Muslims in Britain identified themselves as British.[7] Similarly, research by Hopkins (2007) found that 42 per cent of young Muslim men from Scotland had a stronger Scottish than British identity and 36 per cent defined themselves as being Scottish rather than British, indicating young Muslims' willingness to also ascribe to regional identities alongside their religious identity.

Research by the Muslim Youth Helpline (MYH) indicates that Muslim youth see 'being a Muslim' as an integral part of their identity, affecting all aspects of their lives, with Islam acting as 'a means for establishing parameters amidst competing values' (Malik, Shaikh and Suleyman, 2007, p. 43). These competing values represent both the wider society and those of their parents, whose cultural values are sometimes critiqued as 'un-Islamic' by their children. Such sentiments can lead to feelings of alienation and may also extend towards other, less religiously observant Muslim youth, who may, for example, be drinking alcohol (Hopkins, 2004). Other Muslim youth see their Muslim identity as linked to practising their religion. For instance, Hopkins (2007) found that the young Scottish Muslim men he interviewed were more concerned with 'doing Islam through adherence to the five pillars, rather than being Islamic' (p. 75).

But what of British Muslim identity in practice? Different Muslim groups offer different perspectives on how British Muslim youth should interact with the wider British society. For instance, organizations such as the Muslim Council of Britain (MCB), the Islamic Society of Britain (ISB) and the Muslim Association of Britain (MAB) encourage a British Muslim identity that fosters a sense of shared values[8] and also encourage political participation, whereas on the other end of the spectrum groups such as Hizb ut-Tahrir and Al-Muhajiroun reject the British political system (Greaves, 2005). We can also see that in reality, British Muslims do positively integrate into British society as doctors, lawyers, teachers, nurses, business people, footballers and so forth.

For many Muslim youths, their sense of identity is also linked to seeing themselves as part of a part of a global Muslim community, or *ummah*. Events such as the Bosnian War, Gulf wars and Kashmir have engendered a spiritual link based on a sense of justice (Ramadan, 2004), but for some Muslim youth, events in these countries can potentially feed into a 'victim mentality' which can lead to extremism (Lewis, 2007). The Muslim philosopher Tariq

Ramadan (2004) argues that Western Muslims should see themselves as part of the wider community and not as a minority. Arguably, if one perceives oneself as a minority, then one will be obsessed by one's rights and how one is wronged rather than one's duties towards the wider society. Birt (2009) points to the anti-war activist Salma Yaqoob, highlighting how young Muslims, and especially women, through their involvement in the anti-war coalition with the political left, from 2002, represented a rejection of 'victimhood', and instead developed a 'broad, humanitarian Islam that no longer focuses on Muslim-only causes' (Birt, 2009, p. 222).

However, anti-Muslim sentiment, or Islamophobia[9] is a reality faced by many young British Muslims. A survey of Muslim students by the Federation of Student Islamic Societies (FOSIS) found that 47 per cent of Muslim students in their sample had experienced Islamophobia. Of these, 77 per cent described it as 'direct' and 68 per cent describing it as verbal. The effects of racism and Islamophobia can result in a sense of alienation and low self-esteem, which can, in some cases, lead to mental health issues. The media was also criticized for being very negative about Muslims. Ninety per cent of the students in the FOSIS study believed that that the media portrayal of Muslims needed to be changed. The Peace Direct Report (2006) also reached similar conclusions. Salgado-Pottier (2008) has argued that events such as the riots in Bradford 1995, and in Oldham and Burnley in 2001, the London bombings of 7 July 2005 and the Danish cartoons incident have created a 'moral panic' about British Pakistani and Bangladeshi youth, which is often linked to their Muslim identity.

As the discussion below elaborates, the aims of the MYF are to work with Muslim youth facing some of the above challenges in ways that enhance perceptions of self-worth and help to create a positive British Muslim identity.

The values of the Muslim Youth Foundation

The MYF was initially established by a group of Muslim academics and businessmen in the city centre of Manchester and began as a weekly study circle in the Victoria Park Mosque in the mid-1970s. It later grew to become the MYF in 1983. The MYF believes that we need to empower Muslim youth by developing them into leaders. Since its inception, the MYF has striven to do this and has developed youth who are active within the Muslim community. For example, two of the present trustees of the MYF are young people who have been involved in MYF programmes. There are also other young people active in other Muslim organizations within Manchester who studied at the MYF.

Initially, the work of the MYF was predominately with Muslim youth and focused on raising awareness of Islam in the wider community. Thus, there were various educational, social and spiritual programmes. These included study circles for different age groups (from children to university students), help with homework, qiyam ul-layl (spiritual programmes[10]), IT classes, sports activities (e.g. weight-training, karate, football, table tennis, squash, etc.), day-outings, camps (including in London, Glasgow, Dublin, Paris, Turkey and Morocco), and short courses (e.g. management[11]). A magazine called the Islamic Banner was also introduced in order to both publicize the work of the MYF and to educate Muslim youth in various aspects of Islam and the contribution of Muslims to science. In relation to raising awareness of Islam in wider society, there were weekly Islam information stalls in the city centre plus exhibitions about Islam (for example, on the Hajj) and so on. The philosophy of the Muslim Youth Foundation is to encourage a British Muslim identity and to make positive contributions to society as a whole.

Although the MYF is not as active as it used to be in direct work with youth on its premises – for instance, there is no longer a gym, martial arts lessons or as many study circles or youth camps – the MYF still hosts a weekly study circle, which is attended mainly by young people. The speaker is one of the Khateebs on the 'Khateeb rota' (see below) who is also a qualified counsellor (providing free counselling sessions for predominately Muslim youth at the MYF at least once a week). There is also a programme of monthly lectures and occasional seminars. The MYF maintains its links with the Islamic societies at local universities through the Khateeb programme, running workshops on da'wah (the preaching of Islam) at FOSIS conferences and facilitating lectures with FOSIS of well-known Muslim scholars such as Dr Jamal Badawi from Canada.

A number of the MYF's projects relate to working with children and youth. The Schools Programme is one of the MYF's major projects dating back to the early days of the organization. As well as hosting visits from both schools and trainee teachers to the MYF, the school project has developed to include producing educational materials for schools. The first of these is a DVD entitled 'Muslims in Britain', which is in its final stages of development, targeted at Key Stage Three in the curriculum. Two other projects of the MYF are the Bosnian Children's Project (BCP) and Deaf Group. The Bosnian Children's Project (BCP), which was established in 2000, raises funds for youth work with Muslim children and youth within Bosnia. This project was established after the Bosnian War, with the largest refugee camp near Tuzla. The BCP has recently expanded its work to employ a full-time youth worker to work with children in seven refugee camps around Tuzla. In addition, the MYF has also facilitated yearly trips by British Muslim Youth in the summer to Bosnia, which includes on its programme visits to see the work of the BCP, and to attend the National Remembrance Day on 11 July.[12] The MYF, although being creative with ambitious plans, is often hindered by a lack of finance. The MYF also holds occasional social, cultural and educational programmes for a Muslim Deaf group which have included *Eid* parties, an outdoor camp in Wales, day trips (for example, to Manchester's Old Trafford football ground) and hosts Islamic education programmes run by deaf Muslims.

Another way the MYF aims to encourage a positive British Muslim identity is through its work supporting converts, or reverts to Islam to negotiate their faith with their British identity. We do this by advising converts not to change their names (unless the meaning in Arabic is undignified or disrespectful) and to maintain Western-style clothing while respecting Islamic boundaries for modesty. Similarly, through positive engagement in Islam awareness programmes and inter-faith dialogue, the MYF demonstrates a commitment to the promotion of community cohesion.

The MYF believes that the best way to prevent extremism is through education to give the youth a balanced and comprehensive understanding of Islam, which should include making Islam relevant to the daily lives of the youth, plus developing their Muslim identity through education about their heritage,[13] programmes to develop their spirituality and social programmes including sports. At the same time, Muslim institutions should develop the youth to be proactive British citizens with the appropriate skill sets.

The MYF is non-partisan in that it aims to bring together Muslims of different backgrounds. Thus, the MYF is multicultural, it does not cater for one specific ethnic group, and the congregation of the MYF is multicultural (e.g., Arab, Pakistani, Bengali, African). The MYF also does not promote one particular school of thought but accommodates them all, so, for example, there could be a Hanafi, Shafi', Maliki or Salafi leading the *salah* (the MYF does not have one particular imam).

Developing Muslim youth – the MYF *Khateeb* project

The *Khateeb* rota was established by the MYF in the late 1980s, providing regular speakers to local universities, hospitals and schools across Manchester for the Jumah (Friday) prayer. Currently there are twelve *Khateebs* covering seven locations on the rota, two mosques, four prayer-halls at universities and a local hospital. The aims of the *Khateeb* programme are to deliver a positive, balanced Islamic message in the language that the youth understand (English). This includes the promotion of British Muslim identity and addressing issues that are relevant to British Muslims. Another aim of the rota is to prevent personality cults developing around a specific sheikh (religious leader), which can sometimes occur.

Mosques have been partly blamed for the radicalization of the small number of Muslim youth through alienating them and not making Islam relevant to them. The estimated number of British mosques in 2003 was 1,493 (Fetzer and Soper, 2005). Dyke's (2009) research on over 500 mosques in the UK found that 97 per cent of imams come from abroad and 92 per cent of imams studied abroad. How then can we expect these scholars to understand the issues facing the Muslim youth who have grown up in Britain? In the same study it was found that almost half of the mosques (46 per cent) had no prayer facilities for women, thus also alienating young British Muslim women. Language, as has already been mentioned, is another issue in mosques. The vast majority of the Jumah *khutbahs* tend to be in Arabic, despite the fact that many British Muslims are not fluent in Arabic. Prior to the *khutbah*, many mosques tend to have a lecture but only 9 per cent of them conduct this solely in English; 47 per cent of mosques have no English content in this lecture (this tends to be in Urdu or Bengali), while 44 per cent of mosques conduct the lecture in English plus one or two other languages (Dyke, 2009). Second,and third-generation Muslims are generally not as fluent as the first generation in their mother tongues, thus adding to a sense of marginalization from the mosque. This could be a contributory factor in the radicalization of some Muslim youth, as extremist groups tend to communicate in English. (Panja, 2005) Muslim youth themselves have argued that mosques do not address the issues they face in the UK such as drugs, alcohol, relationships, forced marriages, identity, Islamophobia, and extremist right-wing organizations such as the British National Party (see Iqbal, *the Revival*, 17 Dec 2008).

The *Khateeb* programme was developed in response to this lack of engagement by many mosques in order to encourage dialogue and positive relationships between British Muslim youth and local faith leaders. This is fostered through an emphasis on encouraging the language of discourse within British Muslim organizations, study circles, lectures and *khutbahs* to be in English, not in Urdu or Arabic, as is predominately the case in most mosques. The MYF believes that communication between religious scholars and young people should address issues that young people relate to and should be in a language they understand.

The *Khateeb* programme consists of several elements.

First there is a *Khateeb* rota where *Khateebs* give English-based *khutbahs* at Jumah at the locations on the rota. The *Khateebs* are selected from different ethnic backgrounds, such as Asian, Arab and African, with the aim of promoting unity across ethnic lines, in contrast with other local mosques not on the rota that cater for specific ethnic groups. The *Khateebs* also represent different schools of thought in matters of Islamic jurisprudence (*fiqh*), again with the aim of promoting unity.

In addition to the *Khateeb* rota, the MYF is developing an online 'Khateeb forum', a *khutbah* feedback system plus a *Khateeb* guidebook. The aim of the *Khateeb* forum is to facilitate discussions between the *Khateebs* on the rota, including discussions related to *khutbahs*. *Khutbahs* can also be assessed on the presentation and relevance of their delivery by mosque congregations on the rota via an online feedback system. This ensures that *Khateebs* receive regular feedback. This was the result of a pilot questionnaire on the *khutbah* feedback system which was conducted at the MYF as part of a developmental process for the *Khateebs*. The questionnaire covers issues of both content and delivery of the *khutbah*. It is planned to launch this system at all the locations on the *Khateeb* rota in a paper version in order to give regular feedback to the *Khateebs*. Other aspects of the *Khateeb* programme include seminars for *Khateebs* and training for new *Khateebs*.

New *Khateeb* Training Workshop February 2009

The MYF held a one day training workshop in 'How to be a *Khateeeb*' in February 2009 for male Muslim youth active in Islamic work. The workshop was attended by 22 youths who were predominately active within an Islamic organization, such as local branches of two national Muslim youth groups, undergraduates and postgraduates from Islamic societies at local universities, a Muslim sports group and a teacher in a local boys' Islamic high-school. Two of the speakers had previously studied at the famous Islamic universities, Al-Azhar in Cairo, Egypt and Madinah University in Madinah, Saudi Arabia. The attendees were mainly from Asian or Arab ethnic backgrounds, with one white Muslim. The MYF received very positive feedback on both the content and the organization of the workshop, with two of the attendees later joining the *Khateeb* rota.

The main speaker at the event was a local Muslim scholar (*shaykh*). Although his presentations were in Arabic, they were translated into English by one of the *Khateebs*, and attendees received translated copies of his detailed PowerPoint presentations on the *fiqh* (jurisprudence) of delivering a *khutbah*. These sessions were on comparative jurisprudence from various schools of thought on matters related to Jumah prayer and *khutbahs*. Subjects covered included issues such as how many people are required for Jumah, where one can pray Jumah, the language of the *khutbah*, the time of Jumah and a section on the obligatory and optional parts of a *khutbah*.

There are five 'pillars' of the *khutbah* (which the majority of Islamic scholars agree should be delivered in Arabic and which consist of praising God), the reciting of at least one verse from the Qur'an, a reminder to the congregation to maintain taqwa (an awareness that God is watching, which should lead to piety), asking God to bestow peace on the Prophets and final supplications.

However, there are differences over the issue of the language of the overall khutbah that are worth highlighting for a moment. While the majority of Islamic scholars believe the khutbah should be in Arabic because 'the Jumah prayer is only valid if performed in Arabic except in case of a need', there is an alternative – albeit a minority opinion (proposed by the scholar Abu Hanifah) – that allows for the khutbah to be delivered in any other language as the purpose of the khutbah is to teach the congregation and this can 'only take place in the language of the listener'. As already mentioned, this is the perspective adopted by the MYF (although the recitation of the five pillars of the khutbah should be in Arabic), since the vast majority of attendees to mosques tend to occur on Fridays and Eid celebrations. As there is limited attendance at lectures and other mosque-based educational programmes, the khutbah represents the ideal opportunity to educate Muslims about Islam and to address their concerns.

Other presentations were delivered by Khateebs (very experienced in youth work) on the Khateeb rota and a consultant specializing in self-development and strategic thinking. The workshop was chaired by another Khateeb, a youth who had grown up attending programmes at the MYF. These sessions included guidance on preparing for a khutbah, including recommended topics to be covered in the khutbah and some du'as (supplications), which can be used as part of the khutbah. Preparation for the khutbah is divided into three phases – intellectual preparation (this can be aided by the use of reminder cards), spiritual preparation (this refers to a statement of intention, or niyah) and the physical preparation (the need to take bath or shower prior to prayer). The art of public speaking is also taught, which includes the Sunnah (actions and sayings of the Prophet Muhammad), who influenced the practice of repeating something three times, plus other hints for public speaking such as the use of rhetorical questions, using pauses effectively, speaking from the heart and maintaining eye contact with the audience. The training workshop also included a presentation on the characteristics of a Khateeb. This focused on ten qualities including sincerity, taqwa, (God consciousness), good manners and ethics, deep knowledge, courage and emotional intelligence. This latter presentation highlighted that the emphasis of the *khutbah* should be to bring about change in ways of thinking and behaving among the congregation.

The workshop also provided an opportunity for some of the youth to give a mini-khutbah in front of the group, which was evaluated by two of the *Khateebs* using an evaluation form which considered the structure, content and delivery of the *khutbah*. All trainee *Khateebs* were given a training manual, which included a selection of *du'as* that could be used in a *khutbah*, sample topics for *khutbahs* and two sample *khutbahs*. Each attendee was also given a copy of the FOSIS *Khutbah* Guide. There was also information on common pitfalls in the delivery of a *khutbah*, such as avoiding topics that might disunite and cause *fitnah* (discord), and a guide on translating Arabic terminology into English. These examples illustrate the philosophy of the MYF in striving for unity, training youth in leadership skills and speaking to the mosque audience in a language they understand.

The role of the *Khateeb* in working with Muslim youth

Post-workshop questionnaires with the attending *Khateebs* and trainees on their views on the challenges facing Muslim youth, what they felt their roles as *Khateebs* were in addressing these and their views on the role of Muslim organizations, revealed a number of overlapping themes. These ranged from concerns over extremism, social deprivation, the role of the media in demonizing Muslims, alienation and a need to imbibe a sense of spirituality in young Muslims.

Extremism

The lack of a balanced and comprehensive teaching of Islam was mentioned as a challenge facing Muslim youth. As one respondent put it, there was a need for a teaching of Islam that was 'rooted in (an) orthodoxy that is neither a rejection of Eastern (traditional values) nor Western values'. Another referred to the 'manifestations of extremism' identified by the scholar Yusuf Al-Qaradawi, by noting that:

The *Fard* (obligations) have been replaced by the *Sunnah*, and this also causes conflict and confusion.

In other words, optional issues (where there can be a difference of opinion among Muslims) have become confused with obligatory ones. Consequently, these obligatory matters can become neglected due to a lack of proper Islamic knowledge. There was an emphasis on the need of Muslim organizations to better develop a more balanced and informed understanding of Islam among Muslim youth, or 'good *tarbiyyah*', referring to the theoretical, practical, physical and spiritual development of individuals. The British government's foreign policy and the influence of certain Muslim groups were also cited as potential sources of extremism among Muslim youth.

Spirituality

The issue of spirituality was raised as significant with *Khateebs* and trainees citing the need for Muslim organizations to work on cultivating the spirituality of Muslim youth. For instance:

One of the most important challenges is the spiritual development of a young Muslim who lives in a very materialistic society [in order to] hold spiritual activities, i.e., fasting and extra fasting days, *qiyam ul-layl*, a campaign to encourage reciting Qur'an on daily basis and so on.

The need for study circles was also mentioned.

Alienation

Racism, Islamophobia and stereotyping by the media were also cited as contributory factors in the increased alienation and marginalization of Muslim youth. Some viewed its collective impact as leading to an attraction with drugs and gang culture, which in

turn was weakening family and community bonds and resulting in
a loss of identity:

> The loss of identity, together with the demonizing of Muslims in
> the media, and an increase in racism and religious discrimination
> have given younger Muslims a sense of marginalization from
> main stream society and the Muslim community. Perhaps in their
> despair and peer pressure they turn to drugs and crime. This in
> turn leads them to living in a gang culture which has replaced
> their bonds of family and community.

Another respondent cited social deprivation and poor education
leading to a lack of ambition as significant:

> Education – the vast majority of Muslim youth are under-
> educated and lack ambition and lofty aims. Especially in inner
> cities, young people can aspire to be like local "gangsters"' or
> emulating the lifestyles of celebrities.

Role of the *Khateeb*

The vast majority of the respondents felt that it was the *Khateeb's*
responsibility to make Islam relevant to the youth; that is, to
communicate in their language, both in the general sense of spoken
English and the specific sense of being aware of youth-related
issues:

> The *khutbah* has to be in English because many younger people
> do not fully understand the language of their parents.

> Address the day-to-day issues the youth are facing (speaking
> their language), fostering a message that allows the youth to
> tackle their issues and create a true identity that is both Islamic
> and British in nature.

Another respondent felt that it was the duty of the *Khateeb* to
address issues of self-esteem to Muslim youth as this was significant
in maintaining a positive sense of identity.

Many also believed that the *Khateeb* had to be a role model who could inspire the youth by referring to their Islamic legacy, provide them with vision and leadership or to assist youth in identifying their main concerns and help provide spiritually inspired solutions. Others felt that the *Khateeb's* role went beyond the *khutbah* in working with the youth, either as a 'confidant' or as an 'advisor':

The *khutbah* is only a first step to encouraging younger people to learn about their faith. The real learning can be done in study circles. Within those study circles the youth can be monitored and given greater responsibility where as the *Khateeb* acts as a mentor and a role model.

Role of Muslim organizations in addressing the challenges facing Muslim youth

There were two types of responses to this issue. One was outlining what programmes should be provided by Muslim organizations for youth. The second was concerned with empowering the youth. Respondents felt that it was very important to be sensitive to the needs of the youth through consulting, listening and involving them in their activities. One went as far to say:

The youth are the future, and so need to be the focus of the Muslim organization.

As mentioned earlier, respondents felt that Muslim organizations should provide spiritual programmes for the youth. Other suggestions were that Muslim organizations should provide social activities such as sports, trips and camps. Virtually all the respondents felt that Muslim organizations should have educational programmes to promote better understandings of Islam (with one respondent also adding Arabic). The promotion of critical thinking was also mentioned in order to:

create a social psychology within the Muslim community that promotes innovation, investigation and creativity that is balanced and adheres to Islamic thought. Muslim organizations should base their activities on the propagation of knowledge and tools that will foster the social psychology and enable individuals to tackle modern concepts with the guidance of Islamic thought.

Thus we can see a range of responses, from a general raising of awareness of Islam to a more specific intellectual aspect that addresses modern concepts within an Islamic framework.

Muslim organizations were also expected to play a mentoring role, or to act as 'dynamic mentors' with members acting as role models to Muslim youth. 'Dynamic mentors' were referred to as:

> People who have a deep understanding of Islam through a good "*tarbiyyah*", as well as being well educated with a good understanding of the people/issues. These people can have a profound impact by being inspiring, and through their character inspire people to live better lives.

Thus, members of Muslim organizations should positively motivate Muslim youth and be role models to them. One respondent said that there should also be more cooperation between Muslim organizations, and they should 'share good practice'. The empowerment of Muslim youth by Muslim organizations was another theme mentioned by the respondents. For instance, organizations should:

> produce a new generation of leaders to take on the vast array of challenges faced by youth.

Others said that Muslim youth that should be given responsibility in organizations. As one respondent put it:

> Youth work needs input by the youth, and the youth need to be given a place of importance.

Conclusion

British Muslim youth face several challenges, some that they share with other British youth, and others that are more particular to themselves. This chapter has outlined some of the ways the work of MYF has tried to engage with Muslim youth in addressing some of these concerns and challenges, with a particular emphasis on the training of leadership skills through the *Khateeb* Project. A common factor uniting these challenges is a sense of alienation as a result of both Islamophobia/racism and the generation gap. This sense of alienation is based on low self-esteem and the lack of a balanced understanding of their religion (which can be expressed in a negative way), through to family discord, criminal acts (including those related to gangs and drug use) and being vulnerable to extremist influences. In order to address these issues, Muslim youth believe that Muslim organizations need to better communicate with the youth in a language that they understand. This involves consulting with young people to find out the challenges facing them; not presuming what they are and also consulting with them about the solutions. Muslim youth also need to be empowered within the Muslim community to take on leadership roles and address the issues facing their peers. The Muslim Youth Foundation believes the *Khateeb* programme to be one way of achieving this.

References

Ahmed, S. (2009), *Seen and Not Heard: Voices of Young British Muslims.* Markfield: Policy Research Centre, Islamic Foundation.

Al-Lami, M. (2009), 'Legitimising the discourses of political radicalisation: political violence in the new media ecology', *Politics and International Relations Working Papers*, 11, London: Royal Holloway, University of London.

Alam, M. Y., and Husband, C (2006), British Pakistani men from Bradford: linking narratives to policy. York: Joseph Rowntree Foundation.

Alexander, C. (2008), *Rethinking Gangs.* London: Runnymede Trust.

Anwar, M. (2003), 'British Muslims: socio-economic position', in M. S. Seddon, D. Hussein and N. Malik (eds), *British Muslims: Loyalty and Belonging.* Markfield: The Islamic Foundation.

Bari, A. M. (2005), *Race, Religion & Muslim Identity in Britain.* Swansea: Renaissance Press.

Birt, Y. (2009), 'Islamophobia in the construction of British Muslim identity politics', in P. Hopkins and R. Gale (eds), *Muslims in Britain: Race, Place and Identities,* Edinburgh: Edinburgh University Press.

Dyke, A. H. (2009), *Mosques Made in Britain.* London: The Quilliam Foundation.

Fetzer, J. S., and Soper, J.C. (2005), *Muslims and the State in Britain, France and Germany*. Cambridge: Cambridge University Press.

FOSIS (2005), 'The Voice of Muslim Students: A report into the attitudes and perceptions of Muslim students following the July 7th London attacks'. London: Federation of student Islamic Societies.

Gale, R., and Hopkins, P. (2009), 'Introduction: Muslims in Britain-race, place and the spatiality of identities', in P. Hopkins and R. Gale (eds), *Muslims in Britain: Race, Place and Identities*. Edinburgh: Edinburgh University Press.

Greaves, R. (2005), 'Negotiating British citizenship and Muslim identity', in T. Abbas (ed.), *Muslim Britain: Communities Under Pressure*. London: Zed Books Ltd.

Hamid, S. (2006), 'Models of Muslim youth work: between reform and empowerment', *Youth & Policy*, 92. Leicester: National Youth Agency.

Hassan, M. A., Samater, H. M., Van Liempt, I., Oakes W. J., and Obsiye M. (2009), *In Search for a United Voice: Establishing a London Somali Youth Forum*. London: Somali Youth Development Resource Centre.

Hopkins, P. (2004), 'Young Muslim men in Scotland: inclusions and exclusions' *Children's Geographies*, 2, (2), pp. 257–72.

— (2007), '"Blue squares", "proper" Muslims and transnational networks: narratives of national and religious identities amongst young Muslim men living in Scotland', *Ethnicities*, 7, (1), pp. 61–81.

Iqbal, S. (2008), 'Get with the Times Dude!' (Editorial), *the Revival*, 14, http://www.therevival.co.uk/editorial-get-times-dude. Date accessed: 24 December 2010.

Khan, H. (2005), 'Eid not weed', *the Revival*, 3, http://www.therevival.co.uk/eid-not-weed. Date accessed: 24 December 2010.

Lewis, P. (2007), *Young, British and Muslim*. London: Continuum.

Malik, I. H. (2004), *Islam and Modernity: Muslims in Europe and the United States*. London: Pluto Press.

Malik, M. (2003), 'Muslims and Participatory Democracy' in M. S. Seddon, D. Hussein and N. Malik (eds), *British Muslims: Loyalty and Belonging*. Markfield: The Islamic Foundation.

Malik, R., Shaikh, A., Suleyman, M. (2007), *Providing Faith and Culturally Sensitive Support Services to Young British Muslims*. London: Muslim Youth Helpline and National Youth Agency.

Modood, T. (2009), 'Muslims and the politics of difference' in P. Hopkins and R. Gale (eds), *Muslims in Britain: Race, Place and Identities*. Edinburgh: Edinburgh University Press.

Panja, T. (2005), 'Mosques should be saving lost souls', *the Observer*, Sunday 17 July.

Peace Direct (2006) *Young Muslims Speak*. London: Peace Direct.

Peach, C. (2005), 'British Muslim population: an overview', in T. Abbas (ed.), *Muslim Britain: Communities Under Pressure*. London: Zed Books.

Ramadan, T. (2004), *Western Muslims and the Future of Islam*. Oxford: Oxford University Press.

Salgado-Pottier, R. (2008), 'A modern moral panic: the representation of British Bangladeshi and Pakistani youth in relation to violence and religion', *Anthropology Matters*, 10, (1). http://www.anthropologymatters.com/index.php?journal = anth_matters&page = article&op = view&path%5B%5D = 44. Date accessed: 24 December 2010.

Younis, M. (2010), 'Young British Muslims and relationships', Muslim Youth Helpline. Leicester: National Youth Agency.

13

Engaging with young Muslims: some paradigms from the Qur'an and *Sunnah*

MOHAMMAD S. SEDDON

Introduction

In his book *Religion in Modern Britain* (1995) Steve Bruce made an astonishing claim regarding young people in the UK, stating that:

> The post-war period has also seen the invention of youth. Raising standards of living and the expansion of higher education (63,000 university students in 1938: 383,000 in 1989) have created a charmed space in which young people are given opportunities to act as autonomous individuals as yet unconstrained by the responsibilities that go with work, a family and a mortgage. (p. 30)

Beyond Bruce's contentious charge that young university students act autonomously as a result of being unconstrained by the usual adult responsibilities, his observation of the 'invention' or, rather, rise in 'youth culture' is particularly noteworthy. The phenomenon of 'youth' is, as Bruce suggests, a creation of late-modern societies. Previously, children, in all societies, passed from their childhood directly into adulthood via puberty. In the process, children where often under-educated, exploited by industry and married with children as young as 13. Changes in UK and western governments' legislation relating to education, employment and marriage have both protected children and at the same time reflected the development of youth culture. These protective laws have increased the age of state education, employment and marriage (with parental consent) currently to the age of 16 in the UK. Youth culture has had a profound impact on modern societies in the realms of popular music, fashion and liberal and radical attitudes to drugs, sex, religion and politics. The combined effects of 'youth cultures' on modern societies can be said to have given young people many rights but, as Bruce and many others assert, few responsibilities. The result of this perceived lack of social responsibility means that young people often become 'scapegoats' for wider society's ills, rendering them as generally 'anti-social', 'defiant', 'problematic' and 'rebellious'. These prevalent attitudes towards young people mean that they are also frequently ignored and neglected. Unfortunately, engaging with young people has increasingly been relinquished to under-staffed and poorly-funded youth work agencies at the local government and voluntary community association levels.

Muslim youth in Britain and the West

Young people from most societies in the modern world are faced with a never-ending series of complex challenges and experiences that bring into question their moral, cultural and religious beliefs and practices as a daily consequence of interaction with life. Negotiating these awkward and difficult situations can be perplexing enough for any young person, but what happens when one's particular religious beliefs and cultural traditions are not those of the wider society in which one lives? In this case, the challenges and experiences of the individual are exacerbated by underlying tensions already existing as a result of religious and cultural differences. Such is the situation facing many young Muslims living as minorities in Britain and the West and where an increasing majority of Muslims are now born.[1] In Islamic countries, where Muslims represent a majority, the youth population of those societies is generally well over 50 per cent. In both the minority and majority situations, societies are undergoing rapid changes that are challenging traditional ideas regarding the family, cultural belonging and national identity. Furthermore, as western-emanating globalization imposes an ever-increasing consumerism and materialism, religious and spiritual orientations are gradually eroding. Young Muslims are invariably expected to overcome all of these modern temptations and instead become the future guardians of Muslim integrity and religious fidelity. However, the idealism and optimism of Muslim youth is often manifested in two counter-distinctive realities: spiritual maturity, intellectual engagement and social interaction; or emotional rejectionism, narrow identity politics and religious extremism. These broader questions of identity and 'belongingness' often overshadow the real issues facing young Muslims (particularly those living as minorities) such as, alcohol and drugs, sexuality and gender, educational underachievement, social responsibility, violence, racism and Islamophobia and employment expectations. The perennial question facing those seeking to engage with young Muslims through the provision of youth work is: what practices and methodologies can be best employed to 'reach out' and evoke positive influence and change to affect the lives of young Muslim people? Almost a generation ago, Khurram Murad (1932–96), the former Director General of The Islamic Foundation, Leicester, UK, posed a very perplexing question directed at the youth population for the then burgeoning post-World War Two Muslim community in Britain. The introductory paragraph of his pamphlet, 'Muslim Youth in the West: Towards a New Education Strategy' (1986) bluntly asks:

> What future awaits the Muslim youth in Britain, or, for that matter in any similar predominantly non-Muslim secular society? This crucial question haunts every sensitive and concerned Muslim mind. We are desperately looking for an answer, for a proper viable strategy, an education strategy as we put it, to ensure that our children grow up and remain Muslims. This is a desideratum of the utmost urgency and importance. For the future of the Ummah[2] here, of our families, traditions, and institutions, of the numerous mosques that have come to dot the landscape today, some of them built at huge costs. (p. 3)

Twenty-five years on and little seems to have changed in terms of the Muslim communities' attitudes and accommodations for their youth. And, although there are a number of youth initiatives that have recently sprouted in response to the previous Labour government's counter-terrorist initiative, 'Contact 2: Preventing Violent Extremism', the established pattern for dealing with 'youth issues' has been to leave the youth problems to either the local authorities, nearby mosques or overtly Islamic groups and associations. In short, no serious effort has been made that engages the Muslim communities to address the issues, concerns and anxieties faced by Muslim youths in Britain and the West. This chapter will seek to offer 'best practices' through a faith-based approach to Muslim youth work from the paradigms of the primary sources of Islamic learning: the Qur'an, as the sacred text of Muslims; and the *Sunnah*, the life example of the Prophet Muhammad, as contained within the *ahadith* (Prophetic narrations). In its limited capacity, this chapter will examine two particular underlying issues and concerns facing Muslim youths in the minority context of Britain and the West: i) alcohol and drugs, and ii) sex and relationships, seeking to offer Qur'anic and Prophetic solutions through the use of applied traditional methodologies of *tarbiyyah* (educational training) and *tazkiyyah* (spiritual self-development). This particular approach is consciously meant to appeal to the religious facets of British Muslim youth identity, and is proposed as a complimentary strategy to existing youth work practices.

The Qur'an and *Sunnah*: The 'Time-Space' context

In order to employ the most appropriate application of the teachings of the Qur'an and *Sunnah*, as a means of providing a comprehensive methodology for engaging with Muslims youths, it is important to understand these primary sources within a particular 'time-space' context. By this phrase, we mean to establish a set of principles and approaches in dealing with the very real issues and concerns that young Muslims face, living as minorities, in their daily interactions. If we are to address their issues and concerns in a faith-based and faith-sensitive way, then it is imperative that the Qur'an and *Sunnah* are comprehended holistically, as a universal divine text and Prophetic guidance from which the relevant wisdoms, advice and solutions specifically relating to young people are correctly extracted and effectively employed. The important inter-relatedness of the Qur'an and Prophetic teachings is established in the following verses:

> And we sent you not (Muhammad) but as a mercy for all created beings. (Qur'an, 21:107)

> We sent you as a messenger to mankind: God suffices as a witness. Anyone who obeys the messenger has obeyed God, and whosoever turns away; then We have not sent you as a guardian over them. (Qur'an, 4:79–80)

> In God's messenger you have a perfect example for someone who seeks to return to God and the Last Day, and remembers God frequently. (Qur'an, 33:21)

Taha Jabir al-'Alwani and Imad al-Din Khalil (1999), inform us, regarding the revelation of the Qur'an's verses, that:

> The Qur'an was revealed in separate instalments. Most of these were connected with specific situations and events, in order to prepare the people's hearts, minds and souls to accept, understand and meditate on it at the time of revelation. (p. 12)

The divine process of a slow, gradual and well-arranged revelation of the Qur'anic text was so that people would have enough time to understand, absorb, memorize and fix the meanings of the divine verses and directives permanently within their collective consciousness. They could also internalize the spiritual dimensions of the divine text within their hearts and souls, thus understanding the revelations both exoterically and esoterically. In this way they could receive the divine revelations as both a practical religious instruction and spiritual guidance. Al-'Alawani and Khalil elucidate the relevance of this gradual process of revelation stating: 'The Qur'an contains basic conceptions and general rules, guidance and advice valid for all human beings in every place and time and every realm of life.(p.12)' They go on to explain that if the revelations were merely restricted to the specific events and minor details and issues relevant to the period of its particular revelation, then the Qur'an and the Prophetic teachings could not have acquired its uniqueness of time-space universality (ibid.). Establishing the importance of the Islamic primary sources is essential to developing a methodology for engaging with Muslim youths that encompasses their cultural and religious sensitivities as well as their psychosocial well-being. Scholars such as Tariq Ramadan, Taha Jabir al-'Alawani and Imad al-Din Khalil, argue that a two-approach 'reading' of the primary texts needs to be developed in order to apply a time-space context to the texts. The first approach, al-'Alwani and Khalil assert, is to read the texts as a primary source for the past history of nations whose particular narratives were transmitted for the purposes of admonition and warning as well as revealing details concerning the Hereafter and the Unseen, with the *ahadith* literature providing the much-needed minutia relevant for *fiqh* rulings (ibid., p. 14). Such a reading has, albeit unintentionally, lead to a restricted 'reading' of the texts which confined the miracles of the Qur'an to the levels of literary elegance, inimitable poetic style and rhetoric. This limited approach, al-'Alawani and Khalil argue, 'curbs the enthusiasm to seek those aspects that are renewable and applicable for every time and space.' (ibid.) In order for Muslims to engage effectively and contextually with their primary sources, they need to develop a 'reading' of the text that goes beyond the three general aims of the first approach: 1) acquiring knowledge of earlier peoples and nations, 2) the Hereafter and the Unseen, and 3) *fiqh* rulings. The second approach or 'stage' proposed by al-'Alawani and Khalil points to other essential aims:

i)   To obtain general guidance in human affairs and the sciences that deal with individual and social behaviour as well as with *fitrah* [innate nature].

ii) To acquire knowledge of the basic rules and guidelines for reforming society as well as its political system - in a manner consistent with its view of both human and social nature – and to endeavour to discover how this can be achieved. (ibid., p. 15)

For the purposes of this particular chapter we need not detail the extended discussions relating to *tafaasir* (exegetical approaches) or arguments dealing with the particularities of *usul al-fiqh* (Islamic legal theory). However, utilizing al-'Alawani and Khalil's 'second stage' reading of the primary texts, employing its general principles

and methodology, we need to survey the Qur'an and *Sunnah* in
relation to its injunctions, advice and approaches to young people
and the specific issues and problems they currently face as minority
Muslims in Britain and the West.

Muslim youth issues and concerns

Identifying what are the pressing issues and concerns facing young
Muslims in modern Britain and the West is not as easy as it seems.
This is because often what are claimed to be issues relating to young
people are actually projected onto them by wider society. As a
result, these perceived problems tend to reflect a general pathology
of young people in which youths are viewed largely in terms of
their defiance and rebellion towards their parents, community
leaders and elders and society at large. In respect of young British
Muslims, their perceived problems are compounded by a series of
external factors that range from realizing the particular religious and
cultural aspirations of their parents to being profiled as confused,
belligerent and extremist in regards to identity, religious practices
and matters of faith. All of the above imposing issues and problems
have produced a particular stereotype of young Muslims as both
dysfunctional and highly problematic. Psychologists would affirm
that this negative, accusatory approach towards young people is
extremely counter-productive and that focusing or reiterating
deficiencies and faults in young people invariably produces a 'self-
fulfilling prophecy' of negativity, underachievement and alienation.
For the majority of young Muslims the issues and problems they
face in their difficult and formative adolescent years are perhaps
relatively mundane in comparison to the perceived problems of
laxity (*dhalalah*) and extremism (*ghuluw*) imposed upon them, but
they are by no means less important for the youngsters who have
to negotiate their way through them. The charge of *dhalalah* is
often levelled at young Muslims by their parents and elders of the
community, who believe that youths are failing in their religious
and cultural observances and that as a result they are 'going
astray'. Often these concerns are misplaced and are as a direct
result of mounting 'peer pressure' on parents and elders to be seen
to be doing the right thing. As Ruqaiyyah Waris Maqsood (1995)
suggests:

If you are a deeply spiritual person, the whole thing [parenting teenagers] is complicated by feelings of guilt if you are not producing the kind of young adult you think you aught to be producing. Will your off-spring cause scandal at the mosque, and be badly thought of by the Imam? If your son or daughter goes wrong, will others at the mosque start pointing the finger at you, and assuming that you have failed or done something wrong? (p. 7)

Clearly, the need to conform to community expectations can be a worrying concern for many parents, but this concern can often manifest in a gross mishandling and flawed approach with one's own children. Equally, the policy-driven assertions that young Muslims in general present a 'real and immanent danger' to society at large because of their misguided religious beliefs and practices, which are steeped in *ghuluw* (extremism) and *tashdid* (bigotry), is seriously defective and potentially perilous. A leaked MI5 report in August 2008 by the security service's Behavioural Science Unit revealed that possible would-be Muslim terrorists in Britain are not religious extremists; rather, they are largely 'demographically unremarkable'.[3] Of those arrested and charged for acts of terrorism it was found that very few came from religious households and some are even known to have taken drugs, consumed alcohol and visited prostitutes. However, they were not prone to mental health problems or pathological personality traits. They came from diverse ethnic backgrounds including Pakistani, Middle Eastern and Caucasian, and the proportion of converts to Islam among this particular group is above average. The report also claimed that radical clerics have less of a role in radicalizing youths. Most terrorists appeared to have become radicalized in their early to mid-20s and, overall, they are: 'a diverse collection of individuals, fitting no single demographic profile, nor do they follow a typical pathway to violent extremism. (*Daily Mail*, 21/11/2008)' The MI5's 'restricted' briefing note concluded that there is evidence that a well-established religious identity actually protects many young Muslims against violent radicalization.

However, the realities on the ground are often far removed from the negative representations, perceptions and headline-grabbing media depictions of young Muslims in Britain. This is not to deny

the existence of a fringe minority of young Muslims who are drawn
to religious extremism and terrorist violence, but, rather, to highlight
the realities that the majority experience for British Muslim youths
are ignored or overshadowed by the continued charge of 'identity
crisis' and the current intermittent acts of wrongly named 'Islamic
terrorism'. What is needed when addressing the concerns of young
Muslims is an empathetic, tolerant, moderate and proportional
response, rather than a hostile, confrontational, emotional and
heavy-handed approach. As with all worldly affairs and dealings,
Islam encourages believers to develop a position of moderation, and
the religious duty of the universal Muslim community (*ummah*) as
a 'nation of moderation' (*ummatan wasatan*) is:

> Thus We have brought you forward as a moderate nation so
> that you may act as witnesses to mankind, as the Messenger is a
> witness over you. (Qur'an, 2:143)

Moderation (*wasta*) occupies the balanced central position between
laxity (*dhalalah*) on the one hand and extremism or excessiveness
(*ghuluw*) on the other. This position of moderation when engaging
with young Muslims is critical in developing a dialogue and
an understanding with young people who often claim that their
concerns and voices are usually left ignored when it comes to
discussions regarding their particular predicaments. That is to say,
our approach in dealing and engaging with young Muslims needs
to be both balanced and measured, one that is neither too remote,
disengaged and apathetic nor, equally, interfering, severe or over-
burdensome when confronted with their needs, desires, concerns,
problems, issues, aspirations and anxieties. Making mistakes is
often a consequence of life and usually something we would not
do with the benefit of hindsight or experience, which is quite often
the predicament of young people. This is why young people are
often exposed and vulnerable to many temptations and deviant
distractions that might appear to them as exciting and intriguing
activities and experiences. The Qur'an refers to these alluring
distractions of worldly life in numerous verses:

> What is the life of this world but play and amusement? But best
> is the home in the Hereafter, for those who are righteous, will
> you not then understand? (Qur'an, 6:32)

The life of this world is but play and amusement: And if you believe and guard against evil, He (God) will grant you your recompense, and will not ask you to give up your possessions. (Qur'an, 47:36)

Know you (all) that the life of this world is but play and amusement, pomp and mutual boasting and multiplying (in rivalry) amongst yourselves, riches and children. (Qur'an, 57:20)

Without doubt, you (mankind) love the fleeting life! (Qur'an, 75:20)

There are a number of important issues that are common to British Muslim youths regardless of their particular ethnic and cultural origins. This has less to do with the specific ways in which they understand and manifest their distinctive geo-cultural religious identities, through the varied forms of 'Muslimness' which are present within the very diverse British Muslim landscape, and more to do with what they experience and observe within wider British society, through their everyday lives in school, at college or work, and in their social and recreational realms. Many of these issues, although often encountered by personal experience or observed at very close proximity, are largely taboo subjects that often cannot easily be discussed with parents or community elders because they are deemed *haram* (prohibited) or *makruh* (objectionable) subjects and activities according to Islamic law. However, their religious prohibition does not prevent nor avoid them from being real issues faced by young Muslims brought up and living in non-Muslim environments. For this reason it is only right that these issues and problems are not only identified and discussed rationally and sensitively, but that a suitable approach in how to address these particular concerns is gleaned from the primary religious sources as a means of confirming Islam's claim to provide: i) a solution for all human problems: 'We sent down (in stages) in the Qur'an that which is a healing and a mercy to those who believe' (Qur'an, 17:82); ii) that encompasses all epochs: 'Verily, this is no less than a message to (all) the worlds. (A profit) to whoever among you desires to go straight' (Qur'an, 81:27–8); and iii) in every situation: 'A Guide and a Mercy to the doers of good' (Qur'an, 31:3). In this particular context this chapter intends to explore how Islamically derived solutions as a practical methodology can be applied to two

distinct areas affecting Muslim youths – alcohol and drugs, and sex
and relationships.

Alcohol and drugs

Many of the biggest social problems in Britain and in the West are
associated with the use of alcohol and drugs. The direct affects are
primarily to do with abuse and addiction and related crimes; from
violence and abuse to petty theft and organized drugs trafficking.
Whenever economic recession increases so too does alcohol and
drug dependency, as people seek a temporary, if not dangerous,
escape from their financial difficulties and social burdens. As
a result, what occurs is a downward spiral of social decline and
civic disorder. Islam seeks to develop a preventative approach
to the problem by forbidding the availability and partaking of
alcohol and drugs in society. In divine law (*shari'ah*) and canonical
jurisprudence (*fiqh*) all substances that contaminate the body and
spirit by befogging the mind are known collectively by the single
definition, *khamr*. The word literally means 'to cover the head'
and the word 'headscarf' (*khimar*) comes from the same root. In
a *hadith* the Prophet Muhammad said: 'Every intoxicant is *khamr*
and all *khamr* is *haram* [forbidden]'.[4] As if to clarify the Prophet's
instruction and clarify the prohibition of all intoxicating substances,
the second caliph (*khalifah*), 'Umar ibn al-Khattab (circa 586–644
CE), is reported to have declared: '*Khamr* is (everything) that befogs
the mind.'[5] For young Muslims living in non-Muslim spaces such as
the UK, avoiding proximity to the consumption of alcohol can be
very difficult. Furthermore, the use of so-called 'recreational drugs'
such as marijuana, cocaine, amphetamines and opiates has become
widespread and tolerated to the point that it is no longer considered
a crime or social taboo. This prevalent attitude compounds the
problem for Muslims who are guided not only to avoid partaking
in *khamr*, but are also forbidden to engage in associated activities
such as, growing, fermenting, producing, transporting and trading
in *khamr*, and also serving and handling it along with sitting with
those who consume it. While the *fiqh* categories concerning the
prohibition of *khamr* are clear and agreed upon by the majority
('*ijma*) of Islamic scholars ('*ulama*), it is not surprising that many
young Muslims raised in the West are quite ignorant of the collective

idea of *khamr* as that which includes both alcoholic drinks and narcotic substances. Conversely, many Muslim youths actually mistakenly believe that while alcohol is *khamr* and therefore prohibited, marijuana, bush, skunk, hashish, grass, weed, blow and so on,[6] because of their non-fermented or 'natural' state, are not *khamr*, and are thereby permissible. By the same inclination, this erroneous belief also extends to synthetically produced narcotics such as cocaine, opium, LSD, ecstasy, whizz, speed and crack.[7] Thus, because of a limited understanding and definition of the term *khamr*, a significant number of young Muslims have wrongly become 'recreational users' of narcotic substances, ignorantly believing that they are not defined as *khamr* along with alcoholic drinks, which are widely known to be *haram*.

How then do we effectively engage with this social reality and how do we deal with *khamr* (intoxicants) abuse among young Muslims? In addressing this growing serious issue, it is pertinent to begin by exploring how the Qur'an and Prophetic narrations tackle this particular issue while at the same time considering the 'time-space' factor of the revelation process. This approach is extremely important in identifying an appropriate methodology for engaging with the contemporary problem of alcohol and drug abuse among young Muslims. Shaykh Yusuf al-Qaradawi, a leading contemporary Islamic jurist, informs us that the pre-Islamic Arabs were fond of drinking wine and other forms of alcoholic drinks. So great was their love and indulgence of alcohol that their language had almost 100 names for it and their poetry was littered with references to wine and drinking parties (al-Qaradawi, 1997, p. 90). How, then, does God's revelation approach the problem of widespread alcoholism? Al-Qaradawi addresses this question in clear and concise terms, informing us that God 'adopted a wise course of education [*tarbiyyah*] and training [*tazkiyyah*] prohibiting it [*khamr*] in measured stages' (ibid.). The method of adopting a measured approach to a social problem that has become an embedded cultural practice is a specific methodology that was employed for the staged revelation of the Qur'an:

And the unbelievers say: 'Why is not the Qur'an revealed to him at once?' (It is revealed) in this manner that We may strengthen your heart thereby, and We have rehearsed it to you in slow well-arranged stages, gradually. (Qur'an, 25:32)

(It is) a Qur'an which We have divided (into parts from time to time), in order that you might recite it to men at intervals: We have revealed it by stages. (Qur'an, 17:106)

Al-Qaradawi also informs us that the first stage in weaning the early Muslims from *khamr* was to initially clarify that the harm caused by it is far greater than that of its limited benefits. The second stage advises Muslims that they should not offer their prayers (*salat*) while they are in the state of intoxication. Finally, God revealed the two verses in Chapter Five prohibiting *khamr* completely:

O you who believe, truly intoxicants and gambling and idol worship and divination by arrows are an abomination of Satan's doing: avoid it in order that you may prosper. Assuredly Satan desires to sow enmity and hatred among you with intoxicants and gambling and to hinder you from the remembrance of Allah and from prayers. Will you then not desist? (Qur'an, 5:90–1)

Just as these two verses explicitly forbid intoxicants and gambling, equating them with the greater evil of *shirk* (polytheism), through worshipping idols and fortune-telling, they also spell out the social evils associated with intoxicants and gambling – enmity and hatred. The preceding associated verses relating to the prohibition of *khamr* provide an incremental distancing from the habit of intoxicants by first offering a rational response:

They ask you concerning intoxicants and gambling. Say: 'In each of them there lies serious vice as well as some benefits for mankind. Yet their vice is greater than their benefits.' (Qur'an, 2:219)

Clearly the verse concludes by reasoning that the harmful effects of both intoxicants and gambling far outweigh any perceived benefits. This first verse regarding *khamr* appeals to the higher moral and ethical conscience of believers, while at the same time avoiding any outright condemnation of partaking in intoxicants. The effect is to create doubt regarding intoxicants by urging believers to rationally weigh the 'pros and cons' of intoxicants and gambling, implying in conclusion that the best option is voluntary abstention. Equally, by the time the second verse regarding *khamr* is revealed, for those not already convinced by the rational arguments and moral encouragement of the first verse, a specific prohibition is ordained which prohibits Muslims from offering their prayers (*salat*) while under the influence of *khamr*:

> O you, who believe, do not attempt to pray while you are intoxicated until you know what you are saying. (Qur'an, 4:43)

This specific prohibition carries a deeper wisdom that effectively curtails the partaking of intoxicants for Muslims by ensuring that they are fit to offer their daily obligatory prayers in a sober state of mind. Further, because the ordination of the five daily prayers was established at the time of the Prophet's night journey and accession (*al-isr'a wa al-mi'raj*), which occurred before the *hijrah* (migration) from Makkah to Madinah, it became practically impossible for Muslims to take *khamr* and also attend their five daily prayers. However, reaching this level and degree of devotion and fidelity to the commands of God was not instantly achieved, and as the staged revelatory process suggests, it took some time for Muhammad's first community to reject its established cultural traditions and practices and undertake the radical social reforms instituted by Islam. Throughout this transformation the Prophet remained patient and empathetic towards his followers, supporting them physically, emotionally, psychologically and spiritually. There are a number of sound narrations in which the Prophet referred specifically to the drinks of paradise which included references to fountains of pure water, milk and honey, along with heavenly wines free from intoxicants and drinks of camphor and *zanjabil* (a ginger-based beverage), all served in ornate golden and silver goblets. These many descriptions of heavenly offerings provide both an encouragement and reward for the patience and constancy of Muslims in their obedience of God's commands. What is clear from the staged revelations regarding the prohibition of *khamr* is that:

i) The first verse (Qur'an, 2:219) was both empathetic and non-judgemental of intoxicants. It acknowledged the limited benefits of *khamr* while reasoning that the vices far exceeded them. It encouraged Muslims to consider the moral and ethical implications of intoxicants.

ii) The second verse (Qur'an, 4:43) restrained the use of *khamr* by commanding Muslims not to offer their prayers while intoxicated. This made it practically impossible to both consume intoxicants and attend prayers, thus forcing Muslims to make a moral choice between prayer and *khamr*.

iii) The final verses (Qur'an, 5: 90–1) reduce intoxicants and gambling to the most debased acts (*rijs*) comparing them to worshipping idols and fortune-telling, acts of *shirk* (polytheism) considered to be an unforgivable sin in Islam.

This three-staged methodology of: i) empathy and non-judgemental attitudes, ii) encouraging restraint and moral propriety, and iii) exercising rejection and condemnation, displays what Muslims believe to be a divine wisdom in dealing with a real social problem that allows for personal reform and betterment while displaying empathy and kindness through the process of recovery and amelioration before imposing rejection and condemnation. This staged approach in dealing with a serious social problem encompasses a number of distinct ways of dealing with a problem that is both differentiated and holistic, allowing to move from empathy to encouraging propriety before imposing rejection and condemnation where needed, in the case of no effort to self-reform or abate indulging in *khamr*. This useful and comprehensive three-stage methodology can be applied to any number of other difficult issues and problems relating to young Muslims. Results would not be instantaneous or necessarily guaranteed, but this particular methodology allows a religiously empathetic and faith-based approach in engaging with young Muslims.

Sex and relationships

Possibly one of the most challenging problems faced by Muslim youths and parents alike living in both non-Muslim and Muslim environments is the issue of sex. In the case of non-Muslim societies this is largely due to the wider cultural attitudes to sex in modern, liberal, secular societies. As with the changing lax attitudes to alcohol and drugs in the West, many European societies have developed what they term an 'open-minded' view on sex and sexual relations. We need not discuss in detail the reasons for this shifting social attitude to sex, accept to say that increasing secularity has generally eroded the former dominant Judaeo – Christian values and morals regarding sex and marriage, shifting attitiudes away from religious teachings that encouraged chastity and preferred marriage towards a 'free' attitude to sex without the restraints of religion, morality or ethics. Kecia Ali (2006) states: 'sex is paradoxically both the most private, intimate act humans can undertake and a profoundly social activity' (p. 56). It is for this reason that she asserts that all civilizations and societies regulate sexual activity among their members. However, she is quick to add that the particular ways in which pre-modern Muslim jurists configured the formulations of lawful and unlawful sexual acts, 'does not match Muslims living in the west' (ibid., p. 57). She makes this claim on the strength that the rising age of marriage for both sexes living in both Muslim and non-Muslim societies has precipitated alternative de facto forms of sexual relations 'notwithstanding the continuing importance of female virginity in many communities'(ibid., p. 58). This is despite the willingness on the part of most Muslims to confront the reality of sex outside of marriage. However, beyond the cultural shifts in the later age of marriage, due largely to the importance placed on higher education, Ali suggests that there has been a developed change in the views towards sex 'as an activity that is primarily about the mutual consent and individual attachment of the persons involved', a view which she claims is quite prevalent among minority Muslim youths in the West (ibid., p. 59). In conclusion, Ali observes that 'if everyone refuses to publicly discuss the fact that, with the disappearance of early marriage, many [young] Muslims are not waiting for marriage to have sex, the problem continues' (ibid., p. 73).

How then do Muslims guide and council their youths through the prevalent irreligious and liberal attitudes to sex and marriage within the non-Muslim societies in which they live? Do they develop and advocate a reactionary approach to sex by imposing a suppression of a natural, God-given appetite by encouraging severe religious asceticism and virtual monasticism by locking-up their adolescents away from the temptations in the outside world? Or do they adopt a more realistic and rational approach that accepts the sexual appetite as a divine gift to humans as a means of procreation, physical satisfaction and emotional fulfilment that is to be enjoyed only within the bond of marriage? Al-Qaradawi (1997) informs us that:

'Islam duly recognises the role of the sexual drive, facilitates its
satisfaction through lawful marriage, and just as it prohibits
sex outside of marriage and even what is conducive to it, it also
prohibits celibacy and the shunning of women [and in the case
of women, men].' (p. 196)

If Islam encourages a wholesome and pure attitude to sex that
is without excess and devoid of deprivation and suffering, it is
appropriate that a proper sex education for young Muslims is
developed which clearly explains the spiritual aims and propagates
a religious understanding of the issue so that these desires can be
properly fulfilled in due course (Maqsood, 1995). The Qur'an
commands Muslims: 'And do not come near *zina*, indeed it is an
abomination and an evil way' (Qur'an, 17:23). The word *zina*
means 'illicit sex', which includes both fornication and adultery,
and the verse not only prohibits the acts of fornication and adultery,
but 'it [also] closes all the avenues of approach to it' (al-Qaradwi,
1997, p. 197). In so doing, Islam thereby forbids whatever evokes
sexual passions, promotes indecency and obscenity and opens ways
for illicit sexual relations. These prohibited activities include:

i) *Khalwah*–literally, 'seclusion', but used to denote both a
'spiritual retreat' and a 'secret liaison' between people. In
the specific context of *zina*, it is used to mean a place where
a non-*mahram*[8] male and female might be in privacy. This
prohibition is meant as a protection for individuals from the
possibility of wrongful thoughts and sexual feelings that may
arise as a result of being alone without the fear of intrusion by
a third person. A Prophetic *hadith* carefully reminds Muslims:
'Whoever believes in Allah and the Last Day must never be
in privacy with a woman who is without a *mahram* present,
for otherwise Satan will be the third person [present].'[9] This
Prophetic advice warns against both married and unmarried
people from the dangers of such intimate liaisons that might
stir emotional and physical feelings of desire.

ii) Lustful gazes – the Qur'an instructs: 'Tell the believing men that
they should lower their gazes and guard their sexual organs;
that is purer for them. Indeed, Allah is well-acquainted with
what they do. And tell the believing women that they should
lower their gazes and guard their private parts and not display

their adornment except that which is apparent of it'(Qur'an, 24:30–1). It is often said that sexual desire begins with a particular glance or gaze that 'sparks a flame of passion'. The Prophet advised the young 'Ali ibn Abu Talib, saying: 'Ali, do not let the second glance follow the first. The first look is allowed to you but the second is against you [prohibited].'[10] In this context the idea of 'lowering the gaze' does not mean that one should not look at the opposite sex, but instead, avoid lustful glances and gazes, as the Prophet also said: 'the eyes also commit *zina* and their *zina* is the lustful gaze.'[11]

iii) Looking at the *'awrah* – *'awrah* means 'that which is to be hidden', and it refers to the parts of the male and female body that are to be covered in front of others (male and female) in Islam. Looking at the *'awrah* of others has been expressly forbidden by the Prophet, who said: 'a man should not look at the *'awrah* of another man, nor a woman of a woman, nor should a man go under one cloth with another man, nor a woman with another woman.'[12] The *'awrah* of a man is generally considered to be from his navel to his knees, although some jurists exclude the knee. For a woman, the *'awrah* is generally considered to be her entire body except her hands and face. Although, for women, this complete idea of the *'awrah* differs for her *mahram* males: her husband, children, nephews, father and brothers and so on. Shaykh al-Qaradawi (op.cit) has explained: 'what is *haram* to look at is also of course *haram* to touch with the hands or any other part of the body' (p. 203). It is not necessary or expedient to discuss the particular *fiqh* rules and classifications relating to *'awrah* and dress in the wider *mahram* contexts in this chapter.[13]

While the introductory discussion above sets out the wider moral and ethical philosophy regarding sex and sexual relations in Islam, the reality for many Muslim youths is that while they are experiencing the physical and emotional feelings of the sexual drive, they may not be in a position to marry and, therefore, fulfil their sexual desires. In this situation we need to explore how the Qur'an and *Sunnah* advises single young adults to deal with their sexual feelings. Islam's insistence on the institution of marriage at an early youthful age was not problematic in pre-modern societies in which the concept of 'youth' and 'adolescence' was biologically, rather than legally, defined. In such a cultural understanding, marriage consent was not prescribed by a particular age; it was instead determined by an individual's puberty. In other words, the age of consent was usually considered to be post-puberty. The legal term for 'post-puberty' in Islamic jurisprudence is *baligh*, meaning 'adulthood'. In these particular social conditions and customs, the general expectation was that as soon as one reached adulthood (*baligh*), marriage would naturally follow. This custom was also commonly practised in Europe as recently as the late nineteenth century, a historical detail giving some credence to Bruce's claim of the 'invention of youth' as a post-World War Two phenomenon.[14] For young Muslims acculturated into the modern western tradition of 'youth culture', they find themselves in a precarious position in which they are physically and biologically adult, according to Islamic law, but, in terms of British law, unable to marry legally until the age of 18.[15] Let us then consider that the majority of young British Muslims do not have the means to marry, even if parental consent is given, other social factors – cultural, economic, social and so on – may mean that marrying is impractical, if not impossible. A Prophetic *hadith* advises: 'Young men, those of you who can support a wife should marry, for it lowers your gaze (protects you from lustfully looking at women) and preserves your chastity; but those who cannot should fast for it is a means of cooling sexual passion.'[16]

This *hadith* is extremely important in understanding the dilemma facing young people who are unable to marry yet have a naturally developed sexual urge. In such difficult circumstances young people may resort to masturbation as a means of relieving their sexual tension. For the majority of Islamic scholars masturbation is considered *haram* based on a particular understanding of the following verse:

> Those who guard their sexual organs except with their spouses or those who their right hands possess, for (with regards to them) they are without blame. But those who crave something beyond that are transgressors. (Qur'an, 23:5–7)

Jurists argue that the phrase, 'those who crave something else' refers to fornicators and adulterers but also includes masturbators.

However, a significant number of scholars, including Imam Ahmad Ibn Hanbal, regard semen as an excretion of the body, like other excreta such as urine, faeces and blood; and just as blood-letting is permitted, so too is masturbation. Conditionally, jurists permit masturbating in limited circumstances: i) fear of committing fornication and adultery, and ii) not having the means to marry. Al-Qaradawi (1997) prefers this ruling, particularly where young people are in a situation where 'there is sexual excitement and danger of committing *haram*' (p. 224). He goes on to say that in situations where young people may be encountering many temptations that: 'he [or she] fears he will be unable to resist may resort to this method [masturbation] of relieving sexual tension provided he does not do it excessively or makes it into a habit' (ibid.). It is important here that we refer back to the *hadith* quoted above in order to establish a preference regarding the issue of young Muslims, sex and marriage:

i)   The Prophet advises all young people who are able to marry to do so.

ii) Marrying both 'lowers the gaze' and protects the chastity of young people.

iii) Young people unable to marry are advised to fast regularly.

iv) Fasting for young unmarried people 'cools sexual passion'; that is, sexual desires are naturally tempered through the religious observance of *sawm* (fasting).[17]

With regards to marriage, it is worth reiterating that Islam elevates the institution of marriage as exampled by the Prophet's life. Conversely, celibacy is strongly discouraged as humankind's primordial parents, Adam and Eve, were created to live together in peace and harmony. Thus, they present the paradigm for every believing couple entering into marriage. Because sex outside of marriage is prohibited, Islam upholds that marrying completes half of a Muslim's faith, and that sex and procreation within marriage are not base acts, but natural pleasures that even carry spiritual rewards. The primary consideration when choosing a marriage partner is *taqwah* (a heightened awareness of God) because *nikah* (marriage) is a civil contract (*aqd*) in which both consenting partners are bound by its mutually agreed terms. Without the expressed consent of both partners and the attestation of the contract by two witnesses, the *nikah* is invalid according to Islamic *shari'ah*.[18] The husband has the responsibility of financial maintenance and although the wife is free to pursue a career, she is seen as the source of peace and comfort in the family home (Bokhari and Seddon, 2010).

Conclusion

I have endeavoured to illustrate throughout this chapter that, by the application of the Qur'anic and *Sunnah* (Prophetic) paradigms to two specific and pertinent Muslim youth-related issues, it is possible to extract appropriate methodological approaches to particular concerns that are empathetic to the pervading cultural conditions, are correctly extrapolated and are effectively employed. On the basis of the particular 'time-space' contextual 'reading' of the relevant verses and *ahadith* relating to the issues and problems tackled in this chapter, I would argue that it has been possible to comply with al-'Alawani and Khalil's 'second stage reading' of the Islamic primary sources that provides both:

   i) 'a general guidance in human affairs and the sciences that deal with individual social behaviour as well as the *fitrah* [innate nature].' In this case, that is a particular approach or educational training (*tarbiyyah*) of how to engage with young people's specific issues and concerns.

And,

   ii) 'knowledge of the basic rules and guidelines for reforming society as well as its political system – in a manner consistent with its view of human and social nature – and to endeavour to discover how this can be achieved.' In this particular context, a spiritual and psychosocial reform (*tazkiyyah*) is offered through the incremental methodology instructed by the Qur'anic and Prophetic teachings relating to the specific youth issues and concerns explored in this chapter.

Based on the primary source paradigms explored in this chapter, I would confidently suggest that other pressing issues relating to Muslim youths in Britain and the West – such as educational underachievement, social responsibility, violence and religious extremism, employment expectations and so forth – could be tackled by employing the same methodology: a 'time-space' contextualization of the relevant primary source teachings relating to the particular youth issues listed above. Further, I would also suggest that what is also needed is a greater articulation and propagation – which would encompass the collective works of academics, religious scholars and youth work practitioners – of a faith-based and faith-sensitive approach in engaging with young Muslims as a complimentary approach to existing generic methods and practices in youth work.

References

Al-'Alwani, Taha Jabir, and Khalil, Imad al-Din (1999), *The Qur'an and Sunnah: The Time-Space Factor*. Herndon, Virginia and London: International Islamic Publishing House and International Institute of Islamic Thought.

Al-Qaradawi, Yusuf (1997), *The Lawful and the Prohibited in Islam*. Cairo: El-Falah Publishing.

Ali, Kecia (2006), *Sexual Ethics and Islam: Feminist Reflections on Qur'an, Hadith and Jurisprudence*. Oxford: Oneworld Publications.

Bokhari, Raana, and Seddon, Mohammad (2010), *The Illustrated Encyclopedia of Islam*. London: Lorenz Books.

Bruce, Steve (1995), *Religion in Modern Britain*. Oxford: Oxford University Press.

The Daily Mail, 'Islamic terrorists could be from any race, warns secret MI5 report', 21 September 2008. (http://www.dailymail.co.uk/news/article-1047577/Islamic-terrorists-race-warns-secret-MI5-report.html, accessed 26/5/11.)

Hogget, Brenda M., and Pearl, David S. (1987), *Family Law and Society: Cases and Materials*. London: Butterworths.

Maqsood, Ruqaiyyah Waris (1995), *Living With Teenagers: A Guide for Muslim Parents*. London: Ta Ha Publishers Ltd.

Murad, Khurram (1986), 'Muslim youth in the west: towards a new education strategy'. Leicester: The Islamic Foundation.

Seddon, Mohammad Siddique, Malik, Nadeem, and Hussain, Dilwar (eds) (2003), *'British Muslims: Loyalty and Belonging'*. Leicester: The Islamic Foundation and the Citizen Organizing Foundation.

WEBSITES, ADDRESSES AND CONTACTS OF PROMINENT AGENCIES, INSTITUTIONS AND ORGANISATIONS DEDICATED TO MUSLIM YOUTH WORK

NATIONAL (UK)

Amal Trust (**Light of the Youth**), 15h Bourne House, London, 020 7727 5882, www.amaltrust.org

Islamic Youth Movement, 425 Cheetham Hill Road, Manchester, 0161 205 6662, www.islamicyouthmovement.20m.com

Muslim Youth Foundation, Clydesdale House, Manchester, 0161 832 5352, www.myf.org.uk

Muslim Youth Helpline, 18 Rosemont Road, London, 0808 808 2008, www.myh.org.uk

Muslim Youth League (London), 292-296 Romford Road, London, 020 8257 1786, www.muslimyouth.org.uk

Muslim Youth Northern Ireland, 38 Wellington Park, Belfast, UK, 2890 664465, www.myni.org.uk

Muslim Youth Organisation, 7 Sefcote Road, Enfield, 020 8443 2140,

Muslim Youth Work Foundation, P.O. Box 15649, Birmingham, B2 2QG, www.mywf.org.uk

Noor ul Islam Youth Group, 713 High Road Leyton, London, www.noorulislam.co.uk

SMYLe - Swansea Muslim Youth League, C/O Blackstone Books, Swansea, 07092 021093

World Assembly of Muslim Youth (WAMY UK), 46 Goodge Street, London, 020 7636 7010, www.wamy.co.uk

Young Muslims UK, info@ymuk.net, 0805 087 8766, www.ymuk.net

Youth and Women Educational Trust, 273 Charles Road, Birmingham, 07990 512005, www.ywet.org.uk

INTERNATIONAL

Sufi Youth International, www.sufiyouth.org

WAMY (World Assembly of Muslim Youth), King Fahd Street, Opp. AlOwais Market, Riyadh Mil, Central 11443, Saudi Arabia, www.wamy.org

NORTH AMERICA

Islamic Society of North America, www.isna.net

Muslim Youth Canada Project, www.muslimyouthcanada.wordpress.com

Muslim Youth Group of The Islamic Center of Southern California, www.myg.org

SOUTH AMERICA

WAMY (World Assembly of Muslim Youth - South America Office), General Deheza 680 - P.O. Box 1091, Córdoba, Argentina - C.P. 5000, Tel/Fax: (0054) 51 - 52 7099

EUROPE

Aktivna Islamska Omladina (Active Islamic Youth), Brace sehia bb, Cazin, Bosnia Herzegovina, 77220 Cazin

Forum of European Muslim Youth and Student Organisations (FEMYSO), The European Students' Union, 20 Rue de la Sablonnière,1000 Bruxelles, Belgium, + 32 2 502 23 26, www.femyso.net

Islamic Forum of Europe, 3rd Floor, West Wing, London Muslim Centre, 38 - 44 Whitechapel Road, London E1 1JX, 020 7456 1062, www.islamicforumeurope.com

Muslim Youth of Ireland, www.muslimyouthireland.wordpress.com

Muslimische Jungen in Deutschland (MJD) Muslim Youth of Germany, www.mjd-net.de

SOUTH AFRICA

Muslim Youth Movement of South Africa, www.mym.za.org
WAMY (World Assembly of Muslim Youth), South Africa, www.org.za

AUSTRALIA

Islamic Youth Movement, 128 Haldon Street, Lakemba NSW 2195, Australia, (02) 9740 4460
Sydney Muslim Youth, www.sydneymuslimyouth.com

SOUTH ASIA

Pakistani Youth Organisation, L-113, 13/G Block. 2, Gulshan-e-Iqbal, Karachi – 75300, Pakistan, www.pyo.org.pk
Students Islamic Organisation of India, www.sio-india.org
WAMY (World Assembly of Muslim Youth), Bangladesh, www.wamy.org.bd

FAR EAST

Angkatan Belia Islam Malaysia (Muslim Youth Movement of Malaysia), www.abim.org.my
Asian Federation of Muslim Youth, www.afmy.typepad.com
Himpunan Belia Islam (Muslim Youth Assembly), 27A Guillemard Road, Singapore, 399697, Singapore Post Centre Post Office, P.O. Box 248, Singapore 914009
www.hbi.org.sg
Young Muslim Association of Thailand, www.ymat.org

NOTES

CHAPTER 2

1 http://www.neighbourhood.statistics.gov.uk/dissemination/ LeadKeyFigures.do?a=7&b=276807&c=bradford&d=13&e=16& g=379237&i=1001x1003x1004&m=0&r=1&s=1315336556727 &enc=1. (Accessed 5/9/11)

2 The construction of 'home' has important ramifications to identity, a sense of belonging and enfranchisement as well as attitudes toward others similarly situated. Even today, a common criticism of first-generation South Asians is that 'home' is not the country of residence or citizenship (i.e. Great Britain), but rather Pakistan. As a further complication, the Pakistan that is 'home' is often an imagined Pakistan that is ossified in the consciousness of the subscriber from a prior era (Anwar, 1998).

3 Muhammad Anwar's *The Myth of Return* provides excellent coverage of the phenomenon of migration of young, single male migrants to Great Britain following the conclusion of World War II.

4 British society expects a certain level of conformity to 'Britishness.' One example is evident in the statements of British Member of Parliament, Norman Tebbit, who proffered a test to determine whether South Asian Britons were primarily loyal to Great Britain or to the country of their ethnic origin. If, as Tebbit claimed, they supported India, Pakistan or Bangladesh in a cricket match against the England team, it proved that they were dual loyalists at best, or were primarily loyal to South Asia over Britain. This test has been used to prove and disprove the hypothesis that South Asian Muslims may not be primarily loyal to Britain despite it being their country of domicile. For the South Asian migrants who do root against England, it is often argued that they do so because Britain has never made them feel like they are 'part of the team' anyway, and so they support South Asian teams out of a sense of comfort and pride as well as for sentimental reasons. This pressure is also visited upon the young who are viewed with derision by South Asian elders as being sell-outs if they support England and as traitors by the British is they support

India or Pakistan, for example. This seemingly insurmountable conflict wears upon the identity construction and psyche of an entire generation of young South Asian Muslims in Britain, as they try to 'fit in' to which ever society they can, often trying to reconcile both communities (*Los Angeles Times*, April 1990).

5 The Droogs were the nihilistic youth depicted in the 1962 novella by Anthony Burgess, *A Clockwork Orange* (also made famous by the 1971 movie of the same title, directed by Stanley Kubrick).

6 Nietzsche's describes nihilism 'as a condition of tension, as a disproportion between what we want to value (or need) and how the world appears to operate' (Carr, 1992).

7 Robert Lambert and Jonathan Githens-Mazer in 'Prevent is Dead. What Next?' (The *Guardian*, 14 July 2010).

8 Douglas Murray in 'The Prevent Strategy: A Textbook Example of How to Alienate Just about Everybody' (*Telegraph*, 31 March 2010).

CHAPTER 3

1 Oliver Roy (2008, p. 3) concurs with this: 'The success of Osama Bin Laden is not to have established a modern and efficient Islamist political organisation, but to have invented a narrative that could allow rebels without a cause to connect with a cause.'

2 www.jamestown.org/images/pdf/st_002_008.pdf [accessed 22.10.2010]

3 For instance, the party published a book on the clash of civilizations, titled *The Inevitability of the Clash of Civilisations* (HT, 2002).

4 For an academic overview of HT's early campus activism see Taji-Farouki (1996, p. 172–7).

5 For instance, a recent HT publication states that 'to promote the correct relationship with non-Muslims in Britain, upon an Islamic basis. This means engaging with people upon our distinct Islamic values. These values should be manifest in our character and behaviour, showing others what it really means to live by Islam. We should take every opportunity to explain the Islamic message, also correcting the misconceptions and refute the false propaganda that is all too prevalent in the media' (HT, 2009, p. 11).

6 McLoughlin (2005, p. 58) notes that 'a number of younger Muslim 'alims (scholars) in the Deobandi tradition, who combine the classical training of al-Azhar with higher degrees from British universities, now speak on community affairs in their localities and work through the MCB on a national level'.

7 The term generally refers to political Islam, ideologization of religion and instrumentalist use of Islam in politics. Islamism is a set of

ideologies enunciating the view that Islam is not only a religion but also a political system. Islamists' discourse is based on the rejection of the West. Islamism is a hybrid product of modernity, anti-modernity and a literalist interpretation of Islam which is cut off from its tradition.

8 See 'Egypt jails Islamic group members', BBC News, 25 March 2004, available at http://news.bbc.co.uk/2/hi/middle_east/3567961.stm [accessed 22.10.2010]; see also 'Freed UK three return to families', BBC News, 1 March 2006, available at http://news.bbc.co.uk/2/hi/uk_news/4763056.stm [accessed 22.10.2010].

9 HT Turkey's official website address is: http://www.turkiyevilayeti.org/. It has several other websites in Turkish: http://site.mynet.com/darulummah/; http://www.kokludegisim.net/; http://www.elfurkan.kk5.org/; http://www.islamdevleti.org/; and http://www.darulkitap.com/muhtelif/takiyyuddinennebhani/indexana.htm

10 http://turkiyevilayeti.org/html/rsclr/trrs/ylmzclk.html.

11 It is possible to download 23 different HT books published in Turkish, http://turkiyevilayeti.org/html/ktplr/ktplr.html, in addition to several papers in Turkish http://turkiyevilayeti.org/html/mkllr/mkllr.html.

CHAPTER 4

1 'Ecological factors' refers to social and environmental dynamics that directly impact the subject at the center of the study, as defined by ecological theory.

CHAPTER 5

1 AKDN is an abbreviation of the Aga Khan Development Network.

2 *Didar*, literally means 'meeting', and refers to a religious gathering in which the Isma'ili Imam meets with his followers.

3 Meaning, literally, 'command' or 'word of command'. In the Isma'ili context, *farman* refers to the Isma'ili Imam's speech, which is specifically addressed to the Isma'ili community and contains guidance for both the spiritual and material life of the community.

CHAPTER 7

1. At the moment, there is not enough evidence to assess how recent changes in university fees in the UK will affect Muslim women's participation in higher education. Although Hussain and Bagguley (2007) suggest fees will act to deter Pakistani and Bangladeshi women's HE participation, an ESF study specifically on Muslim

women in HE did not find this to be the case (Tyrer and Ahmad, 2006).
2. See Shiner and Modood (2002); Modood (2006).
3. See Brah and Shaw (1992); Dale, Shaheen, Fieldhouse and Kalra (2002, 2002b); Ahmad et al., (2003); Modood (2006).
4. The work of Claire Alexander (2000, 2006) is particularly instructive here for the ways in which social policies have continued to objectify and pathologize young Muslim men.
5. There are several references in the British press about Shabina Begum, the 15-year-old Luton schoolgirl who embarked on a two-year court battle with her school, Denbeigh High, after she was suspended for wearing the *jilbab* in 2004. Following an initial ruling in favour of the school, Shabina took her case to the Appeal Courts and won. However, the school then took the case to the House of Lords, which ruled in the school's favour. See BBC News, 'School wins Muslim dress appeal', Wednesday 26 March 2006, http://news.bbc.co.uk/1/hi/education/4832072.stm (accessed 20 November 2010).
6. For an example of such perspectives, see Bhopal (1997a, 1997b).
7. An example of this media discourse can be found in Malik (2005) and Coleman (2005).
8. For a critique of the above, see Tyrer and Ahmad (2006).
9. There are some problematic aspects to the term 'non-traditional students' that extend beyond the context of this study. To imply that students, especially those from racialized minorities are 'non-traditional' can inadvertently create a pathologized reading of students who are not from white, middle-class backgrounds. This in turn deflects attention away from structural issues around access to higher education and re-focuses it on the marginalized group as lacking in the appropriate social profile. I will therefore distinguish between 'A-level entrants' and 'non-A- level entrants' where possible. I am grateful to D. Tyrer for drawing this to my attention.
10. Both Hazel Carby (1982/1997) and Avtar Brah (1996) have voiced scepticism of universalistic concepts of gender relations, such as patriarchy theory, with Brah suggesting that we think instead of 'patriarchal relations' as a way to move beyond Western feminist understandings of the term while allowing for the recognition of the ways women's lives are influenced by male-female relations.
11. These offer more vocationally oriented degrees and are often attended by students from the local populations (Modood and Shiner, 1994). Social class plays a role in influencing which students study at which institutions; students from ethnic minorities are more likely to attend these new universities (Modood, 2006). They are also likely to

aggregate around vocational subjects such as biomedical sciences (or related careers), law, engineering, IT and business (Modood, 1998, 2003, 2006; Shiner and Modood, 2002; Connor et al., 2004) so the pattern of higher education is quite differentiated.

12. I refer to 'class' here loosely; South Asian social structures cannot be assumed to hold the same meanings as they do within Western capitalist 'class' societies, and many families experienced profound changes in their socio-economic positions when settling in the UK. However, the references here are based on women's own class-based identifications.

13. While in her teens, Jahanara used to wear the full face covering (*niqab*) and cloak (*jilbab*) until she began attending sixth-form college.

CHAPTER 12

1 The word '*Khateeb*' in Arabic means a preacher or speaker, and usually refers to the person giving the sermon (*khutbah*) as part of the Jumah (Friday congregational prayer).

2 http://www.nya.org.uk/information/100592/careerinyouthwork/.

3 http://www.nyc.pa.gov.sg/1147748707222/1152153441990.html.

4 Wilmslow Road in Manchester is a long road of Asian shops, takeaways and restaurants. In the North-West of England it acts, along with Blackpool, as a magnet to Muslim Youth for *Eid*, where there is a substantial amount of anti-social behaviour exhibited by the Youth, who also hire out expensive cars for the day.

5 'British-Pakistani men from Bradford: Linking narratives to policy,' by M. Y. Alam and Charles Husband (2006).

6 Over-use of the word *bid'ah* is an example of extremism, as mentioned in the next section. However, it is undeniable that there are some cultural practices of some Muslims that are clearly against the religion, such as honour killings.

7 http://news.bbc.co.uk/1/hi/uk/8038398.stm.

8 Malik (2003) defines national identity as 'a sense of belonging to a political community [. . .] that relies on citizens identifying with the common legal and political structures in the state' (Malik, 2003, p. 74). This sense of belonging is expressed as a sense of common good.

9 The term 'Islamophobia' came into the public domain in the UK with the publication of the Runnymede Trust's Report (1997), entitled 'Islamophobia', but the term was first used in an American Journal called *Insight* in 1991 'with reference to Soviet policy in Afghanistan' (Malik, 2004, p. 101).

10 A *qiyam ul-layl* is a spiritual night-stay programme which comprises
    of extra acts of worship such as prayer, *dhikr* (a devotional act
    focussed on the remembrance of God), reading the Qur'an, plus
    lectures, short talks about Islam, and may include other activities
    such as quizzes, role plays, public speaking, games and so on.

11 This management course was organized with the International
    Institute of Islamic Thought (IIIT), which is based in the US.

12 The European Parliament has made 11 July a Day of Remembrance
    of the genocide of the Bosnian Muslims in Srebrenica: in July 1995,
    Serb soldiers separated over 8,100 Bosnian men and boys from
    their families and then murdered them over a period of two weeks,
    dumping their corpses in mass graves.

13 The MYF was one of the founding organizations of '1001
    Inventions', which initially established an exhibition (with an
    accompanying book) showing the contribution of Muslims to science.

CHAPTER 13

1 In the UK, Professor Muhammad Anwar estimates that over 60 per
   cent of Britain's 1.65 million Muslims are British-born. See, Anwar,
   M. (2003), 'British Muslims: Socio-Economic Position', in Seddon,
   M. S., Malik, N. and Hussian, D., (eds), *British Muslims: Loyalty and
   Belonging*, p. 59.

2 *Ummah*, the universal Muslim community.

3 'Islamic terrorists could be from any race, warns secret MI5 report',
   the *Daily Mail*, 21 September 2008.

4 Reported in al-Muslim. Cited in al-Qaradawi (1997), *The Lawful
   and the Prohibited in Islam*, p. 92.

5 Reported in al-Muslim and al-Bukhari. Ibid., p. 93.

6 All words commonly used for various forms of herbal narcotics.

7 Common words for various synthetic narcotic substances.

8 *Mahram* denotes a relationship through marriage or close blood-
   ties whereby marriage would be permanently prohibited according
   to *shari'ah*. In the case of a female Muslim, a *mahram* is either her
   husband or any male relative that is permanently prohibited from
   marriage.

9 Reported by Ahmad on the authority of 'Amir ibn Rabi'ah. Cited
   in al-Qaradawi, (1997), p. 198.

10 Reported by Ahmad, Abu Dawoud and Tirmidhi. Ibid, p. 201.

11 Reported by al-Bukhari and others. Ibid, p. 202.

12 Reported by al-Muslim, Abu Dawoud and Tirmidhi. Ibid, p. 203. The *hadith* also expresses the prohibition of both male and female homosexuality in Islam.

13 For a detailed discussion on this subject see al-Qaradawi (1997), *The Lawful and the Prohibited in Islam*, pp. 203–44.

14 W. J. Goode asserts that: 'Prior to the twentieth century, marriages of girls aged 15–17 were not disapproved of providing that the man was sufficiently well-to-do . . . Prior to the French Revolution, the legal minimum age for marriage in France was 14 years for boys and 12 years for girls.' See Goode, W. J., cited in Hogget, Brenda M., and Pearl, David S., (1987), *Family Law and Society: Cases and Materials*, p. 25.

15 Young adults in the UK may legally marry at 16 providing they have expressed parental permission.

16 Reported by al-Bukhari. Cited in al-Qaradawi (1997), p. 224.

17 The Arabic term *sawm* is usually translated as 'fasting', but the term has a wider meaning in Arabic beyond simply abstaining from food and drink as the word fasting is contemporarily understood. *Sawm* includes all forms of abstention: food, drink, back-biting, gossiping and vain talk, anger and being belligerent, controlling the sexual desires and libido and so forth.

18 The Prophet Muhammad is known to have annulled marriages conducted without the mutual consent of the bride and the groom.

BIBLIOGRAPHY

Abbas, T. (2005), *Muslim Britain*. London: Zed Books.

—. (2007a), 'Muslim minorities in Britain: Integration, multiculturalism and radicalism in the Post-7/7 period', *Journal of Intercultural Studies*, 28(3), pp. 287–300.

—. (2007b), 'Ethno-religious identities and Islamic political radicalism in the UK: A case study', *Journal of Muslim Minority Affairs*, 27(3), pp. 429–42.

—. (2007c), 'British Muslim minorities today: Challenges and opportunities to Europeanism, multiculturalism and Islamism', *Sociology Compass*, 1(2), pp. 720–36.

—. (ed.) (2005), *Islamic Political Radicalism*. Edinburgh: Edinburgh University Press.

—. (ed.) (2005), *Muslim Britain: Communities Under Pressure*. London: Zed Books.

Abdo, G. (2006), 'America's Muslims aren't as assimilated as you think', *Washington Post*, 27 August, B30.

Abdul Bari, M. (2005), *Race, Religion & Muslim Identity in Britain*. Swansea: Renaissance Press.

Abu-Bader, S. (2006), *Using Statistical Methods in Social Work Practice*. Chicago, IL: Lyceum Books Inc.

Abu-Lughod, L. (1991), 'Writing against culture', In Richard G. Fox (ed.), *Recapturing Anthropology: Working in the Present*. Santa Fe, NM: School of American Research, pp. 137–62.

Adamec, L. W. (2001), *Historical Dictionary of Islam*. London: The Scarecrow Press, Inc.

Ahmad, F. (2001), 'Modern traditions? British Muslim women and academic achievement', *Gender and Education*, 13(2), pp. 137–52.

—(2003), 'Still "in progress?" – methodological dilemmas, tensions and contradictions in theorizing South Asian Muslim women', in N. Puwar and P. Ranghuram (eds), *South Asian Women in the Diaspora*. Oxford: Berg, pp. 43–65.

—(2006), *Modern traditions? British Muslim women, higher education and identities*, unpublished Ph.D. thesis, University of Bristol, UK.

—(2007), 'Muslim women's experiences of higher education in Britain', *American Journal of Islamic Social Sciences*, Special Issue on Higher Education, 24(3), pp. 46–69.

—(2009), ' "We always knew from the year dot that university was the place to go": Muslim women and higher education experiences in the UK', in F. N. Seggie and R. O. Mabokela (eds), *Islam and Higher Education in Transitional Societies*. Rotterdam: Sense Publishers, pp. 65–82.

Ahmad, F., Modood, T. and Lissenburgh, S. (2003), *South Asian Women and Employment in Britain: The Interaction of Gender and Ethnicity*. London: PSI.

Ahmed, A. (1994), *Islam, Globalization and Postmodernity*. London: Routledge.

—(2004), *Postmodernism and Islam*. London: Routledge.

Ahmed, A. S. and Donnon, H. (1994), *Islam, Globalisation and Identity*. London: Routledge.

Ahmed, H. and Stuart, H. (2009), *Hizb ut-Tahrir: Ideology and Strategy*. London: The Centre for Social Cohesion.

Ahmed, S. (2000), *Strange Encounters: Embodied Others in Post-Coloniality*. London: Routledge.

Ahmed, S. (2009), *Seen and Not Heard: Voices of Young British Muslims*, Markfield: Policy Research Centre, Islamic Foundation.

Al-'Alwani, Taha Jabir and Khalil, Imad al Din (1999), *The Qur'an and Sunnah: The Time-Space Factor*, Herndon, Virginia and London: International Islamic Publishing House and International Institute of Islamic Thought.

Al-Johar, D. (2005), 'Muslim marriages in America', *The Muslim World*, 95, pp. 557–74.

Al-Lami, M. (2009), 'Legitimising the discourses of political radicalisation: Political violence in the new media ecology', *Politics and International Relations Working Papers*, 11, London: Royal Holloway, University of London.

Al Qaradawi, Y. (1987), *Islamic Awakening Between Rejection and Extremism*. Herndon: The International Institute of Islamic Thought.

—(1997), *The Lawful and the Prohibited in Islam*, Cairo: El-Falah Publishing.

Alexander, C. (2000), *The Asian Gang*, Oxford: Berg.

—(2006), 'Imagining the politics of BrAsian youth', in N. Ali, V. S. Kalra and S. Sayyid (eds), *Postcolonial People, South Asians in Britain*. London: Hurst and Company, pp. 258–71.

—(2008), *Rethinking Gangs*. London: Runnymede Trust.

Ali, K. (2006), *Sexual Ethics and Islam: Feminist Reflections on Qur'an, Hadith and Jurisprudence*. Oxford: Oneworld Publications.

Ali, N., Kalra, V. S. and Sayyid, S. (eds) (2008), *A Postcolonial People*. London: Hurst and Co.

Allen, C. (2010), *Islamophobia*. London: Ashgate.

Ameli, S., Elahi, E. and Merali, A. (2004), *British Muslims' Expectations of the Government: Social Discrimination Across the Muslim Divide*. London: Islamic Human Rights Commission.

Amer, M. M. and Hovey, J. D. (2007), 'Socio-demographic differences in acculturation and mental health for a sample of 2nd generation/ early immigrant Arab Americans', *Journal of Immigrant and Minority Health*, 9, pp. 335–47.

Ansari, H. (2002), *Muslims in Britain*. UK: Minority Rights Group International.

—(2004), *The Infidel Within*. London: Hurst & Company.

Anthias, F. and Nira Yuval-Davis (1993), *Racialised Boundaries: Race, Nation, Gender, Colour and Class and the Anti-Racist Struggle*, London: Routledge.

Anwar, M. (1979), *The Myth of Return*. London: Heinemann.

—(1998), *Between Cultures: Continuity and Change in the Lives of Young Asians*. London: Routledge.

—(2003), 'British Muslims: Socio-economic position' in M. S. Seddon, D. Hussein and N. Malik (eds), *British Muslims: Loyalty and Belonging*. Markfield: The Islamic Foundation.

—(2008), 'Muslims in Western States: The British experience and the way forward', *Journal of Muslim Minority Affairs*, 28(1), pp. 125–37.

Arab American Institute (2003), *Healing the Nation: The Arab American Experience After September 11*, retrieved from http://aai.3cdn. net/64de7330dc475fe470_h1m6b0yk4.pdf

Archer, L. (2002), 'Change, culture and tradition: British Muslim pupils talk about Muslim girls' post-16 "choices"', *Race Ethnicity and Education*, 5(4), pp. 359–76.

Archer, L. and Francis, B. (2006), *Understanding Minority Ethnic Achievement: 'Race', Class, Gender and 'Success'*. London: Routledge.

Archer, L., Hutchings, M. and Ross, A. (2003), *Higher Education and Social Class, Issues of Exclusion and Inclusion*. London: Routledge Falmer.

Aronowitz, M. (1985), 'The social and economical adjustment of immigrant children. A review of literature', *International Migration Review*, 18(2), pp. 237–57.

Asmar, C. (2005), 'Internationalising students: Reassessing diasporic and local student difference', *Studies in Higher Education*, 30(3), pp. 291–309.

Asmar, C., Proude, E. and Inge, L. (2004), ' "Unwelcome sisters"? An analysis of findings from a study of how Muslim women (and Muslim men) experience university', *Australian Journal of Education*, 48(1), pp. 47–63.

Aspinall, P. (2000), 'Should a question on "Religion" be asked in 2001 British Census? A public policy case in favour', *Social Policy & Administration*, 34(5), pp. 584–600.

Aswat, Y. and Malcarne, V. L. (2007), 'Acculturation and depressive symptoms in Muslim University students: Personal-family acculturation match', *International Journal of Psychology*, 1(11), pp. 1–11.

Ayers, W. (2005), *Teaching Toward Freedom: Moral Commitment and Ethical Action in the Classroom*. Boston: Beacon Press.

—(2006), *To Become a Teacher: Making a Difference in Children's Lives*. New York: Teachers' College Press.

Ayers, W. and Alexander-Tanner, R. (2010), *To Teach: The Journey, in Comics*. New York: Teachers' College Press.

Ayers, W. and Ford, P. (2008), *City Kids, City Teachers: Reports from the Front Row*. New York: The New Press.

Ayers, W., Quinn, T. and Stovall, D. (eds) (2009), *Handbook of Social Justice in Education. New York:* Routledge.

Bagby, I, Perl, M. P. and Froehle, B. T. (2001), *The Mosque in America: A National Portrait*. Washington, DC: Council on American-Islamic Relations.

Ball, S., Reay, D. and David, M. (2002), ' "Ethnic choosing": Minority ethnic students, social class and higher education choice', *Race, Ethnicity and Education*, 5(4), pp. 333–57.

Baran, Z. (2004b), *Hizb ut-Tahrir: Islam's Political Insurgency*. Washington, DC: The Nixon Centre.

—(ed.) (2004a), *The Challenge of Hizb ut-Tahrir: Deciphering and Combating Radical Islamist Ideology*. Washington, DC: The Nixon Centre.

Barazangi, N. H. (1988), *Perceptions of the Islamic Belief System: The Muslims in North America*, Ph.D. Thesis, Cornell University, Ithaca.

—(1991), 'Islamic education in the United States and Canada: Conception and practice of the Islamic belief system', in Y. Haddad (ed.), *The Muslims of America*. New York: Oxford University Press, pp. 157–74.

—(1996), 'Parents and youth: Perceiving and practicing Islam in North America', in B. C. Aswad and B. Bilge (eds), *Family and Gender Among American Muslims: Issues Facing Middle Eastern Immigrants and Their Descendants*. Philadelphia, PA: Temple University Press, pp. 129–42.

Barth, F. (1969), *Ethnic Groups and Boundaries*. Boston: Little, Brown and Company.

—(2000), 'Enduring and emerging issues in the analysis of ethnicity',
   in, H. Vermeulen and C. Govers (eds), *Anthropology of Ethnicity:
   Beyond 'Ethnic Groups and Boundaries'*. Amsterdam: HET Spinhuis
   Publishers, pp. 11–32.
Basit, T. N. (1995), ' "I want to go to college": British Muslim girls and
   the academic dimension of schooling', *Muslim Education Quarterly*,
   12, pp. 36–54.
—(1996), ' "I'd hate to be just a housewife": Career aspirations of British
   Muslim girls', *British Journal of Guidance and Counselling*, 24,
   pp. 227–42.
—(1997), *Eastern Values; Western Milieu: Identities and Aspirations of
   Adolescent British Muslim Girls*, Aldershot: Ashgate.
Ba-Yanus, B. and Siddiqui, M. M. (1998), A report on the Muslim
   population in the United States of America, New York: Center for
   American Muslim Research and Information.
Bayat, A. (1998), 'Revolution without Movement, Movement without
   Revolution: Comparing Islamic Activism in Iran and Egypt',
   Comparative Studies in Society and History, 40(1), pp. 136–69.
BBC (2011), 'State multiculturalism has failed, says David Cameron', 5
   February 2011, http://www.bbc.co.uk/news/uk-politics-12371994,
   accessed 27 May 2011.
BBC News (2005), 'Plans to Erase University Bias', *BBC News*, http://news.
   bbc.co.uk/1/hi/education/4484540.stm, accessed 05 January 2009.
BBC News (2006), 'School wins Muslim dress appeal', 26 March 2006,
   http://news.bbc.co.uk/1/hi/education/4832072.stm, accessed 20
   November 2010.
BBC News (2007), Internet used to target extremism, 31 October 2007.
   http://news.bbc.co.uk/1/hi/uk/7070416.stm, accessed 29 May 2011.
Beckford, R. (2000), *Dread and Pentecostal: A Political Theology for the
   Black Church in Britain*. London: S. P. C. K.
—(2004), *God and the Gangs. An Urban Toolkit for Those Who Won't
   Be Bought Out, Sold Out or Scared Out*. London: DLT.
Berg, L. (1972), *Look at Kids*. London: Penguin.
Berry, J. W. (1986), 'The acculturation process and refugee behavior',
   in C. L. Williams and J. Westinmeyer (eds), *Refugee Mental Health
   in Resettlement Countries*. Washington, DC: Hemisphere Publishing
   Corp, pp. 25–37.
—(1997), 'Immigration, acculturation and adaptation', *Applied
   Psychology*, 46, pp. 5–68.
Berry, J. W., Phinney, J., Sam, D. L. and Vedder, P. (2006), *Immigrant
   Youth in Cultural Transition: Acculturation, Identity, and Adaptation
   Across National Contexts*. Mahwah, NJ: Lawrence Erlbaum
   Associates, Inc.

Bhabha, H. (1996), 'Unsatisfied: Notes on Vernacular composition', L. Moreno and P. Pfeiffer (eds), *Text and Nation: Cross-Disciplinary Essays on Cultural and National Identities*. New York: Camden House.

Bhattacharrya, G. and Gabriel, J. (1997), 'Racial formations of youth in late twentieth century England', in J. Roche and S. Tucker (eds), *Youth in Society*. London: Sage, pp. 68–80.

Bhopal, K. (1997a), *Gender, 'Race' and Patriarchy, A Study of South Asian Women*. Aldershot: Ashgate.

—(1997b), 'South Asian women within households: Dowries, degradation and despair', *Women's Studies International Forum*, 20, pp. 483–92.

Billis, D. (1984), *Welfare Bureaucracies*. London: Heinemann.

—(1991), 'The roots of voluntary agencies', in *Non Profit and Voluntary Sector Quarterly*, 20(1), pp. 57–70.

Birt, Y. (2009), 'Islamophobia in the construction of British Muslim identity politics', in P. Hopkins and R. Gale (eds), *Muslims in Britain: Race, Place and Identities*. Edinburgh: Edinburgh University Press.

Blasi, A. (1988), 'Identity and the development of the self', in D. K. Lapsley and F. C. Power (eds), *Self, Ego, and Identity: Integrative Approaches*. New York: Springer-Verlag, pp. 226–42.

Bloom, B. S. (1956), *Taxonomy of Educational Objectives, Handbook I: The Cognitive Domain*. New York: David McKay Co Inc.

Bokhari, R. and Seddon, M. (2010), *The Illustrated Encyclopedia of Islam*. London: Lorenz Books.

Bourhis, R. Y. and Barrette, G. (2004), 'Notes on the Immigrant Acculturation Scale', *Working Paper, LECRI*, Department of Psychology, University of Quebec, Montreal, Canada, November.

Brah, A. (1993), 'En-gendered racisms, ethnicities and nationalisms in contemporary Western Europe', *Feminist Review*, 45, pp. 9–29.

—(1996), *Cartographies of Diaspora, Contesting Identities*. London: Routledge.

Brah, A. and Phoenix, A. (2004), 'Ain't I a woman? Revisiting intersectionality', *Journal of International Women's Studies*, 5(3), pp. 75–86.

Brah, A. and Shaw, S. (1992), *Working Choices: South Asian Young Muslim Women and the Labour Market*, Research Paper No. 91. London: Department of Employment.

Briggs, R. and Birdwell, J. (2009), *Radicalisation Among Muslims in the UK, MICROCON Policy Working Paper 7*. Brighton: MICROCON.

Brighton, S. (2007), 'British Muslims, multiculturalism and UK foreign policy: 'integration' and 'cohesion' in and beyond the state', *International Affairs*, 83(1), pp. 1–17.

Bronfenbrenner, U. (1989), 'Ecological systems theory', in R. Vasta (ed.), *Six Theories of Child Development, Annals of Child Development, 6*. Greenwich, CT: JAI press, pp. 187–249.

Brubaker, R. (2005), 'The "diaspora" diaspora', *Ethnic and Racial Studies*, 28(1), pp. 1–19.

Bruce, S. (1995), *Religion in Modern Britain*. Oxford: Oxford University Press.

Bukhari, Z. H. (2001), 'Demography, identity, space: Defining American Muslims', in P. Strum and D. Tarantolo (eds), *Muslims in the United States*. Washington, DC: Woodrow Wilson International Center for Scholars, pp. 7–20.

Bunglawala, Z., Halstead, M., Malik, M. and Spalek, B. (2004), *Muslims in the UK: Policies for Engaged Citizens*, Open Society Institute, EU Monitoring and Advocacy Program.

Burgess, A. (1962), *A Clockwork Orange*. London: Heinemann.

Butler, J. (1997), *The Psychic Life of Power: Theories of Subjection*. Stanford: Stanford University Press.

Caglar, A. (1997), 'Hyphenated identities and the limits of culture', in T. Modood and P. Werbner (eds), *The Politics of Multiculturalism in the New Europe*. London: Zed Books, pp. 169–85.

Cakir, R. (2004), 'The rise and fall of Turkish Hizb ut-Tahrir', in Z. Baran (ed.), *The Challenge of Hizb ut-Tahrir: Deciphering and Combating Radical Islamist Ideology*. Washington, DC: The Nixon Centre, pp. 37–9.

Cantle, T. (2001), *Community Cohesion – A Report of the Independent Review Team*. London: Home Office.

Carby, H. (1982), 'White woman listen! Black feminism and the boundaries of sisterhood', reproduced in H. S. Mirza (ed.) (1997), *Black British Feminism, A Reader*. London: Routledge.

—(1999), *Cultures in Babylon: Black Britain and African America*. New York: Verso Books.

Carmichael, S. and Hamilton, C. V. (1967), *Black Power*. New York: Random House.

Carr, K. (1992), *The Banalization of Nietzsche*. New York: SUNY Press.

Carter, R. B. and El Hindi, A. E. (1999), 'Counseling Muslim children in school settings', *Professional School Counseling*, 2(3), pp. 183–8.

Cashmore, E. (1985), *Rastaman: The Rastafarian Movement in England* (2nd edition). London: Unwin Paperbacks.

Cassidy, C., O'Connor, R. and Dorrer, N. (2006), *Young People's Experiences of Transition to Adulthood. A Study of Minority Rthnic and White Young People*. York: Joseph Rowntree Foundation.

Center for American Islamic Relations (2006), *American Muslim Voters: A Demographic Profile and Survey of Attitudes*, Washington, DC.

Choudhury, T. A. (ed.) 2005. *Muslims in the UK Policies for Engaged Citizens*. Budapest: Open Society Institute.

Clark, D. B. (1973), 'The concept of community: A re-examination', *Sociological Review*, 21, pp. 398–416.

Clark, J. A. (2004), *Islam, Charity, and Activism: Middle-Class Networks and Social Welfare in Egypt, Jordan, and Yemen*. Bloomington: Indiana University Press.

Cleaver, E. *Soul on Ice*. New York: Bantam Doubleday Day Publishing Group.

Coleman C. (2005), 'Amazing double life a growing trend among Muslim girls', *The Daily Mail*, April.

Collins, P. H. (1991), *Black Feminist Thought: Knowledge, Consciousness and the Politics of Empowerment*. New York: Routledge.

Collins-Mayo, S., Mayo, B., Nash, S. and Cocksworth, C. (2010), *The Faith of Generation Y*. Church House Publishing.

Commins, D. (1991), 'Taqi Al-Din Al-Nabhani and the Islamic Liberation Party', *The Muslim World*, 81(3–4), pp. 194–211.

Connor, H., Tyers, C., Modood, T. and Hillage, J. (2004), *Why the Difference? A Closer Look at Higher Education Minority Ethnic Students and Graduates*, Research Report 552, Institute for Employment Studies, Department for Education and Skills.

Connor, K. (2005), 'Islamism' in the West? The life-span of the Al-Muhajiroun in the United Kingdom', *Journal of Muslim Minority Affairs*, 25(1), pp. 119–35.

Cooke, M. and Lawrence, B. (ed.) (2005), *Muslim Networks: From Hajj to Hiphop*. Chapel Hill: The University of North Carolina Press.

Council on American-Islamic Relations (2001), *American Muslims: Population Statistics*, retrieved 5 June 2006, from http://www.cair.com/asp/populationstats.asp

Cox, D. R. (1983), 'Religion and the welfare of immigrants', *Australian Social Work*, 36(1), pp. 3–10.

Crawford, K. (1996), 'Vygotskian approaches to human development in the information era', *Educational Studies in Mathematics*, 31, pp. 43–62.

Cressey, G. (2007), *The Ultimate Separatist Cage? Youth Work with Muslim Young Women*. Leicester: National Youth Agency.

Cusworth, L., Bradshaw, J., Coles, B., Keung, A. and Chzhen, Y. (2009), *Understanding the Risks of Social Exclusion Across the Life Course: Youth and Young Adulthood*, London: Social Exclusion Task Force, Cabinet Office.

The Daily Mail, 'Islamic terrorists could be from any race, warns secret MI5 report', 21 September 2008.

Dale, A., Shaheen, N., Fieldhouse, E. and Kalra, V. (2002a), 'Labour
   market prospects for Pakistani and Bangladeshi women', *Work,
   Employment and Society*, 16(1), pp. 5–26.
—(2002b), 'Routes into education and employment for young Pakistani
   and Bangladeshi women in the UK', *Ethnic and Racial Studies*, 25(6),
   pp. 942–68.
Daniels, H. (2007), 'Discourse and identity in cultural-historical activity
   theory: A response,' *International Journal of Educational Research*,
   46(1–2), pp. 94–9.
Davies B. (1999), *A History of the Youth Service in England* (Vols 1
   and 2). Leicester: National Youth Agency.
Denny, F. M. (1995), 'Islam in Americas', in J. L. Esposito (ed.), *The
   Oxford Encyclopedia of the Modern Islamic World*, New York:
   Oxford University Press, pp. 296–300.
Deuchar, R. (2009), *Gangs, Marginalised Youth and Social Capital*. Stoke-
   on-Trent: Trentham Books.
DiCaprio, N. S. (1983), *Personality Theories: A Guide to Human Nature*
   (2nd edition). Winston: CBS College Publishing..
Didier, C. (2006), 'Hizb ut-Tahrir: An Islamist Threat to Central Asia?'
   Journal of Muslim Minority Affairs, 26(1), pp. 113–25.
Dwyer, C. (1999a), 'Contradictions of community: Questions of identity
   for young British Muslim women', *Environment and Planning A*, 31,
   pp. 53–68.
—(1999b), 'Veiled meanings: British Muslim women and the negotiation
   of differences', *Gender, Place and Culture*, 6(1), pp. 5–26.
—(2000), 'Negotiating diasporic identities: Young British South Asian
   Muslim women', *Women's Studies International Forum*, 23(4),
   pp. 475–86.
Dwyer, C., Modood, T., Sanghera, G., Shah, B., and Thaper-Bjorkert, S.
   (2006), 'Ethnicity as social capital? Explaining the differential
   educational achievements of young British Pakistani men and
   women', Paper presented at the Mobility, *Ethnicity and Society
   Conference*, Thursday 16 and Friday 17 March 2006, University of
   Bristol.
Dwyer, C. and Shah, B. (2009), 'Rethinking the identities of young
   British Muslim Women', in P. Hopkins and R. Gale (eds), *Muslims in
   Britain: Race, Place and Identities*. Edinburgh: Edinburgh University
   Press.
Dyke, A. H. (2009), *Mosques Made in Britain*. London: The Quilliam
   Foundation.
Eck, D. L. (1997), *On Common Ground: World Religions in America*.
   New York: Columbia University Press.

Edelman, M. W. (1996), 'Foreword', in L. Lantieri and J. Patti (eds), *Waging Peace in Our Schools*. Boston: Beacon Press.

Emberling, G. (1997), 'Ethnicity in complex societies: Archaeological perspectives', *Journal of Archaeological Research*, 5(4), pp. 295–344.

EMCRX (2005), *The Impact of 7 July 2005 European Monitoring Centre of Racism and Xenophobia. 2005. London Bomb Attacks on Muslim Communities in the EU*. Vienna: European Monitoring Centre of Racism and Xenophobia.

Equal Opportunities Commission (2006), *Moving on Up? Bangladeshi, Pakistani and Black Caribbean Women and Work*. Manchester: EOC.

Erikson, E. H. (1950), *Childhood and Society*. New York: Norton.

—(1958), *Young Man Luther: A Study in Psychoanalysis and History*. London: Faber & Faber Ltd.

—(1968), *Identity: Youth and Crisis*. London: Faber & Faber Ltd.

Esposito, J. L. (2003), *The Oxford Dictionary of Islam*. Oxford: Oxford University Press. Faber & Faber Ltd.

Fahmy, E. 'Youth, Poverty and Social Exclusion', in D. Gordon, R. Levitas and C. Pantazis (eds), *Poverty and Social Exclusion in Britain: The Millennium Survey*. Bristol: Policy Press, pp. 347–73.

Faist, T. (2000), *The Volume and Dynamics of International Migration and Transnational Social Spaces*. Oxford: Oxford University Press.

Fanon, F. (1965), *The Wretched of the Earth*. London: MacGibbon & Kee.

—(1967), *Black Skin White Masks*. New York: Grove Press.

Farrar, M. (2006), 'When alienation turns to nihilism: The dilemmas posed for diversity post 7/7', *Conversations in Religion and Theology*, 4(1), pp. 99–109.

Favell, A. (2001), 'Integration policy and integration research in Europe: A review and a critique', in T. A. Aleinikoff and D. Klusmeyer (eds), *Citizenship Today: Global Perspectives and Practices*. Massachusetts: Brookings Institution Press.

—(2003), 'Integration nations: The nation-state and research on immigrants in Western Europe', in G. Brochmann (ed.), *The Multicultural Challenge*. Oxford: Elsevier.

Federation of Student Islamic Societies (2005), *The Voice of Muslim Students, FOSIS Muslim Student Survey*. London: FOSIS.

Fennema, M. (2004), 'The concept and measurement of ethnic community', *Journal of Ethnic & Migration Studies*, 30(3), pp. 429–47.

Forman, M. T. (2001), Straight outta Mogadishu': Prescribed identities and performative practices among Somali youth in North American high schools, *Topia*, 5, pp. 20–41.

FOSIS (2005), *The Voice of Muslim Students: A Report into the Attitudes and Perceptions of Muslim Students Following the July 7th London attacks*. London: Federation of student Islamic Societies.

Foucault, M. (1969), *The Archaeology of Knowledge*. London: Routledge.

—(1973), *The Birth of the Clinic*, London: Tavistock Publications Limited.

—(1984), 'The order of discourse', in M. Shapiro (ed.), *Language and Politics*, Oxford: Blackwell, pp.108–38.

Frischauer, W. (1970), *The Aga Khans*. London: The bodley head, from http://www.irr.org.uk/2002/april/ak000001.html, accessed 20 August 2010.

Gale, R. and Hopkins, P. (2009), 'Introduction: Muslims in Britain-race, place and the spatiality of identities', in P. Hopkins and R. Gale (eds), *Muslims in Britain: Race, Place and Identities*. Edinburgh, Edinburgh University Press.

Gammell, C. (2010), 'Stephen Timms knife attack: CCTV shows moment Muslim woman stabs MP', *The Telegraph*, 02 November http://www.telegraph.co.uk/news/uknews/crime/8105085/Stephen-Timms-knife-attack-CCTV-shows-moment-Muslim-woman-stabs-MP.html

Gerges, F. A. (2005), *The Far Enemy: Why Jihad Went Global*. New York: Cambridge University Press.

Ghuman, P. A. S. (1997), 'Assimilation or integration? A study of Asian adolescents', *Education Research*, 39(1), pp. 23–35.

Gillborn, D. (1997), 'Racism and reform: New ethnicities/old inequalities', *British Education Research Journal*, 23, pp. 345–60.

Gilliat-Ray, S. (2000), *Religion in Higher Education: The Politics of the Multi-faith Campus*. Wiltshire: Ashgate.

—(2010), *Muslims in Britain*. Cambridge: Cambridge University Press.

Gilroy, P. (1987), *There Ain't no Black in the Union Jack: The Cultural Politics of Race and Nation*. Hutchinson: London.

—(1997), 'Diaspora and the detours of identity', in K. Woodward (ed.), *Identity and Difference*. London: Sage, pp. 299–343.

Glees, A. and Pope, C. (2005), *When Students Turn to Terror: Terrorist and Extremist Activity on British Campuses*. London: Social Affairs Unit.

Goodman, L. E. (1972), 'Ibn Khaldun and Thucydides', *Journal of the American Oriental Society*, 92(2), pp. 250–70.

Gordon, M. M. (1964), *Assimilation in American Life*. New York: Oxford University Press.

Graves, T. (1967), 'Pyschological acculturation in a tri-ethnic community', *South-Western Journal of Anthropology*, 23, pp. 337–50.

Greaves, R. (2005), 'Negotiating British citizenship and Muslim identity', in T. Abbas (ed.), *Muslim Britain: Communities Under Pressure*. London: Zed Books Ltd.

Gruen, M. (2004), 'Demographics and methods of recruitment', in Z. Baran (ed.), *The Challenge of Hizb ut-Tahrir: Deciphering and Combating Radical Islamist* Ideology. Washington, DC: The Nixon Centre, pp. 116–23.

Haddad, Y. (ed.) (2002), *Muslims in the West*. New York: Oxford University Press.

Haddad, Y. Y. (1997), 'Make room for the Muslims?', in W. H. Conser Jr. and S. B. Twiss (eds), *Religious Diversity and American Religious History*. Athens: University of Georgia Press, pp. 218–61.

Haddad, Y. Y. and Lummis, A. T. (1987), *Islamic Values in the United States*. New York: Oxford University Press.

Haddad, Y. Y. and Smith, J. I. (1996), 'Islamic values among American Muslims', in B. C. Aswad and B. Bilge (eds), *Family and Gender Among American Muslims*. Philadelphia: Temple University Press, p. 19.

Hall, S. (1989), *Ethnicity: Identity and Difference*. Available from https://pantherfile.uwm.edu/wash/www/102/stuarthall.htm#2, accessed 20 August 2010.

—(1992), 'New Ethnicities', in J. D. Rattansi (ed.), *'Race', Culture and Difference*. London: Sage Publications, pp. 252–8.

—(1994), 'Cultural identity and Diaspora', in P. Williams and L. Chrisman (eds), *Colonial Discourse and Post-Colonial Theory: A Reader*. New York: Columbia University Press.

Hamid, S. (2006), 'Models of Muslim youth work: Between reform and empowerment', *Youth & Policy*, 92. Leicester: National Youth Agency.

Haqqani, H. and Hillel F. (2008), 'Islamist parties: Going back to the origins', *Journal of Democracy*, 19(3), pp. 13–18.

Harker, K. (2001), 'Immigrant generation, assimilation, and adolescent psychological well-being', *Social Forces*, 79(3), pp. 969–1004.

Harris, D. (ed.) (1995), *Multiculturalism from the Margins*. Westport: Bergin & Garvey.

Hassan, M. A., Samater, H. M., Van Liempt, I., Oakes W. J. and Obsiye M. (2009), *In Search for a United Voice: Establishing a London Somali Youth Forum*. London: Somali Youth Development Resource Centre.

Hellyer, H. A. (2008), 'Engaging British Muslim communities in counter-terrorism strategies', *The RUSI Journal*, 153(2), pp. 8–13.

Hendry, L. B., Mayer, P. and Kloep, M. (2007), 'Belonging or opposing? A grounded theory approach to young people's cultural identity in a majority/minority societal context', *Identity: An International Journal of Theory and Research*, 7(3), pp. 181–204.

Henry, J. and Donnelly, L. (2008), 'Female Muslim medics "disobey hygiene rules" ', *The Telegraph*, 03 February, http://www.telegraph.co.uk/news/uknews/1577426/Female-Muslim-medics-disobey-hygiene-rules.html, accessed 11 November 2010.

Hesse, B. (2001), *Un/Settled Multiculturalisms: Diasporas, Entanglement, Transruptions*. London: Zed Books.

Higher Education Statistic Agency (2004), *Higher Education Statistics for the UK*, Cheltenham: Higher Education Statistic Agency.

Hizb-ut-Tahrir, (2000), *The Method to Re-establish the Khilafah and Resume the Islamic Way of Life*. London: Al-Khilafah Publications.

—(2002), *The Inevitability of the Clash of Civilisation*. London: Al-Khilafah Publications.

—(2007), *Radicalisation, Extremism & 'Islamism' Realities and Myths in the 'War on Terror, A Report by Hizb ut-Tahrir Britain*. London: HT.

—(2008), *The British Government's 'Preventing Violent Extremism' & 'Community Cohesion' Agenda A Strategy for Control over the Muslim community in Britain and the Reformation of Islam*. London: HT.

—(2009), *A Positive Agenda for Muslims in Britain*. London: HT.

—(2010), *Media Pack*. London: HT.

Hodge, D. R. (2002), 'Working with Muslim youths: Understanding the values and beliefs of Islamic discourse', *Children and Schools*, 24(1), pp. 6–20.

Hogget, B. M. and Pearl, D. S. (1987), *Family Law and Society: Cases and Materials*. London: Butterworths.

Holt, J. (1964), *How Children Fail*. New York: Pitman Publishing Corporation.

Hooks, B. (2003), *Teaching Community: A Pedagogy of Hope*. New York: Routledge.

Hopkins, P. (2004), 'Young Muslim men in Scotland: Inclusions and exclusions', in *Children's Geographies*, 2(2), pp. 257–72.

—(2007), ' "Blue squares", "proper" Muslims and transnational networks: Narratives of national and religious identities amongst young Muslim men living in Scotland', *Ethnicities*, 7(1), pp. 61–81.

Hopkins, P. and Gale, R. (2009), (eds), *Muslims in Britain*. Edinburgh: Edinburgh University http://www.saneworks.us/uploads/application/87.pdf, accessed 29 May 2011.

Hussain, D. (2004a), 'British Muslim identity', in M. S. Seddon, D. Hussain and N. Malik (eds), *British Muslims Between Assimilation and Segregation: Historical, Legal and Social Realities*. Markfield: The Islamic Foundation.

—(2004b), 'The Impact of 9/11 on British Muslim Identity', in
R. Geaves, T. Gabriel, Y. Haddad and J. Idleman Smith (eds), *Islam &
The West: Post 9/11*. Aldershot and Burlington, VA: Ashgate,
pp. 115–29.

Hussain, E. (2007), *Islamist: Why I Joined Radical Islam in Britain, What
I Saw Inside and Why I Left*. London: Penguin Books.

Hussain, Y. and Bagguley, P. (2007), *Moving On Up: South Asian Women
and Higher Education*. Stoke-on-Trent: Trentham Books.

Ibn Khaldun, Abd al-Rahman ibn Mohammad (1967), *The Muqaddimah:
An Introduction to History*. Translated into English by F. Rosenthal,
edited and abridged by N. J. Dawood. Princeton, NJ: Princeton
University Press.

—(1971), *Al-Muqaddimah*. Bayrut: Dar Ihya'al-Turath al-Arabi.

—(1980), *Muqaddimah*. Translated into Persian by P. Gunabadi. Tehran:
Bungah-e Tarjomah wa Nashr-e Kitab.

Ignatieff, M. (1997), *The Warrior's Honour: ethnic war and the modern
conscience*, Oxford: Blackwell.

Ijaz, A. and Abbas, T. (2010), 'The impact of inter-generational change on the
attitudes of working-class South Asian Muslim parents on the education
of their daughters', *Gender and Education*, 22(3), pp. 313–26.

International Crisis Group (2003), *Radical Islam in Central Asia:
Responding To Hizb ut-Tahrir, ICG Asia Report No.58*. Osh/Brussels:
ICG.

Iqbal, S. (2008), 'Get with the Times Dude!' (Editorial), *the Revival*, 14,
http://www.therevival.co.uk/editorial-get-times-dude, accessed 24
December 2010.

Islamic Human Rights Commission (2006a), *'You Only Have the Right
to Silence, A Review of Concerns Regarding Security Discourse on
Muslims on Campus in Britain'*, IHRC: London.

—(2006b), *You Only Have the Right to Silence: A Briefing on the
Concerns Regarding Muslims on Campus in Britain*. Available at
www.ihrc.org.uk/file/YouONLYhavetheRighttoSilence.doc, accessed
23 August 2010.

Issawi C. (1950), *An Arab Philosophy of History: Selections from the
Prolegomena of Ibn Khaldun of Tunis (1332–1406)*. London: John
Murray.

Iyer, D. S. and Haslam, N. (2003), 'Body image and eating disturbances
among South Asian-American women: The role of racial teasing',
International Journal of Eating Disorders, 34, pp. 142–7.

Jafar, A. (2006), 'Promoting good campus relations: Dealing with hate
crimes and intolerance' Issues affecting Freedom of Expression', in *A
Response to the Ebdon Report*, Parliamentary University Group.

James, D. C. S. (1997), 'Coping with a new society: The unique psychosocial problems of immigrant youth', *The Journal of School Health*, 67, pp. 98–102.

Jameson N. (2003) 'British Muslims – Influencing UK Public Life: A Case Study', in M. S. Seddon, D. Hussein and N. Malik (eds), *British Muslims: Loyalty and Belonging*, Markfield, The Islamic Foundation.

John, M. (2003), *Children's Rights and Power: Charging up for a New Century*. London: Jessica Kingsley Publishers.

Jones, D. M. and Smith, M. L. R. (2010), 'Beyond belief: Islamist strategic thinking and international relations theory', *Terrorism and Political Violence*, 22(2), pp. 242–66.

Jupp, V. and Norris, C. (1996), 'Traditions in documentary analysis', in M. Hamersley (ed.), *Social Research: Philosophy, Politics and Practice*. London: Sage in Association with the Open University.

Kalanov, K. and Alonso, A. (2008), *Sacred Places and 'Folk Islam', in Central Asia, UNISCI Discussion Papers* 17. Zurich: UNISCI.

Karagiannis, E. and McCauley, C. (2006), 'Hizb ut-Tahrir al-Islami: Evaluating the Threat Posed by a Radical Islamic Group That Remains Nonviolent', *Terrorism and Political Violence*, 18(2), pp. 315–34.

Kaya, A. (2007), 'German–Turkish transnational space: A separate space of their own', *German Studies Review*, 30(3), pp. 1–20.

Keller, H. and Sigron, M. (2010), 'State security v freedom of expression: Legitimate fight against terrorism or suppression of political opposition?', *Human Rights Law Review*, 10(1), pp. 151–68.

Khan, H. (2005), 'Eid Not Weed', *the Revival*, 3, http://www.therevival.co.uk/eid-not-weed, accessed 24 December 2010.

Khan, M. (1990), 'Macroeconomic policies and the balance of payment in Pakistan: pp. 1972–86', *International Monetary Fund Working Paper: WP/90/78*. Washington, DC, pp. 9–15.

Khan, M. G. (2006), 'Introduction: Responding to lives, not events', *Youth & Policy*, Special issue, Muslim Youth Work, no. 92.

Khanum, S. (1995), 'Education and the Muslim girl', in M. Blair, J. Holland and S. Sheldon (eds), *Identity and Diversity: Gender and the Experience of Education*. Clevedon: Multilingual Matters Ltd.

Khusnidinov, Z. (2004), 'The Uzbek response', in *The Challenge of Hizb ut-Tahrir: Deciphering and Combating Radical Islamist Ideology*, edited by Z. Baran, Washington, DC: The Nixon Centre, pp. 140–50.

King, W. L. (1987), 'Religion', in M. Eliade (ed.), *The Encyclopaedia of Religion*. New York: Macmillan Publishing Company.

Kohl, H. (1991), *I Won't Learn From You*. New York: The New Press.

Kosmin, B. A., Mayer, E. and Keysar, A. (2001), 'American religious identification survey', *The Graduate Center of the City University of New York*, retrieved 5 June 2006, from http://www.gc.cuny.edu/faculty/researchstudies/aris.pdf.

Kukhareva, M., Eames, J., Sinclair, T., Kendall, S., Chakravorty, M. and Watts, M. (2007), *Ethnic Minority Participation in Higher Education in the East of England*. Cambridge: Association of Universities in the East of England.

Kundnani, A. (2002), 'The death of multiculturalism', *Institute of Race Relations*. http://www.irr.org.uk/2002/april/ak000001.html, accessed 6 May 2011.

—(2008), 'How are think tanks shaping the political agenda on Muslims in Britain?', 2 September 2008, *Institute for Race Relations*, http://www.irr.org.uk/2008/september/ak000003.html, accessed 6 May 2011.

Kymlicka, W. (2007), *Multicultural Odysseys: Navigating the New International Politics of Diversity*. Oxford: Oxford University Press.

Lantieri, L. and Patti. J. (1996), *Waging Peace in Our Schools*. Boston: Beacon Press.

Layard, R. and Dunn, J. (2009), *A Good Childhood: Searching for Values in a Competitive Age*. London: Penguin.

Leiken, R. S. and Brooke, S. (2007), 'The Moderate Muslim Brotherhood', *Foreign Affairs Journal*, 86(2), pp. 107–21.

Lewis, P. (1994), *Islamic Britain*. London: I. B. Tauris.

—(2002), *Islamic Britain: Religion, Politics and Identity Among British Muslims*. London: I. B. Tauris.

—(2006), 'Imams, ulema and Sufis: Providers of bridging social capital for British Pakistanis?', *Contemporary South Asia*, 15(3), pp. 273–87.

—(2007), *Young, British and Muslim*. London: Continuum.

Liberty (2004), *Reconciling Security and Liberty in an Open Society– Liberty Response*. London: Liberty.

Liebkind, K. (2001), 'Acculturation', in R. Brown and S. Gaetner (eds), *Blackwell Handbook of Social Psychology*, Vol. 3: Intergroup processes. Oxford, England: Blackwell, pp. 386–406.

Lindner, E. W. (2004), 'Children as theologians', in P. B. Pufall and R. P. Unsworth, (eds), *Rethinking Childhood*. New Brunswick: Rutgers University Press, pp. 54–69.

MacDonald, R. (2008), 'Disconnected Youth? Social Exclusion, the "Underclass" & Economic Marginality', *Social Work & Society*, Special Issue: Marginalized Youth, Disconnected Youth? Social Exclusion, the 'Underclass' & Economic Marginality, 6(2).

Macpherson, W. (1999), *The Stephen Lawrence Inquiry Report*. Presented to Parliament by the Secretary of State for the Home Department by Command of Her Majesty. February 1999.

Mahmoud, V. (1996), 'African American Muslim families', in M.
  McGoldrick, J. Giordano and J. K. Pearce (eds), *Ethnicity and Family
  Therapy*. New York: Guilford Press, pp. 122–8.
Malik I. H. (2004), *Islam and Modernity: Muslims in Europe and the
  United States*. London: Pluto Press.
Malik, M. (2003), 'Muslims and Participatory Democracy', in M. S.
  Seddon, D. Hussein and N. Malik (eds), *British Muslims: Loyalty and
  Belonging*. Markfield: The Islamic Foundation.
Malik, R., Shaikh, A. and Suleyman, M. (2007), *Providing Faith and
  Culturally Sensitive Support Services to Young British Muslims*.
  London: National Youth Agency.
Malik, S. (2005), 'Girls just wanna have fun', *Q-News*, Issue 36.
Maloof, P. S. and Ross-Sheriff, F. (2003), *Muslim Refugees in the United
  States. A Guide for Service Providers*. Washington, DC: Center for
  Applied Linguistics.
Mandaville, P. (2001), 'Reimagining Islam in diaspora: The politics of
  mediated community', *International Communication Gazette*, 63(2–3),
  pp. 169–86.
Mansfield, E. and Kehoe, K. (1994), 'A critical examination of anti-racist
  education', *Canadian Journal of Education*, 19(4), pp. 418–30.
Maqsood, R. W. (1995), *Living With Teenagers: A Guide for Muslim
  Parents*. London: Ta Ha Publishers Ltd.
Marcia, J. E. (1988), 'Ego identity, cognitive/moral development, and
  individuation', in D. K. Lapsley and F. C. Power (eds), *Self, Ego, and
  Identity: Integrative Approaches*. New York: Springer-Verlag.
Marshall, S. E. and Read, J. G. (2003), 'Identity politics among Arab-
  American women', *Social Science Quarterly*, 84(4), pp. 875–91.
Masood, E. (2006), *British Muslims Media Guide*. UK: British Council.
Mayer, J. (2004), *Hizb ut-Tahrir – The Next Al-Qaida, Really? PSIO
  Occasional Paper 4*. Geneva: IUHEI.
McLoughlin, S. (2005), 'The State, 'New' Muslim Leaderships and
  Islam as a 'Resource' for Public Engagement in Britain', in J. Cesari
  and S. McLoughlin (eds), *European Muslims and the Secular State*.
  Aldershot: Ashgate, pp. 55–69.
McRoy, A. (2005), *From Rushdie to 7/7: The Radicalisation of Islam in
  Britain*. London: Social Affairs Unit.
Milton-Edwards, B. (1996), *Islamic Politics in Palestine*. London and New
  York: Tauris.
Mirza, H. S. (1995), 'Black women in higher education: Defining a space/
  finding a place', in L. Morley and V. Walsh (eds), *Feminist Academics:
  Creative Agents for Change*. London: Taylor & Francis.
Mizruchi, M. S. (1996), 'What do interlocks do? An analysis, critique, and
  assessment of research on interlocking directorates', *Annual Review of
  Sociology*, 22, pp. 217–98.

Modood, T. (1992), 'British Muslims and The Rushdie affair', in
J. D. Rattansi (ed.), 'Race', Culture & Difference. London: Sage
Publications, pp. 260–77.
—(1997), 'The politics of multiculturalism in the New Europe', in
T. M. Werbner (eds), The Politics of Multiculturalism in the New
Europe. London: Zed Books Ltd, pp. 1–25.
—(1998), 'Ethnic minorities' drive for qualifications', in T. Modood and
T. Acland (eds), Race and Higher Education: Experiences, Challenges
and Policy Implications. London: Policy Studies Institute.
—(2003), 'Ethnic differences in educational performance', in D. Mason
(ed.), Explaining Ethnic Differences. Bristol: The Policy Press.
— (2004), 'Capitals, ethnic identity and educational qualifications',
Cultural Trends, 13(2), pp. 87–105.
—(2005), Multicultural Politics: Racism, Ethnicity and Muslims in
Britain. Edinburgh: University Press.
—(2006), 'British Muslims and the politics of multiculturalism',
in T. Modood, A. Triandafyllidou and R. Zapata-Barrero (eds),
Multiculturalism, Muslims and Citizenship: A European Approach.
London and New York: Routledge, pp. 37–56.
—(2006), 'Ethnicity, Muslims and higher education entry in Britain',
Teaching in Higher Education, 11(2), pp. 247–50.
—(2007), Multiculturalism: A Civic Idea. Cambridge: Polity.
—(2009), 'Muslims and the politics of difference', in P. Hopkins and R.
Gale (eds), Muslims in Britain: Race, Place and Identities. Edinburgh:
Edinburgh University Press.
Modood, T. and Acland, T. (eds) (1998), Race and Higher Education:
Experiences, Challenges and Policy Implications. London: Policy
Studies Institute.
Modood, T. and Shiner, M. (2002), 'Favourite colours', The
Guardian, http://www.guardian.co.uk/world/2002/jun/25/race.
newuniversities19922012, accessed 3 January 2009.
Modood, T. and Werbner, P. (eds) (2005), The Politics of Multiculturalism
in the New Europe. Minneapolis: University of Minnesota Press.
Modood, T., Berthoud, R., Lakey, N. J., Smith, P., Verdee, S. and Beishon,
S. (1997), Ethnic Minorities in Britain: Disadvantage and Diversity.
London: Policy Studies Institute.
Monaghan, K., du Plessis, M. and Malhi, T. (2003), Race, Religion and
Ethnicity Discrimination. London: Fretwells Ltd.
Muir, H. and Stone, R. (2004), Islamophobia: Issues, Challenges and Action.
UK and US: The Commission on British Muslims and Islamophobia.
Mukhametrakhimova, S. (2006), Dealing With Hizb-ut-Tahrir. London:
Institute of War and Peace Reporting (IWPR).
Murad, K. (1986), Muslim Youth in the West: Towards a New Education
Strategy, Leicester: The Islamic Foundation.

Murphy, C. (2002), *Passion for Islam*. New York: Simon & Schuster.

Nanji, A. (2008), *Dictionary of Islam*. London: Penguin Books.

Nawaz, M. (2008a), (testimonial) 'The Roots of Violent Islamist Extremism and Efforts to Counter It', *Hearing Before the Committee on Homeland Security and Governmental Affairs*. United States Senate, One Hundred Tenth Congress, Second Session, July 10.

—(2008b), *The Way Back from Islamism, PolicyWatch #1390: Special Forum Report*. Washington, DC: Washington Institute for Near East Policy (WINEP). http://www.washingtoninstitute.org/templateC05. php?CID = 2911, accessed 24 October 2010.

Nebbitt, V. E., Sr. and Lombe, M. (2007), Environmental correlates of depressive symptoms among African American adolescents living in public housing. *Journal of Human Behavior in the Social Environment*, 15(2), pp. 435–54.

Newman, B. M. and Newman, P. R. (2011), *Development Through Life: A Psychosocial Approach*. Belmont, CA: Wadsworth Cengage Learning.

Newman, M. (2008), 'Research into Islamic terrorism led to police response' in *The Times Higher Education*, http://www.timeshighereducation.co.uk/ story.asp?sectioncode = 26&storycode = 402125&c = 2, accessed 01 March 2009.

Noam, G. G. (1988), 'The self, adult development, and the theory of biography and transformation', in D. K. Lapsley and F. C. Power (eds), *Self, Ego, and Identity: Integrative Approaches*. New York: Springer-Verlag.

Nu'man, F. H. (1992), *The Muslim Population in the United States: A Brief Statement*. Washington, DC: The American Muslim Council *of Ethnic and Migration Studies*, 30(3), pp. 429–47.

Office for Public Management (2009), *The Experiences of Muslim Students in Further and Higher Education*, Greater London Authority.

Olcott, M. B. and Ziyaeva, D.(2008), *Islam in Uzbekistan: Religious Education and State Ideology*. Washington, DC: Carnegie Endowment for International Peace.

Olson, D. H., Portner, J. and Lavee, Y. (1985), *FACES III*. St. Paul: University of Minnesota, Department of Family Social Science. (Also in K. Concoran and J. Fischer (2000), *Measures for Clinical Practice*. The Free Press, pp. 247–9.)

Open Society Institute (2005), *Muslims in the UK: Policies for Engaged Citizens*. Budapest: Open Society Institute.

Ouseley, H. (2001), Community pride not prejudice – making diversity work in Bradford, Sir Herman Ouseley, The Ouseley Report.

Panja, T. (2005), 'Mosques should be saving lost souls', *The Observer*, 17 July.

Parekh, B. (2001), *The Future of Multi-Ethnic Britain*. London: Profile Books Ltd.

Peace Direct (2006), 'Young Muslims Speak', London: Peace Direct.

Peach, C. (2005), 'British Muslim Population: An Overview', in T. Abbas (ed.), *Muslim Britain: Communities Under Pressure*. London: Zed Books.

—(2006), 'Muslims in the 2001 Census of England and Wales: Gender and economic disadvantage', *Ethnic and Racial Studies*, 29(4), pp. 629–55.

Peek, L. (2005), Becoming Muslim: The development of a religious identity. *Sociology of Religion*, 66(3), pp. 215–42.

Phillips, A. (2006), ' "Really" equal: Opportunities and autonomy', *Journal of Political Philosophy*, 14(1), pp. 18–32.

Phinney, J., Berry, J. W., Vedder, P. and Liebkind, K. (2006), 'The acculturation experience: Attitudes, identities, and behaviors of immigrant youth', in J. W. Berry, J. S. Phinney, D. L. Sam and P. Vedder (eds), *Immigrant Youth in Cultural Transition: Acculturation, Identity, and Adaptation Across National Contexts*. Mahwah, NJ: Lawrence Erlbaum Associates, Inc., pp. 71–116.

Pine, B. and Drachman, D. (2005), Effective child welfare practice with immigrant and refugee children and their families. *Child Welfare*, 84(5), pp. 537–62.

Plante, T. G. and Boccaccini, M. T. (1997a), Reliability and validity of the Santa Clara Strength of Religious Faith Questionnaire. *Pastoral Psychology*, 45, pp. 375–87.

—(1997b), The Santa Clara Strength of Religious Faith Questionnaire. *Pastoral Psychology*, 45, pp. 301–15.

Poole, E. (2002), *Reporting Islam: Media Representations and British Muslims*. London: I. B. Tauris.

Portes A. and Rumbaut, R. G. (1996), *Immigrant America: A Portrait*. Berkeley: University of California Press.

—(2001), *Legacies*. Berkeley, CA: University of California Press.

Power, C. (1998), The new Islam, *Newsweek*, 16 March, 131, pp. 34–7.

Procidano, M. E. and Heller, K. (1983), Measures of perceived social support from friends and from family: Three validation studies. *American Journal of Community Psychology*, 11, pp. 1–24.

Radcliffe, L. (2004), 'A Muslim lobby at Whitehall? Examining the role of the Muslim minority in British foreign policy making', *Islam and Christian-Muslim Relations*, 15(3), pp. 365–86.

Radloff, L. S. (1977), 'The CES-D Scale: A self-report depression scale for research in the general population', Journal of *Applied Psychological Measures*, 1(3), pp. 385–401.

—(1991), 'The use of the Center for Epidemiologic Studies Depression Scale in adolescents and young adults', *Journal of Youth and Adolescence*, 20, pp. 149–65.

Radloff, L. S. and Locke, B. Z. (1986), 'The Community Mental Health Assessment Survey and the CES-D Scale', in M. Weissman, J. Myers and C. Ross (eds), *Community Surveys*. New Brunswick, NJ: Rutgers University Press.

Radloff, L. S. and Teri L. (1986), 'Use of the Center for Epidemiologic Studies Depression Scale with older adults', *Clinical Gerontologist*, 5, pp. 119–35.

Ramadan, T. (2004), *Western Muslims and the Future of Islam*. Oxford: Oxford University Press.

Rattansi, A. and Phoenix, A. (2005), 'Rethinking youth identities: Modernist and postmodernist frameworks', *Identity: An International Journal of Theory and Research*, 5(2), pp. 97–123.

Read, B., Archer, L. and Leathwood, C. (2003), 'Challenging cultures? Student conceptions of 'belonging' and 'isolation' at a post-1992 university', *Studies in Higher Education*, 28(3), pp. 261–77.

Reay, D., Davies, J., David, M. and Ball, S. J. (2001), 'Choices of degree or degrees of choice? Class, 'race' and the higher education choice process', *Sociology*, 35(4), pp. 855–74.

Renton, D. (2008), 'Document on student extremism seriously flawed', 10 April, Institute for Race Relations, http://www.irr.org.uk/2008/april/ha000019.html, accessed 6 May 2011.

Richards, W. (2009), 'His master's voice', *A Journal of Youth Work*, Issue 2, pp. 7–23.

Ricoeur, P. (1984), *Time and narrative: Volume 1*. Mclaughlin and Pellauer (Trans.), Chicago: University of Chicago Press.

Rosenberg, M. (1979), *Conceiving the Self*. New York: Basic Books. (Also in K. Concoran and J. Fischer (2000), *Measures for Clinical Practice*. The Free Press, pp. 610–11.)

Ross-Sheriff, F. and Husain, A. (2001), 'Values and ethics in social work practice with Asian Americans: A South Asian Muslim Case Example', in Fong, R and Furuto, S. *Culturally Competent Practice*. Boston: Allyn and Bacon, pp.75–88.

Rossenberg, M. (1965), *Society and the Adolescent Self-image*. Princeton, NJ: Princeton University Press.

Rowbottom, R. W. (1977), *Social Analysis*. London: Heinemann Educational.

Roy, O. (2008), *Al Qaeda in the West as a Youth Movement: The Power of a Narrative. MICROCON Policy Working Paper 2*. Brighton: MICROCON.

Rubbin, A. and Babbie, E. R. (2008), *Research Methods for Social Work* (6th edition). Belmont, CA: Thompson Brooks Cole.

Sadat, M. H. (2001), 'The quest for Afghanistan by defining Afghaniyat', *Omaid Weekly*. Available from, http://www.omaid.com/english_section/back_issues_archive/476.htm#item2, accessed 20 August 2010.

—(2008), 'Hyphenating *Afghaniyat* (Afghan-ness) in the Afghan diaspora', *Journal of Muslim Affairs*, 28(3), pp. 329–42.

Salgado-Pottier, R. (2008), 'A modern moral panic: The representation of British Bangladeshi and Pakistani youth in relation to violence and religion', *Anthropology Matters*, 10(1). http://www.anthropologymatters.com/index.php?journal=anth_matters&page=article&op=view&path%5B%5D=44, accessed 24 December 2010.

Samad, Y. (1996), 'The politics of Islamic identity among Bangladeshis and Pakistanis in Britain', in T. Ranger, Y. Samad and O. Stuart (eds), *Culture Identity and Politics: Ethnic Minorities in Britain*, Avebury, Aldershot, pp. 90–8.

Samad, Y. and Sen, K. (2007), *Islam in the European Union: Transnationalism, Youth and the War on Terror*. Oxford: Oxford University Press.

Sardar, Z. and Masood, M. (2006), 'Ziauddin Sardar: Paradise lost, a future found', 15 May, http://www.opendemocracy.net/globalization/sardar_3547.jsp.

Sariibrahimoglu, L. (2009), 'Turkish Counter-Terrorist Police Allege Hizb-ut-Tahrir Link with Ergenekon', *Eurasia Daily Monitor* 6, 147. Washington, DC: The Jamestown Foundation, http://www.jamestown.org/programs/edm/single/?tx_ttnews%5Btt_news%5D = 35349&tx_ttnews%5BbackPid%5D = 485&no_cache = 1, accessed 24 October 2010.

Schmidt, G. (2004), 'Islamic identity formation among young Muslims: The case of Denmark, Sweden, and the United States', *Journal of Muslim Affairs*, 24(1), pp. 31–45.

Searle, J. (1995), *The Construction of Social Reality*. London: Penguin.

Seddon, M. S., et al. (eds) (2003), *British Muslims: Loyalty and Belonging*. Leicester: The Islamic Foundation and the Citizen organising Foundation.

Seddon, M. S., Hussain, D. and Malik, N. (2004), (eds), *British Muslims Between Assimilation and Segregation*. Leicester: The Islamic Foundation.

Shaikh, M. A. (1995), 'Teaching about Islam and Muslims in the public school classroom' (3rd edition). Mountain Valley, CA: *Educational Studies*, 20(1), pp. 69–86.

Shain, F. (2003), *The Schooling and Identity of Asian Girls*. Stoke-on-Trent: Trentham Books.

Shain, Y. (1999), *Marketing the American Creed Abroad: Diasporas in US and their Homelands*. Cambridge: Cambridge University Press.

Shain, Y. and Sherman, M. (1998), 'Dynamics of disintegration: Diaspora, secession and the paradox of nation-states', *Nations and Nationalism*, 4(3), pp. 321–46.

Shaw, A. (2000), *Kinship and Continuity: Pakistani Families in Britain*. Amsterdam: Harwood Academic Publishers.

Sheffer, G. (1986), 'A new field of study: Modern diasporas in international politics', in G. Sheffer (ed.), *Modern Diasporas in International Politics*. London: Croom Helm.

—(1995), 'The emergence of new ethno-national diasporas', *Migration*, 28(2), pp. 5–28.

Shiner, M. and Modood, T. (2002), 'Help or hindrance? Higher education and the route to ethnic equality', *British Journal of Sociology of Education*, 23(2), pp. 209–32.

Siddiqui, A. (2007), *Islam at Universities in England: Meeting The Needs and Investing in the Future*, Report submitted to Bill Rammell MP 9 Minister of State for Lifelong Learning, Further and Higher Education.

Siddiqui, A. H. (1990), (Trans.) *Mishkat-ul-Masabih* (Vol 1). New Delhi: Kitab Bhavan.

Simmons, C., Simmons, C. and Allah, M. H. (1994), 'English, Israeli-Arab and Saudi Arabian adolescent values', *Educational Studies*, 20(1), pp. 69–86.

Smith, J. I. (1999), *Islam in America*. New York: Columbia University Press.

—(2005), 'Patterns of Muslim immigration', *USINFO. STATE.GOV, International Information Programs*, retrieved 26 June 2005 http://uninfo.state.gov/products/pubs/muslimlife/immirat.htm.

Stetsenko, A. and Arievitch, I. M. (2002), 'Learning and development: Contributions from post-Vygotskian research', in G. Wells and G. Cluxton (eds), *Learning for Life in the 21st Century: Sociocultural Perspectives on the Future of Education*. London: Blackwell, pp. 84–97.

Strum, P. (2003), 'Executive summary', in P. Strum and D. Tarantolo (eds), *Muslims in the United States*. Washington, DC: Woodrow Wilson International Center for Scholars, pp. 1–4.

Suárez-Orozco, C. (2004), 'Formulating Identity in a Globalized World', in M. Suárez-Orozco and D. B. Qin-Hilliard (eds), *Globalization: Culture and Education in the New Millennium*. Berkeley, CA: University of California Press.

Tabachnick, B. G. and Fidell, L. S. (2007), *Using Multivariate Statistic* (5th edition). Boston: Allyn and Bacon.

Taji-Farouki, S. (1996), *A Fundamental Quest: Hizb ut-Tahrir and the Search for the Islamic Caliphate*. London: Grey Seal.

Tartar, M. (1998), 'Counseling Immigrants: School contexts and emerging strategies', *British Journal of Guidance Counseling*, 26, pp. 337–52.

Thorne, J. and Stuart, H. (2008), *Islam on Campus: A Survey of UK Student Opinions*. Great Britain: The Centre for Social Cohesion.

Treacher, A. (2006), 'Something in the air: Otherness, recognition and ethics', *Journal of Social Work Practice*, 20(1), pp. 27–37.

Tyrer, D. and Ahmad, F. (2005), 'Those Muslim women are at it again!', *Q-News*, November 2005, Issue 364.

—(2006), *Muslim Women, Identities, Experiences, Diversity and Prospects in Higher Education*. Oxford: Liverpool John Moores University and European Social Fund.

Ulman, C. and Tartar, M. (2001), 'Psychological adjustment among Israeli adolescent Immigrants: A report on life satisfaction, self-concept, and self-esteem', *Journal of Youth and Adolescence*, 30, pp. 4449–63.

Vakil, A. and Sayyid, S. (eds) (2010), *Thinking Through Islamophobia: Global Perspectives*. London: Hurst 2010.

Valentine, S. R. (2010), 'Monitoring Islamic Militancy: Hizb-ut-Tahrir: 'The Party of Liberation', *Policing*, 4(3), pp. 1–10.

Verkuyten, M. (1998), 'Perceived discrimination and self-esteem among ethnic minority adolescents', *The Journal of Social Psychology*, 138(4), pp. 479–93.

Verkuyten, M. and Yildiz, A. A. (2007), 'National (dis)identification, and ethnic and religious identity: A study among Turkish-Dutch Muslims', *Personality and Social Psychology Bulletin*, 33(1448), pp. 1–15.

Vermeulen, F. and Berger, M. (2008), 'Turkish civic networks and political behaviour in Amsterdam and Berlin', in S. K. Ramakrishnan and I. Bloemraad (eds), *Civil Hopes and Political Realities: Immigrants, Community Organizations and Political Engagement*. New York: Russell Sage Foundation, pp. 160–92.

Vermeulen, H. and C. Govers (eds), *Anthropology of Ethnicity: Beyond 'Ethnic Groups and Boundaries'*. Amsterdam: HET Spinhuis Publishers, pp. 11–32.

Vertovec, S. (1997), 'Three meanings of "diaspora", exemplified among South Asian religions', *Diaspora*, 6(3), pp. 277–99.

Vygotsky. L. S. (1978), *Mind and Society: The Development of Higher Mental Processes*. Cambridge, MA: Harvard University Press.

Wahlbeck, Ö. (1999), *Kurdish Diasporas: A Comparative Study of Kurdish Refugee Communities*. London: Macmillan.

—(2002), 'The concept of diaspora as an analytical tool in the study of refugee communities', *Journal of Ethnic and Migration Studies*, 28(2), pp. 221–38.

Weissman, M., Orvaschel, H. and Padian, N. (1980), 'Children's symptom and social function self-report scales: Comparison of mothers' and children's reports', *Journal of Nervous and Mental Disease*, 168, pp. 736–40.

Weller, P, Feldman, A. and Purdam, K. (2001), *Religious Discrimination in England and Wales*. London: Home Office Research, Development and Statistics Directorate.

Werbner, P. (2004), 'Theorising complex diasporas: purity and hybridity in the South Asian public sphere in Britain', *Journal of Ethnic and Migration Studies*, 30(5), pp. 895–911.

Whine, M. (2004), 'Hizb ut-Tahrir in open societies', in *The Challenge of Hizb ut-Tahrir: Deciphering and Combating Radical Islamist Ideology*, edited by Z Baran. Washington, DC: The Nixon Centre.

Wierenga, A. (2001), 'Losing and finding the plot: the value of listening to young people', Conference paper for *Starting Where They Are, International Conference on Young People and Informal Education*, University of Strathclyde. pp. 6–9 September.

Wiktorowicz, Q. (2005), *Radical Islam Rising: Muslim Extremism in the West*. Oxford: Rowman and Littlefield Publishers.

Wimmer, A. and Schiller, N. G. (2002), 'Methodological nationalism and beyond: Nation-state building, migration and the social sciences', *Global Networks*, 2(4), pp. 301–34.

Winter, T. (2003), 'Some reflections on the psychosocial background', in M. S. Seddon, D. Hussain and N. Malik (eds), *British Muslims: Loyalty and Belonging*. Leicester: Islamic Foundation.

YMCA (2009), 'YMCA Movement to Play Key Role in Delivery of myplace Projects', http://www.ymca.org.uk/pooled/articles/BF_NEWSART/view.asp?Q = BF_NEWSART_310609, accessed 29 May 2011.

Young, K. (2006), *The Art of Youth Work* (2nd edition). Lyme Regis: Russell House Publishing Ltd.

Younis, M. (2010), *Young British Muslims and Relationships, Muslim Youth Helpline*. Leicester: National Youth Agency.

Zambelis, C. (2007), 'Egypt's Muslim Brotherhood: Political Islam Without al-Qaeda', Jamestown Foundation, *Terrorism Monitor*, 5, 22. http://www.jamestown.org/programs/gta/single/?tx_ttnews%5Btt_news%5D=4568&tx_ttnews%5BbackPid%5D=182&no_cache=1, accessed 24 October 2010.

Zanca, Rl. (2004), 'Explaining' Islam in Central Asia: An Anthropological Approach for Uzbekistan', *Journal of Muslim Affairs*, 24(1), pp. 99–107.

Zine, J. (2000), 'Redefining resistance: Towards an Islamic subculture in schools', *Race, Ethnicity, and Education*, 3(3), pp. 293–316.

—(2007), Safe havens or religious 'ghettos'? Narratives of Islamic
    schooling in Canada. *Race, Ethnicity, and Education*, 10(1), pp. 71–92.
Zuckerman, P. (2007), 'Atheism: Contemporary Numbers and Patterns', in
    M. Martin (ed.), *The Cambridge Companion to Atheism*, Cambridge:
    Cambridge University Press, pp. 47–65.

INDEX